HAYNES **MAX** POWER Renault

clio

The definitive guide to **modifying**
by **Bob Jex**

HAYNES MAX POWER Renault

clio

The definitive guide to **modifying**
by **Bob Jex**

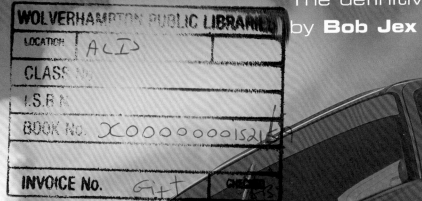

Haynes Publishing

© Haynes Publishing 2006

ISBN 1 85960 989 9

Printed by **J H Haynes & Co Ltd,**
Sparkford, Yeovil, Somerset BA22 7JJ, England.

First printed December 2002
Reprinted 2006

Tel: 01963 442030 Fax: 01963 440001
Int. tel: +44 1963 442030 Fax: +44 1963 440001
E-mail: sales@haynes-manuals.co.uk
Web site: www.haynes.co.uk

Haynes North America, Inc
861 Lawrence Drive, Newbury Park, California 91320, USA

Editions Haynes
4, Rue de l'Abreuvoir
92415 COURBEVOIE CEDEX, France

Haynes Publishing Nordiska AB
Box 1504, 751 45 UPPSALA, Sweden

(3989-3AK1)

It wasn't my idea guv'nor!

1 Advice on safety procedures and precautions is contained throughout this manual, and more specifically on page 210. You are strongly recommended to note these comments, and to pay close attention to any instructions that may be given by the parts supplier.

2 J H Haynes recommends that vehicle customisation should only be undertaken by individuals with experience of vehicle mechanics; if you are unsure as to how to go about the customisation, advice should be sought from a competent and experienced individual. Any queries regarding customisation should be addressed to the product manufacturer concerned, and not to J H Haynes, nor the vehicle manufacturer.

3 The instructions in this manual are followed at the risk of the reader who remains fully and solely responsible for the safety, roadworthiness and legality of his/her vehicle. Thus J H Haynes are giving only non-specific advice in this respect.

4 When modifying a car it is important to bear in mind the legal responsibilities placed on the owners, driver and modifiers of cars, including, but not limited to, the Road Traffic Act 1988. IN PARTICULAR, IT IS AN OFFENCE TO DRIVE ON A PUBLIC ROAD A VEHICLE WHICH IS NOT INSURED OR WHICH DOES NOT COMPLY WITH THE CONSTRUCTION AND USE REGULATIONS, OR WHICH IS DANGEROUS AND MAY CAUSE INJURY TO ANY PERSON, OR WHICH DOES NOT HOLD A CURRENT MOT CERTIFICATE OR DISPLAY A VALID TAX DISC.

5 The safety of any alteration and its compliance with construction and use regulations should be checked before a modified vehicle is sold as it may be an offence to sell a vehicle which is not roadworthy.

6 Any advice provided is correct to the best of our knowledge at the time of publication, but the reader should pay particular attention to any changes of specification to the vehicles, or parts, which can occur without notice.

7 Alterations to vehicles should be disclosed to insurers and licensing authorities, and legal advice taken from the police, vehicle testing centres, or appropriate regulatory bodies.

8 The vehicle has been chosen for this project as it is one of those most widely customised by its owners, and readers should not assume that the vehicle manufacturers have given their approval to the modifications.

9 Neither J H Haynes nor the manufacturers give any warranty as to the safety of a vehicle after alterations, such as those contained in this book, have been made. J H Haynes will not accept liability for any economic loss, damage to property or death and personal injury arising from use of this manual other than in respect of injury or death resulting directly from J H Haynes' negligence.

Contents

Haynes
Max Power

01

Buyer's guide

02

Insurance

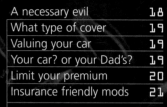

03

08

09

10

Suspension

Brakes

Interiors

Security

Body styling
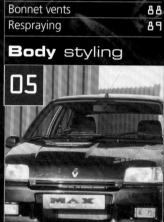
Lights & bulbs

Wheels & tyres

04 05 06 07

11 12 13 14

ICE

Engines

Exhausts

Reference

Haynes
Max Power

What's that then?

Haynes Publishing have, for the last forty years, been helping people keep their cars on the roads in countries all over the world by publishing maintenance manuals. Chances are you've either got one of them yourself or you know somebody who has.

"Lights & bulbs" includes headlight mods, side repeaters, rear light clusters, etc.

Before

After

Remember what it feels like on your birthday, or at Christmas, when you're faced by a pile of pressies? So do we, that gnawing feeling in your gut, what's in them? What did I get? Take that feeling and multiply it by twelve, that's how we felt when we started this project. When we decided that it was time to try something new, we couldn't wait. Because the same theories apply to modifying your car as servicing it, we reckoned we'd better get on and do it ourselves. We don't pay other people to do it for us, and we get the same dodgy instructions with kit as everybody else.

So if you've ever wondered how to fit a universal door mirror properly, smooth a tailgate or just bolt a seat in, this book is for you.

We've picked up a skip full of tips along the way, and they're all here for you to use. We haven't tried to set any trends, but we've covered every possible process we think you'll need. So where we've tinted a front door window, the same rules apply to a rear one, job done.

If you look in the magazines and want some of that, join us, 'cos so do we, and we'll show you how to get it.

Keeping it real

Modifying a car is not without its problems in the 'real world', as opposed to the seemingly fantasy world of the glossy mags. For instance, it's pretty silly to spend hours fitting illegal window tints or smoked lights if you get pulled the first time you're out afterwards. Of course, you can get pulled for all sorts of reasons (and just driving a modified car is reason enough sometimes), but keeping the car actually legal is one of the 'hidden' challenges with modifying. Throughout the book, our tips should give all the help you need to at least appear to be on the right side of the law. The annual MOT test is another favourite time for your mods to get panned, and again, we aim to give you all the help necessary to ensure at least that what you've changed doesn't lead to a fail.

Security is another major issue with a tweaked motor, and the perils of insurance cannot be taken lightly, either. We aim to give down-to-earth advice to help you keep the car in the first place, and to help you in not upsetting your insurers too much if the worst happens.

A word about fashion

In producing this book, we're aware that fashions change. What we show being fitted to our car might well be hideously out of date in 6 months time, or might not be your thing in the first place! Also, some of the stuff we've acquired from our various suppliers may no longer be available by the time you read this. We hope that, despite this, our approach of showing you step-by-step how to fit the various parts will mean that, even if the parts change slightly, the procedures we show for fitting will still be valid.

Our main project car was a 1.4RT, 1995 N reg, with some additional work being carried out on other Clios.

"Wheels & tyres" takes a detailed look at all the options.

"Body styling" shows you how to fit universal mirrors to full body kits.

"Interiors" includes seats, painting trim, gear knobs and loads more.

Clio -
the thinking man's French favourite

Clio owners dare to be different - *vive la différence*, as they probably don't actually say in France. With all the pressure on to buy a Saxo or 106, it's a true individual who buys a Clio instead - and hey - isn't being individual what modding's all about anyway?

In the world of small hatches, many people agree that the Clio was the first "big-car-feel" model the world had seen, when it landed in 1991. Insiders at Renault apparently talk about their build quality in terms of models "before-Clio" and after it, so great a jump was made in how their cars were screwed together. Let's not forget, the Clio replaced the R5, and no-one's going to accuse that of being a quality product (one reason the GT Turbo was so quick was its lightness - draw your own conclusions from that).

The R5 replacement could be described as having slightly bland styling, but we prefer to call

it nicely understated, in a boxy, almost Golf-esque way. Thoroughly modern, it's a low-drag shape with wide track and a long wheelbase, both of which help to explain its excellent handling and ride (at least until you slam it). The engines are modern overhead-cam "Energy" units, and the body's well-protected against rust - it even won Car of the Year in 1991.

The model the world was really waiting for, once the Clio arrived, was the GT Turbo replacement. Renault were very secretive at first, then stories began to leak out that it wouldn't be a turbo-nutter

like the 5. What, no turbo lag? No torque-steer? How could one of the pioneers of turbos even think of not doing a turbo hot hatch? *Sacré bleu!* Still, most people forgave Renault when the chunky Clio 16-valve arrived, late in 1991, sharing the already-acclaimed 1.8 litre motor with the recently-announced 19 16V. Packing an impressive 137 bhp and revving to the moon and back, those who've driven it don't even mention turbos again… This is one pumped-up Clio, in every sense - there's a bonnet power bulge/air scoop, and bulging flared arches front and rear (the fronts are plastic, by the way). And the handling - let's just say this is the French car which saw off the mighty 205 GTi, and leave it at that.

One of the best-known (notorious, even) special-edition models of any hot hatch range first arrived in November 1993. The original "Williams" was supposed to be a strictly-limited run of 400 RHD models - each one had a numbered plaque on the dash, to reinforce the "limited" message. Imagine how those 400 owners must have felt when, less than a year later, Renault brought out the Clio Williams 2, and a year after that, the Williams 3… *"Final Fantasy 26"*, anyone? Rumour has it that some owners took Renault to court over it. Still, you can't deny the Williams easily justifies its existence (several times over). After all, it's not just a standard 16V with gold alloys - the Williams features a 2.0 litre 150 bhp motor, close-ratio gearbox, larger bonnet bulge (nice!), and racing-inspired suspension tweaks.

The most famous thing about the rest of the Clio range were the long-running "Nicole - Papa" tv ads, which we all watched to keep up-to-date with the never-ending facelifts. Oh alright, we were really just checking out Nicole (Estelle Skornik). The "Mark 1" Clio

went through three distinct "Phases" in its life from 1991 to 1998, and the later "Mark 2" has already had its first. Clearly very fashion-conscious, these Frenchies. Most modders agree that the facelift NOT to have was the last of the early models, the "Phase 3", which ran from 1996 to 1998, and featured a very girly headlight makeover. Sorry, we don't do cute. Still, with kit already appearing for the Mk 2 Clio, its future as the more individual choice of modified French motor is assured.

Buyer's guide

What to buy - model guide

'Basic' models

First of all, don't buy a 5-door. Well, okay - if you must, but nobody really buys 5-doors for modifying purposes. If it doesn't say in the advert which it is, ask. You could always de-handle the rear doors to make it a bit less obvious, but you'll still be in a minority! The diesels make nice cars for when you reach the pipe-and-slippers years, and come in attractive colours such as white, and navy blue. Beige too, possibly. The "Baccara" is worth seeking out for its standard leather interior, but might be worth avoiding for the wood veneer trim and equally-unfortunate automatic gearbox, which isn't very Max Power. At all.

As with any car, go for the latest model you can afford (but watch which facelift you're getting). Some of the special editions (and there've been plenty of those) had some useful extra kit, like sunroofs, tints and body-colour bumpers, as well as the obligatory ghastly interior re-trim. Many of the lesser Clios were bought as second cars, for housewives to get in the shopping and for the school run; there's also a fair number in the hands of pensioners. Although some of these will be the less trendy 5-door models, if you can find a 3-door, they can be the best buys of all, provided they've been looked after. Why pay extra for a plusher model, if you're going to gut the interior anyway? Just make sure you've got cash to spare, to start modding immediately - you don't want to be seen driving granny's old Clio for longer than you can help.

Nearly all Clios, except the very earliest ones, had a catalytic converter. Many people think that avoiding a "cat" is a good idea, and we wouldn't disagree - if the "cat" goes wrong, as in failing the MOT emissions test, it'll be big bucks to sort. And no, you can't just take it off - fit that de-cat pipe by all means, but don't say we told you to do it - your car will then be illegal on the road. All "cat" models have fuel injection. Before you run away with the idea that this means more power, think again. Fitting a "cat" means controlling emissions, which means leaning the engine off as far as possible - not a recipe for tyre-shredding torque… Still, even a 1.2 Clio's good for 60 bhp in stock form, so burning-off the odd Fiesta still isn't out of the question, even with the cat.

By far the most common engine size, the 1.2 litre models all fall into Group 4 for insurance. Virtually all the special editions (Oasis, Paris, Fidji, Be Bop, Les Routiers - can I go home now?) had the 1.2 motor - some had a 5-speed 'box thrown in, rather than the standard four-on-the-floor. Now there's nothing wrong with having "just" the 1.2, nothing at all, but can we distract you by pointing out that the 1.4 models are just one group higher on insurance, and have 80 bhp rather than 60 bhp? Yup - that's what we thought. The 1.4 RT models are even quite well-kitted, with leccy windows, rev counter and remote central locking (all useful modifier's stuff). Course, if it's kit you're after, seek out one of the rare Baccaras, which had leather seats and steering wheel, power steering, alloys and electric mirrors (and a rather uncool automatic 'box as standard). One of the best buys only lasted one year in production - the 1.4 S had the 80 bhp engine, rear roof spoiler, front fogs and sports seats; still in Group 5 for insurance, it's a wonder they didn't sell shedloads. The RT also came with a 1.8 litre 95 bhp engine (Group 7), but only as a five-door. Shame.

If you're going to fit fat tyres, try getting a car with power steering (available as an option on early 1.4 models, standard on the auto Baccara, RSi and 16V, fitted to all 1.4/1.8 RTs after November 1993, and 1.2 RN models after March 1994). The non-assisted steering isn't that heavy to start with, but the combination of big rims and small Momo wheel might need a few sessions down the gym! Most models from mid-1993 came with a Renault immobiliser, which might help with the insurance, while Phase 2 models from March 1994 had seat belt tensioners and side impact bars, which might be handy in avoiding a trip to hospital. Airbags arrived on some models from September 1994, but didn't make it across the whole range until the Phase 3 facelift in May 1996.

'Sporty' models

Surprisingly, there aren't really any stand-out insurance-friendly sporty Clios, despite what you might think. The eight-valve RSi seems to fit the bill, with a 110 bhp 1.8 litre motor, virtually all the required kit (alloys, bodykit, electrics, sports bits inside), front and rear discs, but has the same Group 11 insurance rating as the "proper" hot Clio, the 16-valve. Weird or what? The 16-valve engine has another 27 horses, more of a bodykit (flared arches, deeper front bumper) and more goodies inside. Some 16-valvers were specced with a very tasty leather interior, which is well worth seeking out. Out in the real world, we'd be very tempted to check with our brokers whether the official Group 11 rating is fact or fantasy, before handing over the folding for any 16V - it just seems too good to be true. Unofficially, the Clio 16V can apparently be anything from Group 12 to 15.

No surprises when it comes to insuring a Clio Williams. The 2.0 litre daddy of the range, with ultimate levels of va-va-voom, weighs in with a Group 17 rating. Gulp. Still, you can't deny it looks the business in stock form, with the trademark gold wheels and badges against the Monaco blue metallic - this is one tough-looking little beast. Trouble is, you don't often see them now - they only made about a thousand in total, and anyone who hasn't stacked it (or lost it in the night) has perhaps realised the investment potential instead, and never takes it out. Definitely a pukka modern classic car - don't expect to pick (a real) one up cheap.

Don't buy a dog

In general, the Clio is a solid used buy, with only a few problems worth noting. Clios don't rust much, and the interiors generally hang together quite well, considering the reputation of many French cars.

Apart from a few minor electrical gremlins (check, for instance, that the rear wiper works) and a tendency for not liking wet starting, the Clio's a reliable enough little chariot. What you'll be up against on an older car is the price of Renault spare parts - think of a number and double it, then it'll be the wrong bit when it comes… Or maybe we've just been unlucky.

Unless you're planning on spending big money on a Williams, it's far better to buy privately, as long as you know what you're doing. Dealers still think they can charge over the odds for small cars, but all you'll get for the extra money is a full valet and some degree of comeback if the car's a dog. Buying privately, you get to meet the owner, and this can tell you plenty about how the car's been treated. Everyone's nervous when buying a car, but don't ignore your "gut feelings" when you first see the car, or meet its owner. Also, DON'T make the common mistake of deciding to buy the car

Tricks 'n' tips
Tyres can be a giveaway to a car maintained on a shoestring - four different makes of tyre, especially cheap brands, can indicate a penny-pinching attitude which won't have done the rest of the car any favours.

before you've even seen it - too many people seem to make up their minds before setting out, and blindly ignore all the warning signs. Remember, there *are* other cars, and you *can* walk away! Think of a good excuse before you set out.

Take someone who 'knows a bit about cars' along with you - preferably, try and find someone who's either got a Clio, or who's had one in the past.

Never buy a car in the dark, or when it's raining. If you do have to view any car in these conditions, agree not to hand over any money until you've seen it in daylight, and when the paintwork's dry (dull, faded paint, or metallic paint that's lost its lacquer, will appear to be shiny in the rain).

Check that the mileages and dates shown on the receipts and MOTs follow a pattern indicating normal use, with no gaps in the dates, and no sudden drop in the mileage between MOTs (which might suggest the mileage has been 'clocked'). If you are presented with a sheaf of paperwork, it's worth going through it - maybe the car's had a history of problems, or maybe it's just had some nice expensive new parts fitted (like a clutch, starter motor or alternator, for instance).

Check the chassis number (VIN number) and engine number on the registration document AND on the car. Any sign of welding near one of these numbers should be treated with suspicion - to disguise the real number, a thief will run a line of weld over the old number, grind it flat, then stamp in a new number. Other scams include cutting the section of bodywork with the numbers on from another car, then cutting and welding this section into place. The VIN number appears on a plate at the front of the engine compartment, or on the body pillar behind the (open) driver's door. If there is any sign that this plate has been tampered with, walk away - the car could be a "ringer" (a stolen car with a fake I.D.). Later cars also have the VIN etched into the windscreen or tailgate glass - make sure it matches (or has someone covered it with a sticker, to hide it?).

The engine number is stamped onto a shiny aluminium plate at the front of the engine, near the dipstick tube. This plate shouldn't be difficult to spot - if the number's been removed, or if there's anything suspicious about it, you could be buying trouble.

Check the registration document very carefully - all the details should match the car. If buying privately, make sure that it's definitely the owner's name and address printed on it - if not, be very careful! If buying from a dealer, note the name and address, and try to contact the previous owner to confirm mileage, etc, before handing over

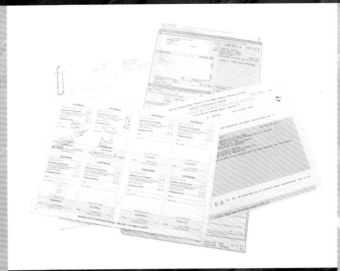

Full service history (fsh)

Is there any service history? If so, this is good, but study the service book carefully:

a *Which garage has done the servcing? Is it a proper dealer, or a backstreet bodger? Do you know the garage, and if so, would you use it?*

b *Do the mileages show a nice even progression, or are there huge gaps? Check the dates too.*

c *Does it look as if the stamps are authentic? Do the oldest ones look old, or could this 'service history' have been created last week, to make the car look good?*

d *When was the last service, and what exactly was carried out? When was the cambelt last changed? Has the owner got receipts for any of this servicing work?*

One sign of a genuine car is a good batch of old MOTs, and as many receipts as possible - even if they're for fairly irrelevant things like tyres.

more than a deposit. Unless the car's very old, it shouldn't have had too many previous owners - if it's into double figures, it may mean the car is trouble, so checking its owner history is more important.

The VIN plate is attached to the bonnet front slam panel . . .

. . . and the VIN is also etched into the windscreen and tailgate glass.

Problem areas

The dreaded rust isn't much of a factor, but check the rear arches and tailgate carefully. Apparently, one unusual place Clios can go is around the opening rear side windows - water gets trapped under the rubber. Keeping this area dry and clean is a must for happy Clio ownership. Major rust anywhere else could be down to badly-repaired crash damage, so walk away.

One of the most expensive bits under the bonnet is electrical, and can end up taking an early bath - what superb design. We're talking about the fuel injection ECU here, which is located under the plastic panels at the base of the windscreen, and can get more than splashed, let's say, if the bulkhead drain holes become blocked. Ask the seller to take out the vehicle jack (this has to come out for access to the ECU), and check the black box for signs of damp - a damp brain is not what you want.

All Clios have a camshaft driven by a rubber timing belt, also known as a 'cambelt'. If the engine's timing belt snaps, the engine could be

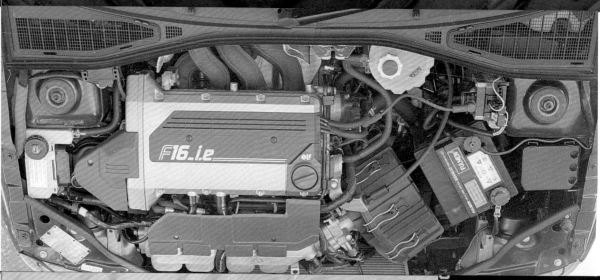

wrecked. Finished. Ruined. Knackered. Without the cambelt, the valves won't move up and down, and the pistons will smash into them (so on 16-valve engines, you could be looking at SIXTEEN bent valves - and maybe, cylinder head and piston damage). One of the most common scenarios for a cambelt to snap is when pulling away from a standstill - burning away from the lights is fun, but could be death to an old cambelt. If you don't know when the belt was last replaced, have a look around the engine bay for a sticker - many garages put a sticker on the engine to say when the belt was fitted, and to say when a new one will be needed. As a guide, fit a new cambelt every 3 years or 30 000 miles - this shouldn't be an expensive job (typically, about £80), and if you drive your car hard, it's a lot cheaper than rebuilding or replacing the engine!

Clios can suffer problems with their engine mountings - there are three altogether, one either side at the top, and a lower link (which looks like a dog's bone) behind the engine, low down. If the lower link wears, the car will tend to jump out of gear; if the engine mounting under the battery tray wears, the engine will droop down on one side (this might also lead to gear selection problems). Check for wear in the mountings by grabbing the top of the engine and trying to rock it; also watch for engine movement while the seller tries to pull away with the handbrake on.

Rattles from the front suspension over bumps may be down to worn strut top bearings (easy enough to replace). Also listen out for rumbling wheel bearings, and clicking driveshafts when the car's driven on full lock in either direction - remember what we said about Renault parts prices…

The last major problem worth mentioning concerns the gearbox, or rather the differential, into which the two driveshafts fit. Apparently, there's a thrustwasher inside the diff which can wear out inside 70,000 miles (and it'll cost shedloads to replace). It's possible to check this, it seems, by jacking up the passenger-side front wheel, and seeing how much play there is when the wheel is pulled/pushed in and out (car in gear). We're not sure this test would actually prove anything, though - best advice is to check that all the gears engage cleanly, that they don't jump out (accelerate in each gear, then back off), and that there isn't excessive gearbox noise.

Check front foglights for damage, or signs of water leaking in, and check (especially) 16V models for excess front brake disc wear. Phew. That's all, folks.

While the trim on a Clio is very durable, it should still be obvious whether the car's been abused over a long period, or whether the mileage showing is genuine or not (shiny steering wheels and floppy window winder handles are a good place to start checking if you're suspicious). Okay, so you may be planning to junk most of the interior at some point, but why should you pay over the odds for a tat car which the owner hasn't given a stuff about?

Although you may feel a bit stupid doing it, check simple things too, like making sure the windows and sunroof open and shut, and that all the doors and tailgate can be locked (if a lock's been replaced, ask why). Check all the basic electrical equipment too, as far as possible - lights, front and rear wipers, heated rear window, heater fan; it's amazing how often these things are taken for granted by

buyers! If your chosen Clio already has alloys fitted, does it have locking wheel bolts? Where's the key?

One thing to check on all Clios is that the catalytic converter ("cat") is working - this is a wickedly expensive part to replace, but the best way to ensure at least one year's grace is to only buy a car with a full MOT (the cat is checked during the emissions test).

Many later Clios will have a driver's airbag fitted - these will have "AIRBAG" or the initials "SRS" (supplementary restraint system) on the steering wheel centre pad. The orange airbag warning light should come on and go off when the engine's started - if the warning light stays on, this counts as an MOT fail, and curing the fault could be mega-bucks (it might also indicate that the airbag's gone off, in a crash!). If the light never comes on, this could still mean there's a fault with the airbag, but your dishonest seller's just taken out the bulb... nice try.

Sports models

Has it been treated well, or thrashed to death? We wouldn't pay top dollar for any sporty Clio without seeing evidence of careful maintenance, because any car will stand a good ranting much better if it's been properly serviced. Even a fully-stamped service book only tells half the story, though. Does the owner look bright enough to even know what a dipstick IS, never mind how to check the oil level between services?

Remember that there's even more to look out for than on a lesser

model. If the car's temptingly cheap (and even if it's not), never take anything just at face value - check everything you can about the car yourself. Getting your hands on a really good sporty Clio is not a simple task - dodgy dealers (and owners!) know there's a market for repaired write-offs and stolen cars ('ringers'), and gullible private punters get ripped every day.

More so than any other model, check for signs of accident damage, especially at the front end. Ask if it's ever been in a shunt - if the seller says no, but there's paint overspray under the bonnet, what's going on? Also check for paint overspray on the window rubbers, light units and bumpers/trim. With the bonnet open, check that the headlight rear shells are the same colour - mis-matched or new-looking ones merit an explanation from the seller. Does the front number plate carry details of the supplying garage, like the back one? If not, why has a new plate been fitted?

Check the glass (and even the head and tail lights) for etched-in registration numbers - are they all the same, and does it match the car's actual registration? A windscreen could've been replaced for any number of innocent reasons, but new side glass indicates a break-in at least - is the car a 'stolen/recovered' (joyridden) example? Find the chassis and engine numbers, as described earlier in this Section, and satisfy yourself that they are genuine - check them against the "logbook" (registration document). An HPI check (or similar) could be well worthwhile, but even this won't tell you everything. If you're at all suspicious, or if the answers to your questions don't ring true, then walk away. Make any excuse you like.

The sporty models tend to get driven hard, and while they're better able to take this than some cars, hard driving will take its toll somewhere. The suspension should feel quite stiff and taut - any sogginess is usually caused by worn shock absorbers (not a problem, if you're fitting a full lowering kit, but use it to haggle the price down). Any vibration or juddering through the steering when braking indicates serious brake wear (warped brake discs), or possibly, play in the suspension/steering joints (fitting a lowering kit will not cure this kind of play, which also eats front tyres!).

It's still worth a bit of insurance discount if an approved (Thatcham Cat 1 or 2) alarm or immobiliser is fitted, and you might find it's an essential fitment, just to get any kind of quote. Make sure that any alarm actually works, that it looks properly installed, with no stray wires hanging out, and that you get the Thatcham certificate or other paperwork to go with it. If the seller fitted it, it's worth finding out exactly how it's been wired in - if it goes wrong later, you could be stranded with no chance of disabling the system to get you home.

Sealing the deal

Everything as expected and the car's just what you want? It's time to start haggling. Never just agree to hand over the full advertised price for the car, but don't be too ambitious, either (it's best to stay friendly at this point - winding-up the owner is the last thing you need). If the ad says "o.n.o.", expect at least 10% off - if not, why bother putting it on the ad? Try a low offer to test the owner's reaction (they can only say no!) then reluctantly increase the offer until you're both happy. Haggling can also include other considerations besides cash - will the owner chuck in the nice stereo and wheels, leave the tax on, or put a new MOT ("ticket") on it?

Bagged a bargain? Sorted! Offer to leave a deposit (this shows you're serious), but before parting with any more cash, it may be worth considering the following.

Ask for time to get in touch with the previous owner shown on the "logbook" (registration document). If you can speak to them, it's a useful exercise in confirming the car's history and mileage.

A wise thing to do is to run a vehicle check on the car with an organisation such as HPI Autodata or the AA. It'll cost you (usually around the 30-quid mark) but could save a lot of hassle in future. They'll need the details of all the identification numbers on the vehicle and documents, as well as the mileage etc. For your money, they'll run the details of the car through their computer database. This database contains the records of all vehicles reported stolen, which have been total losses (ie. have been totalled after a serious accident) or have outstanding finance against them. They can then confirm over the phone the vehicle is straight, and in theory you can proceed with the deal, safe in the knowledge you're not about to purchase a ringer. Not only will you receive a nice certificate through the post with your vehicle details on it, but running the check also gives you financial insurance. The information given is guaranteed (usually to the tune of about ten grand) so if Plod turns up on your doorstep a month later, demanding you return your new vehicle to its rightful owner, you should be able to claim your cash back. No worries.

Tricks 'n' tips

If your understanding of the mechanical workings of the modern automobile is a bit vague and you want a second opinion, it may also be worth considering having the vehicle inspected. The AA and RAC offer this service, but there may be other people in your area too - check in the Yellow Pages. This is a bit pricier than the vehicle check, but will give you peace of mind and some comeback should things not be as expected. If you've got a friendly garage, maybe they could be persuaded to check the car over for a small fee.

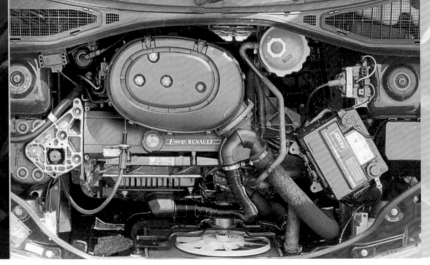

Like many small-car ranges in recent years, the number of "special edition" models offered in the Clio's history has been enormous. The models listed below are a representative selection - to have listed them all would've taken half the book! Don't pay over the odds for a special edition, unless it's genuinely got some extra kit you're interested in having - most are just the 1.2 base model with a sunroof and stickers.

March 1991 (H reg) - Clio "Phase 1" range introduced. 1.2, 1.4 and 1.8 litre "Energy" petrol engines, 1.9 diesel. 1.2 RL models have 4-speed gearbox, RN has 5-speed, tints, sunroof. 1.4/1.8 RT has electric windows, remote locking, rev counter (1.8 available as 5-door only).

May 1991 (H reg) - 1.4 Baccara auto introduced, based on 1.4 RT with luxury trim (leather seats, wood veneer dash, electric mirrors, etc).

July 1991 (H reg) - 1.4 RN models available.

November 1991 (J reg) - 1.8 16V model introduced, with 137 bhp engine. Flared front and rear arches, bonnet power bulge, deep front bumper with front fogs, rear roof spoiler, turbo-vane alloys, sports interior, electric windows/mirrors, remote locking, alarm/immobiliser. 1.4 S model introduced - similar spec to 1.4 RN, but with green bumper inserts, white steel wheels, rear roof spoiler, sports seats and rev counter.

February 1992 (J reg) - Fidji 1.4 limited edition available. Red, white or blue, sunroof, tints, blue bumper inserts.

October 1992 (K reg) - Minor changes: 1.2 RL now known as RL Prima. Models above RL gain tilt/slide sunroof (electric on Baccara and 16V). Fidji 1.2 limited edition available. 1.4 S model discontinued.

April 1993 (K reg) - 1.8 RSi model introduced. 110 bhp engine, front and rear discs, bodykit, alloys, sports interior, electric windows, remote locking.

May 1993 (K reg) - Liberté 1.2 limited edition available (5-door only). Blue/green seat trim (nice!)

July 1993 (K reg) - Oasis 1.2 limited edition available (3/5-door) - tints, sunroof.

November 1993 (L reg) - Clio Williams limited edition introduced - 2.0 litre 150 bhp engine, metallic blue with gold 15-inch alloys, gold "Williams" graphics, otherwise similar to 16V model. Production run of 400, numbered plaque on dash. 1.4 RT models now have power steering.

March 1994 (L reg) - Phase 2 facelift introduced. New front grille, dark tinted rear lights, black tailgate lower trim panel, side impact bars and seat belt tensioners. 1.2 RN models gain power steering. 1.4 RT gains 16V-style dash, with wider instrument pod. 16V models have new rounded five-spoke alloys. 1.8 Baccara introduced (5-door only), replacing 1.4 - 90 bhp, automatic.

June 1994 (L reg) - Be Bop 1.2 special edition introduced. 5-speed gearbox, tints, sunroof.

September 1994 (M reg) - Clio Williams 2 special edition introduced. Driver's airbag standard on 1.4 RT, RSi and 16V.

December 1994 (M reg) - Les Routiers 1.2 limited edition available. 5-speed gearbox, tints, sunroof.

Model history

March 1995 (M reg) - Champs Elysees 1.4 limited edition available. Based on 1.4 RT, with alloys and CD player (Group 6 insurance).

August 1995 (N reg) - Clio Williams 3 special edition introduced, as previous Williams, but with ABS (300 RHD). Oasis limited edition re-introduced. 5-speed gearbox, tints, sunroof.

January 1996 (N reg) - RL Paris, RL Oasis and RL Versailles limited editions introduced.

May 1996 (N reg) - Phase 3 facelift introduced. New front-end treatment with rounder lights, new bumpers, high-level brake light. New steering wheel, interior revisions. 5-speed gearbox and driver's airbag standard across the range. New 1.2 litre engine with multi-point injection (still 60 bhp). 1.4 litre models reduced to 75 bhp, RT models gain body-colour bumpers and mirrors. RSi gains alarm/immobiliser, 16V-style dash with extra gauges. 16V model no longer available.

June 1996 (N reg) - 1.2 RN Club Med limited edition available.

October 1996 (P reg) - 1.4 S Maxim limited edition available, with alloys, tints, roof spoiler, front fogs, electric windows and remote locking (Group 5 insurance).

January 1997 (P reg) - Baccara replaced by 1.8 Initiale - similar spec, with leather interior, twin airbags, 110 bhp with automatic gearbox.

April 1997 (P reg) - 1.2 Zoom limited edition available, with "Easy" semi-automatic gearbox.

May 1997 (P reg) - 1.2 Provence limited edition available. Body-coloured bumpers, remote locking, sunroof, immobiliser.

June 1997 (P reg) - 1.2 Panache limited edition available. Remote locking, tints, sunroof, immobiliser.

October 1997 (R reg) - 1.4 Sport introduced, with alloys, front fogs, roof spoiler, sports seats, electric windows (Group 5 insurance). 1.2 Biarritz limited edition available. Body-coloured bumpers, remote locking, sunroof, immobiliser.

May 1998 (R reg) - Replaced by 2nd generation Clio.

Performance figures

	0-60 (sec)	Top speed (mph)
1.2	14.7	96
1.4	10.5	104
1.8 RT	10.1	108
1.8 RSi	9.3	117
16V	7.8	126
Williams	7.4	130
1.9 Diesel	13.6	101 (Hmm... not that slow, then)

Insurance
A necessary evil

Ah, insurance - an awful lot of money, for a piece of paper you're not really supposed to use! Of course, you MUST have insurance - you're illegal on the road without it, and you won't be able to get the car taxed, either. If you drive without insurance and are caught, you may have great trouble EVER getting an insurance quote again - the insurance companies seem to regard this offence nearly as seriously as drink-driving on your record, so don't do it!

The way the insurance companies work out premiums and assess risks is a mystery to most of us. In general, the smaller the engine you have in your Clio, the less you'll pay for insurance, so hopefully, a Clio 1.2 will be lots less to insure than a "Valver". However, it's possible that, if one company has had a lot of claims on Clios in the past, the Clio 16V factor might 'unfairly' influence the premiums of lesser Clios, too (this is why it's important to shop around). An 'insurance-friendly' 1.4 RT should be a good bet for a sensible premium, but remember that insurance companies aren't stupid - if you turn your RT into a 16V-lookalike, they may well 'load' the premium to nearly 16V level, because the potential car-thief might not spot that it's not actually a hot Clio when parked up at night.

If your annual premium seems like the national debt of a small African country (and whose isn't!), always ring as many brokers and get as many quotes as you possibly can. Yes, there's loads better ways to spend an evening/afternoon than answering the SAME twenty questions over and over again, but you never know what the next quote will be. A few extra minutes spent on the phone (or on the 'net) once a year may result in an extra few hundred quid in your back pocket. Well, you live in hope don't you!

With modified cars, insurance becomes even more of a problem. By putting on all the alloys, trick body kits, nice interiors, big ICE, you're making the car much more of a target for thieves (yes, ok, I know you know this). The point is, the insurance companies know this too, and they don't want to be paying out for the car, plus all the money you've spent on it, should it go missing. There is a

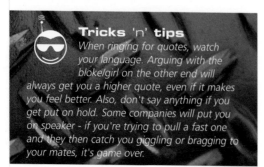

Tricks 'n' tips
When ringing for quotes, watch your language. Arguing with the bloke/girl on the other end will always get you a higher quote, even if it makes you feel better. Also, don't say anything if you get put on hold. Some companies will put you on speaker - if you're trying to pull a fast one and they then catch you giggling or bragging to your mates, it's game over.

temptation 'not to tell the insurance' about the mods you've made. Let's deal with this right now. Our experience has been that, while it can be painful, honesty is best. Generally, the insurance company line is: "...thanks for telling us - we won't put the car 'up a group' (ie charge you more), but we also won't cover the extra cost of your alloy wheels/body kit/tasty seats in the event of any claim...". This is fair enough - in other words, if your car goes missing, you get paid out, based on a standard car, minus all the goodies. If you particularly want all the extras covered, you might have a long hard search - most companies (IF they'll offer you cover at all) will only offer "modified for standard" policies. There are specialist insurers who are more friendly towards fully-loaded cars, but even they won't actually cover the cost of replacement goodies.

What type of cover, Sir?

For most of us, cost means there's only one option - TPF&T (third party, fire and theft). Fully-comp insurance is an unattainable dream for most people until they reach the "magic" age of 25, but what's the real story?

Third Party only

The most basic cover you can get. Basically covers you for damage to other people's cars or property, and for personal injury claims. Virtually no cover for your own stuff, beyond what you get if you take the optional "legal protection" cover.

Third Party, Fire and Theft

As above, with cover for fire and theft, of course! Better, but not much better. This is really only cover in the event of a "total loss", if your car goes missing or goes up in smoke. Still no cover for your car if you stack it into a tree, or if someone breaks in and pinches your stereo (check your policy small-print).

Fully-comprehensive

In theory at least, covers you for any loss or damage. Will cover the cost of repairing or replacing your car, often with discounted windscreen cover and other benefits. If you lose control of the car on an icy road (arguably, not your fault) you get paid. If someone pinches your wheels and drops the car on the floor, you get paid - at least for the damage done to the underside, and for standard wheels and tyres. Most policies include provision of a hire car after a shunt, which is pretty useful. Some offer cheap breakdown cover packages in with the main policy. With a fully-comp policy, you can "protect" your no-claims bonus for a small fee so you don't automatically lose all those hard-earned years' worth of discount if you prang it (generally, you can ONLY do this on fully-comp).

All this extra cover costs, obviously, but how much? You might be surprised what the actual difference is (IF they'll quote you). Think about it, anyway - it's got to be worth a couple of hundred quid more to go fully-comp, if your car's worth into four figures, surely?

Valuing your car

When your insurance pays out in the event of a total loss or write-off, they base their offer on the current market value of an identical standard model to yours. The only way you'll get more than the average amount is to prove your Clio is in above-average nick (with photos?) or that the mileage was especially low for the year.

With this in mind, don't bother over-valuing your Clio in the hope you'll get more in the event of a claim - you won't! The only way to do this is to seek out an "agreed-value" deal, which you can usually only get on classic-car policies (with these, the car's value is agreed in advance between you, not worked out later by the company with you having no say in it). By over-valuing your Clio, you could be increasing your premium without gaining any benefit - sound smart to you?

Equally though, don't under-value, in the hope you'll get a reduction in premium. You won't, and if there's a total loss claim, you won't get any more than your under-valued amount, no matter how loudly you complain.

Work on what you paid for the car, backed up with the sort of prices you see for similar cars in the ads (or use a secondhand car price guide). Add no more than 10% for the sake of optimism, and that's it.

YOUR car? Or your Dad's?

Insurance really costs when you're the wrong side of twenty-five. Ever been tempted to tell your insurance that your full-on sorted Clio belongs to your Dad (old insurance-friendly person), then get him to insure it, with you as a named driver? Oh dear. This idea (known as "fronting") is so old, it's grown a long white beard. And it sucks, too. First of all, insurance companies aren't stupid. They know your Dad (or your Mum, or old Uncle Bert) isn't likely to be running around in a kid's pocket-rocket, and they treat any "named driver" application with great suspicion. Even if they do take your money, don't imagine they've been suckered. In the event of a claim, they'll look into everything very carefully, and will ask lots of awkward questions. If you get caught out in the lie, they've taken your money, and you've got no insurance - who's been suckered now?

This dubious practice also does you no favours in future years. All the time you're living the lie, you're not building up any no-claims bonus of your own - you're just delaying the pain 'til later, and without having real cover in the meantime.

"Legit" ways to limit your premium

If you do enough ringing around for quotes, you'll soon learn what the "right answers" to some of the questions are - even if you can't actually give them (but, as we've already said, DON'T tell lies to your insurance company). Mind you, with a little thought, you can start to play their game and win - try these:

Limit your mileage. Most companies offer a small discount if you only cover a small annual mileage. To get any meaningful reduction, the mileage has to be less than 10,000 per year. Few companies, though, ever ask what the car's current mileage is - so how are they gonna know if you've gone over your self-imposed limit?

Volunteer to increase your excess. The "excess" is put there to stop people claiming for piddling little amounts - when they pay out, it's always the repair/replacement cost MINUS whatever the "excess" is. So, for instance, if you've got a £200 theft excess, it means you'll automatically get £200 less than the agreed value of your car, should it be stolen. Most policies have "compulsory" excess amounts, which you can do nothing about. By increasing excesses voluntarily, you're limiting the amount you'll get still further. Insurance companies like this, and should reduce your premium in return - but this only goes so far, so ask what the effect of different voluntary excesses will be. Don't increase your excess too far, or you'll get paid nowt if you claim!

Make yourself the only driver. Pretty self-explanatory. The more people who drive your car, the greater the risk to the compan, and a car's owner will always drive more carefully (it's their money that bought it) than any named driver. If you've built up 2 years' worth of no-claims, but your partner hasn't, putting them on your insurance will bump it up, due to their relative inexperience

Get a garage - and use it. Where you park can have a big effect on your premium. Parking it on the street is the worst. Park off the road (on a driveway) when you're at home. The best thing is to have a garage of your own (don't pretend you use your Dad's garage) - see if you can rent one locally, even if it means walking a few hundred yards. If you're a student living away from home, tell your company where the car will be parked during term-time - if you're at Uni in London, this is a bigger risk than living at home "in the country", and vice-versa.

Fit an approved alarm or immobiliser. See if you can get a list from your company of all their approved security devices, and fit whatever you can afford. Not all companies approve the same kit, so it might even be worth contacting more than one company for advice. Any device with a Thatcham or Sold Secure rating should be recognised. In some cases, the discounts offered are not that great any more - but an alarm is still a nice way to get peace of mind. Most Clios from mid-1993 had a Renault RAPS immobiliser as standard.

Build up your no-claims bonus. You'll only do this by owning and insuring a car in your own name, and then not making any claims. Simple really. One rather immoral (but not actually illegal) dodge is to buy an old banger, insure it cheap, then never drive it. You'll need to keep it fully road-legal (with tax, MOT) if you park it on the road. For every year you do this, you'll build up another year of NCB.

Hang onto your no-claims bonus. Obviously, the less you claim, the less your insurance will cost. If something happens to your car, don't be in too big a hurry to make a claim before you've thought it all through. How much will it cost to fix? How much is your excess? How much will your renewal premium be, next year? If you have a big enough accident which you're sure isn't your fault, ring your company, but make it quite clear you're NOT claiming yet - just informing them of the accident. It should be down to the other driver's insurance to pay. You don't always lose all your no-claims, either, even if it was your fault - depends how many years you've built up. Once you've got a few years, ask whether you can "protect" your no-claims.

Avoid speed cameras and The Law. Yes, okay, easier said than done! But anything less than a clean licence is not good from the insurance perspective. One SP30 won't hurt much, but the second strike will, so take it easy. Don't get caught on traffic-light cameras, either - a major no-no.

Insurance-friendly mods?

Insurers don't like any changes from standard, but some things you'll do are worse from their viewpoint than others. The guidelines below are just that - for guidance. No two companies will have the same outlook, and your own circumstances will play a big part too.

Golden Rule Number One: Before you spend huge money modifying the car, ring your insurance, and ask them how it will affect things.

Golden Rule Number Two: If in doubt, declare everything. Insurance companies are legally entitled to dispute any claim if the car is found to be non-standard in any way.

Body mods - Even a tiny rear spoiler could be classed as a "bodykit" (yes, it's daft, but that's how it is). Anything which alters the exterior appearance should be declared. As long as the mods don't include a radical full-on bodykit, the jump in premium should be fairly small.

Brakes - The companies view brake mods as tampering with safety-related kit, and modifying the brakes implies that you drive fast and hard. You might get away will standard-sized grooved/drilled discs and pads, but fitting bigger discs and replacement calipers will prove expensive.

Engine mods - "Mild" mods, such as induction kits and exhausts don't give much more power, so don't generally hurt. But "chipping" your Clio will lead to drastic rises in premiums, or a complete refusal of cover. With complete engine transplants, you'll be required to give an engineer's report, and to get your wad out.

Interior mods - Don't assume that tarting up the inside won't interest the insurance company. By making any part of the car more attractive, you're also attracting the crims. Cars get trashed for parts, as often as not - and your racing seats and sexy steering wheel could be worth major money. Still, the effect on premiums shouldn't be too great, especially if you've got an alarm/immobiliser.

Lights - Change the car's appearance, and are safety-related. You'll probably get asked for lots of details, but as long as you've kept it sensible (and legal, as far as possible), the effect on your wallet shouldn't be too harsh.

Security - Make sure you mention all security stuff - alarms, immobilisers (including mechanical devices), locking wheel nuts, large Alsatian in the back seat... But - don't over-sell the car. Tell the truth, in other words. If you've got a steering wheel lock, do you always fit it? If you didn't when your car went missing, you're in trouble. Don't say you've got a Cat 1 alarm if it really came from Argos, and don't tell them you garage the car at night if it's stuck out in the road.

Suspension - Changes the car's appearance, and is safety-related. Some enlightened companies once took the view that modded suspension helps the car corner better, so it's safer. Drops of 30 to 40 mm shouldn't mean bigger premiums.

Wheels - Very appearance-altering, and very nickable. At least show some responsibility by fitting some locking nuts/bolts and an approved alarm/immobiliser. Quite likely to attract a low-to-moderate rise in premium, which still won't cover your wheels properly - you could arrange separate cover for your wheels, then at least you'll get paid. Some companies ask for a photo of the car with the wheels on.

And finally - a new nightmare

Not telling the insurance the whole truth gets a little tricky when you make a claim. If the insurance assessor comes to check your bent/burnt/stolen-and-recovered "standard" Clio, and finds he's looking at a vehicle fitted with trick alloys/bodykit/radical interior, he's not going to turn a blind eye. Has the car got an MOT? Oh, and did you declare those points on your licence? No? You're then very much at the mercy of your insurer, especially if they can prove any mods contributed to the claim. At best, you'll have a long-drawn-out battle with your insurer to get a part-payout, and at worst they'll just refuse to get involved at all.

One more thing - *be careful what you hit.* If your insurance is declared void, they won't pay out for the repairs to the other car you smacked into, or for the lamp-post you knock down (several hundred quid, actually). And then there's the personal injury claims - if your insurance company disowns you, it'll be you who has to foot the bill. Even sprains and bruises can warrant claims, and more serious injuries can result in claims running into lots of zeroes! Without insurance cover, **you'll** have to pay. Probably for a long, long time. Think about it, and we won't see you in court.

Security

Lock me or lose me

It's a sad fact, but making your car attractive to the opposite sex also tends to attract attention of a less-welcome kind, from less-than-human pond life.

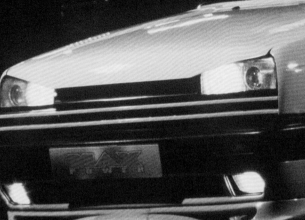

Avoiding trouble

You're modifying your car to look cool and to be seen in. No problem - but be careful where you choose to show your car off, and who to. Be more discreet, the nearer you get to home - *turn your system down* before you turn into your road, for instance, or you'll draw attention to where that car with the loud stereo's parked at night.

Without being too paranoid, watch for anyone following you home. At night, if the car behind switches its lights off, be worried. If you

suspect this is happening, do not drive home - choose well-lit public places until they give up. Believe us - it happens.

If you're going out, think about where you're parking - well-lit and well-populated is good. Thieves hate light being on them, so don't make it easy by parking somewhere dark - think about this if you park up in daylight, knowing you won't be back 'til late.

Hands up, who doesn't lock their car when they get petrol?. Your insurance company has a term for this, and it's "contributory negligence". In English, this means you won't get a penny if your car goes missing when you haven't locked it.

If you're lucky enough to have a garage, use it. On up-and-over garage doors, fit extra security like a padlock and ground anchor.

A clever thief will watch your movements and habits over several days before trying your car. Has it got an alarm, and do you always set it? Do you only fit your steering wheel lock when you feel like it? Do you always park in the same place, and is the car hidden from the house or from the road? Don't make his life easier. Ask yourself how YOU'D nick your car…

A word about your stereo

From the moment you bolt on those nice alloys, it's taken as read that you've also got stereo gear that's worth nicking - and the thieves know it. All the discreet installation in the world isn't going to deter them from finding out what's inside that nice motor.

Please don't advertise your love of ICE around your car. Your nice stereo gear will fit other cars too, and can be ripped out in nothing flat. You may be very proud of your ICE install, but nothing is more of an "invite" than a huge ICE sticker or sunstrip. If you've fitted one just to look cool, replace it now with something less provocative - seriously. Your set might not actually be very expensive, but you could still lose a side window for advertising something better.

You'll have got a CD player, obviously, but don't leave discs or empty CD cases lying around inside the car. A nice pair of 6x9s in full view on the back shelf is an invite to having your rear window smashed - stealth shelf, anyone? When you're fitting your system, give some thought to the clues you could accidentally leave in plain view. Oxygen-free speaker cable is great stuff, but it's also a bit bright against dark carpets, and is all the clue necessary that you're serious about your speakers. Hide amps and CD changers under your front seats.

Most modern sets are face-off or MASK, so if they've got security features like this, use them - take your faceplate off when you leave the car, and take it with you rather than leaving it in the door pocket or glovebox (the first places a thief will look).

Things that go beep in the night

Don't skimp on an alarm, it may never even be put to the test, but if it is, you'll be glad you spent wisely …

The first step to car security is to fake it. Tacky *"This car has an alarm"* stickers won't fool anyone, but why not just fit a flashing LED? We know it's not the real thing, but … An LED is cheap to buy and easy to fit, and can be rigged to a discreet switch inside the car.

Don't overlook the value of so-called "manual" immobilisers, such as steering wheel locking bars and gear-to-handbrake lever locks. These are a worthwhile deterrent - a thief not specifically after your car may move on to an easier target. Some items may be "Sold Secure" or Thatcham Cat 3, which means they've withstood a full-on brute force attack for a useful length of time.

The only way to combat the more determined thief is to go for a well-specified and intelligently-installed alarm. Immobilisers alone have their place, but sadly, even a pro-fitted immobiliser on its own won't stop someone pinching your wheels, or having it away with the stereo gear. Neither, incidentally, will a cheap alarm - you have to know how the thieves operate to stand any chance defeating them. Any alarm you fit yourself probably won't gain you any insurance discount, but it will give you peace of mind, and DIY means you can do a real trick installation, to make it very hard work for the gyppos.

Finally, one other scam to be aware of. If your alarm is suddenly going off a lot at night, when previously it had been well-behaved, don't ignore it. It's an old trick for a thief to deliberately set off your alarm several times, each time hiding round the corner when you come out to investigate, then to wait until the fifth or sixth time when you don't reset it (in disgust), leaving him a clear run. If your alarm does keep false-alarming without outside assistance, find out the cause quickly, or your neighbours will quickly become "deaf" to it.

Thatcham categories and meanings:

1 **Cat 1.** For alarms and electronic immobilisers.

2 **Cat 2.** For electronic immobilisers only.

3 **Cat 2-1.** Electronic immobilisers which can be upgraded to Cat 1 alarms later.

4 **Cat 3.** Mechanical immobilisers, eg snap-off steering wheels, locking wheel bolts, window film, steering wheel locks/covers.

5 **Q-class.** Tracking devices.

Other alarm features

Two-stage anti-shock - means that the alarm shouldn't go off, just because the neighbour's cat jumps on your car roof, or because Little Johnny punts his football into your car. Alarm will only sound after a major shock, or after repeated shocks are detected.

Anti-tilt - detects any attempt to lift or jack up the car, preventing any attempt to pinch alloys. Very unpopular with thieves, as it makes the alarm very sensitive (much more so than anti-shock). Alarm may sound if car is parked outside in stormy conditions (but not if your suspension's rock-hard!).

Anti-hijack - immobiliser with built-in delay. If your motor gets hijacked, the neanderthals responsible will only get so far down the road before the engine cuts out.

Rolling code - reduces the chance of your alarm remote control signal from being "grabbed" by special electronic equipment.

Total closure - module which connects to electric windows/sunroof and central locking, which closes all items when alarm is set. Alarms like this often have other nifty features such as remote boot opening.

Pager control - yes, really - your alarm can be set to send a message to your pager (why not your mobile?) if your car gets tampered with.

Current-sensing disable - very useful feature on some cars which have a cooling fan which can cut in after the ignition is switched off. Without this feature, your alarm will be triggered every time you leave it parked after a long run - very annoying.

Volumetric-sensing disable - basically allows you to manually disable the interior ultrasonics, leaving the rest of the alarm features active. Useful if you want to leave the sunroof open in hot weather - if a fly gets in the car, the alarm would otherwise be going off constantly.

Talking alarms - no, please, please no. Very annoying, and all that'll happen is you'll attract crowds of kids daring each other to set it off again. Unfortunately, these are becoming more popular, with some offering the facility to record your own message!

The knowledge

What people often fail to realise (at least, until it happens to them) is the level of violence and destruction which thieves will employ to get your stuff - this goes way beyond breaking a window.

It comes as a major shock to most people when they discover the serious kinds of tools (weapons) at many professional thieves' disposal, and how brutally your lovingly-polished car will be attacked. Many people think, for instance, that it's their whole car they're after, whereas it's really only the parts they want, and they don't care how they get them (this means that these parts are still attractive, even when fitted to a basic car which has yet to be fully modded). Obviously, taking the whole car then gives the option of hiding it to strip at leisure, but it won't always be the option chosen, and you could wake up one morning to a well-mangled wreck outside.

Attack 1 The first option to any thief is to smash glass - typically, the toughened-glass side windows, which will shatter, unlike the windscreen. Unfortunately for the thief, this makes a loud noise (not good), but is a quick and easy way in. The reason for taking this approach is that a basic car alarm will only go off if the doors are opened (voltage-drop alarm) - provided the doors aren't opened, the alarm won't go off.

Response 1 A more sophisticated alarm will feature shock sensing (which will be set off by the impact on the glass), and better still, ultrasonic sensing, which will be triggered by the brick coming in through the broken window.

Response 2 This kind of attack can also be stopped by applying security film to the inside of the glass, which holds it all together and prevents easy entry.

Attack 2 An alternative to smashing the glass is to pry open the door using a crowbar - this attack involves literally folding open the door's window frame by prising from the top corner. The glass will still shatter, but as long as the door stays shut, a voltage-drop alarm won't be triggered.

Response This method might not be defeated by a shock-sensing alarm, but an ultrasonic unit would pick it up.

Incidentally, another bonus with ultrasonic alarms is that the sensors are visible from outside - and act as a deterrent.

Attack 3 The next line of attack is to disable the alarm. The commonest way to kill the alarm is either to cut the wiring to the alarm itself, or to disconnect the battery, "safely" hidden away under the bonnet. And just how strong is a bonnet? Not strong enough to resist being crowbarred open, which is exactly what happens.

Response 1 If your alarm has extra pin-switches, be sure to fit one to the bonnet, and fit it in the bonnet channel next to the battery, so that it'll set off the alarm if the bonnet is prised up. Also make sure that the wire to the pin-switch cannot be cut easily though a partly-open bonnet.

Response 2 Make sure that the alarm module is well-hidden, and cannot be got at from underneath the car.

Response 3 Make the alarm power supply connection somewhere less obvious than directly at the battery terminal - any thief who knows his stuff will immediately cut any "spare" red wires at the battery. Try taking power from the fusebox, or if you must source it under the bonnet, trace the large red battery lead to the starter motor connections, and tap into the power there.

Response 4 Always disguise the new alarm wiring, by using black insulating tape to wrap it to the existing wiring loom. Tidying up in this way also helps to ensure the wires can't get trapped, cut, melted, or accidentally ripped out - any of which could leave you with an alarm siren which won't switch off, or an immobiliser you can't disable.

Response 5 An alarm which has a "battery back-up" facility is a real kiss of death to the average thief's chances. Even if he's successfully crow-barred your bonnet and snipped the battery connections, the alarm will still go off, powered by a separate battery of its own. A Cat 1 alarm has to have battery back-up.

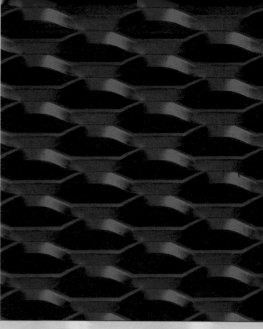

Fitting a basic LED

All you need for this is a permanent live feed, an earth, a switch if you want to be able to turn it on/off, and the flashing LED itself (very cheap, from any car accessory shop).

An LED draws very little current, so you'll be quite safe tapping into almost any live feed you fancy. If you've wired in your ICE, take a live feed from the permanent (radio memory supply) wire at the back of your head unit, or have a delve into the back of the fusebox with your test light (as featured in the full alarm fitting procedure, further on). An earth can easily be tapped again from your head unit, or you can make one almost anywhere on the metal body of the car, by drilling a small hole, fitting a self-tapping screw, then wrapping the bared end of wire around and tightening it.

The best and easiest place to mount an LED is into one of the many blank switches the makers seem to love fitting. The blank switch is easily pried out, and a hole can then be drilled to take the LED (which usually comes in a separate little holder). Feed the LED wiring down behind the dashboard to where you've tapped your live and earth, taking care not to trap it anywhere, nor to accidentally wrap it around any moving parts.

Connect your live to the LED red wire, then rig your earth to one side of the switch, and connect the LED black wire to the other switch terminal. You should now have a switchable LED! Tidy up the wiring, and mount the switch somewhere discreet, but where you can still get at it. Switch on when you leave the car, and it looks as if you've got some sort of alarm - better than nothing!

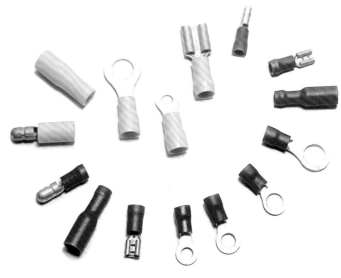

Wiring
basics

With your wires identified, how to tap into them? Before we even get that far, is that wire you're planning on playing with live?

Switch off the ignition at least - and ideally disconnect the battery before you do anything else. On cars with airbags, don't go tapping into any of the airbag wiring, which is usually bright yellow. With that cleared up, how were you planning on joining the old and new wires together? Here's our advice:

The best options are:

Soldering - avoids cutting through your chosen wire - strip away a short section of insulation, wrap your new wire around the bared section, then apply solder to secure it. If you're a bit new to soldering, practice on a few offcuts of wire first - it ain't rocket science! Re-insulate the soldered connection afterwards, with tape.

Bullet connectors - cut and strip the end of your chosen wire, wrap your new one to it, push both into one half of the bullet. Connect the other end of your victim wire to the other bullet, and connect together. Always use the "female" half on any live feed - it'll be safer if you disconnect it than a male bullet, which could touch bare metal and send your motor up in smoke.

Block connectors - so easy to use. Just remember that the wires can come adrift if the screws aren't really tight, and don't get too ambitious about how many wires you can stuff in one hole (block connectors, like bullets, are available in several sizes). Steer clear of connectors like the one below - they're convenient, but they can give rise to problems.

With any of these options, always insulate around your connection - especially when soldering, or you'll be leaving bare metal exposed. Remember that you'll probably be shoving all the wires up into the dark recesses of the under-dash area - by the time the wires are nice and kinked/squashed together, that tiny bit of protruding wire might just touch that bit of metal bodywork, and that'll be a fire...

Fitting an **auxiliary fusebox**

You'll need plenty of fused live feeds from the battery during the modifying process, for stereo gear, neons, starter buttons - and alarms, and it's always a pain working out where to tap into one. If you make up your own little fusebox, mounted somewhere easy to get at, you'll never have this problem again - and it's easy enough to do.

01 Okay, so you've got your large live wire into the car - where to put the fusebox? Our fusebox, by the way, came from our local Lucas store - but you could go for an ICE distribution block. It's got to be accessible, and if we can make it look good, better still - ours is going behind the left-hand sill trim panel, which just unclips at the front. Now there's two huge wiring plugs in the way. On our car, they weren't connected, so they were unclipped and stashed.

02 With the unrequired plugs out of the picture, it's time for the first trial fitting. The idea is to eventually have the fusebox cover sticking out through a hole we'll cut later, in the sill trim panel. The black plastic you can see behind the fusebox was trimmed back . . .

The first job is to run a main supply cable from the battery positive terminal, to inside the car - but don't connect the wire up to the battery terminal just yet. Make sure that the main cable is man enough for all the loads you're likely to put on it - starting with four-gauge wire (available from all good ICE suppliers) will mean you're never short of amps. As for where to feed the cable through, see the section on fitting an alarm (next in this section) or the ICE chapter for some good spots for a hole.

Make a note of which fuse is for which circuit, and carry the paper around in the glovebox (along with some spare fuses). If a fuse ever blows, you won't end up with your head stuck under the dash, trying to remember where you tapped in, and where the fuse is. You'll just pull the cover off, and replace the fuse. Who would've thought electrical safety could be so cool?

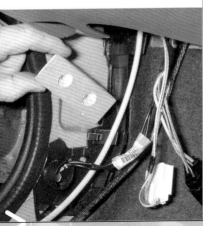

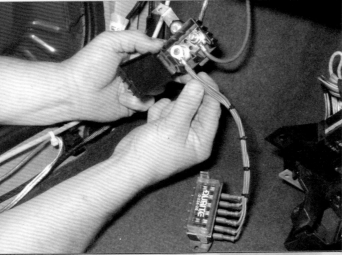

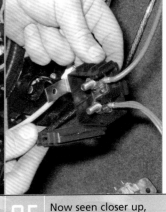

03 . . . to make way for a mounting block, which we lovingly fashioned out of a scrap piece of MDF, for screwing into place.

04 And this is what the other part of our cunning plan looks like. It's a junction box, which takes in the 4-gauge live feed on one terminal, and then splits it off into several feeds for our fusebox - we've done all six here.

05 Now seen closer up, we screwed on a small mounting bracket, so's the junction box can be stowed up under the dash. This little fella has a hinged plastic cover, which must be clipped over the two live terminals for fairly obvious reasons...

Achtung!
MDF dust is nasty stuff to breathe in. Wear a mask when you're cutting, drilling or sanding it.

06 With the junction box in place, it's the turn of the fusebox, which is just a drill-and-screw job.

07 Now for the slightly scary bit - cutting the sill trim panel. Get this wrong, and it's gonna be very obvious - so take your time. All you can really do is mark a rough outline of the fusebox on the panel . . .

08 . . . then get out the Stanley knife, and hope for a result as good as this - not bad for a first effort. A tip is to make the hole slightly smaller than you really want, first time, then try it for fit - you can always make a small hole (that's slightly out) bigger, after all. Fit the right-size fuse for whatever you're connecting up, and you're there.

Alarm fitting

Security

The alarm we've chosen to fit is a MicroScan, which, whilst it isn't a Clifford, still offers a decent level of protection, and a useful array of features for a sensible price. When it goes off, it actually sounds like a Clifford - result!

As with everything else in this book, remember that we're showing you just how this *particular* alarm is fitted. All the same, whatever alarm you fit, it'll still be useful to pick out the fitting principles and tips. Always refer to the instructions which come with your alarm, and don't go joining the red wire to the yellow wire, just because WE say so...

01 Disconnect the battery negative lead, and move the lead away from the battery, or you'll be blowing fuses and your new alarm will go mental the minute it's rigged up.

02 Decide where you're going to mount the alarm/siren. Choose somewhere not easily reached from underneath, for a start, and if you can, pick a location away from where you'll be topping up washers, oil or coolant - fluids and alarm modules don't mix. However, the most suitable spot on our Clio was next to the coolant bottle. Tough. To make fitting the module a bit easier, we unhooked the bottle's rubber mounting strap . . .

03 . . . and moved the bottle to one side. There's no need to go ripping off any coolant hoses, luckily.

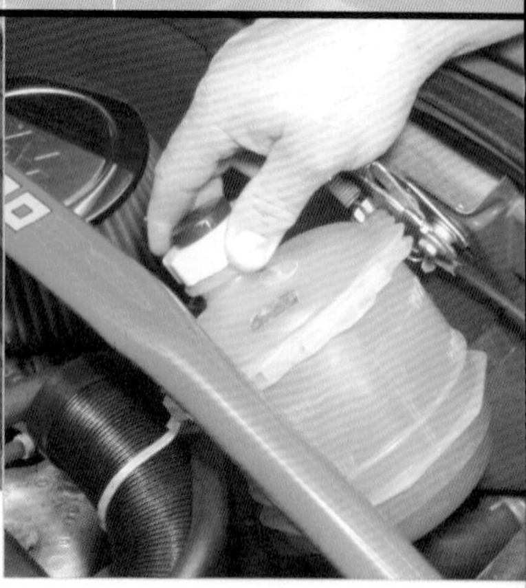

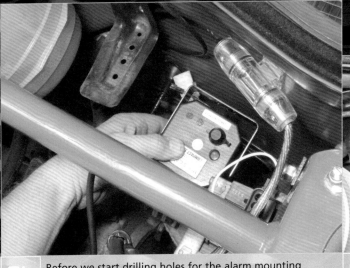
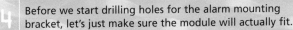

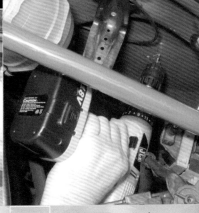

> **04** Before we start drilling holes for the alarm mounting bracket, let's just make sure the module will actually fit.

05 With the exact position of the module established, you can use just the bracket to mark where the holes need to go . . .

06 . . . then in comes the drill. Don't assume you can drill holes into the car just anywhere you like - any lower or nearer the centre of the car than this, and you might just drill through the heater matrix. The trick is to always drill slowly and carefully - pull the drill back as it's about to go through, and try to find out what's behind.

The next thing we need, hole-wise, is one to take the alarm wiring into the car. The Clio is blessed with a superb, easily-removed rubber grommet behind the battery, tucked in behind the suspension strut which is just fine for this. Seen from inside the car, looking up under the passenger side of the dash, this is where any **07** wire poked through the grommet will end up.

According to the instructions for our alarm, the only wire not needed inside the car is a brown wire for the bonnet pin switch. Before trying to feed a huge mass of wires through into the car, a tip is to gather all the wires together, and tape them all together at the end - **08** makes pushing them all through a small hole much easier.

This doesn't have to be done right now, but it's good 'housekeeping' to loom up all those straggly alarm wires before going much further. Where necessary, tape or cable-tie the new loom to the inner wing or bulkhead, to keep it clear of moving **09** parts. Unsecured wiring which can flap about might also work itself out of those connector plugs, in time, causing all sorts of problems.

>>

There's also no reason not to plug the alarm in at this stage, though you could leave this until all the rest of the wiring's connected up. If your alarm module has a master key switch fitted, you could always plug in the wiring and turn off the alarm until you're ready.

10

Okay, before we dive inside, let's fit the bonnet switch, which is essential to the plot. If a thief gets your bonnet open unhindered, he can attack your alarm siren and wiring. Game over. Fit your pin switch close to the battery, to protect the battery connections. To help decide the exact switch position, smear a little copper grease on this bonnet seal strip, and shut the bonnet . . .

11

. . . now open the bonnet again, and check this out - we now have a lovely copper stripe on our bonnet. So why do we want that, then? Well, with a reference point like this on the car's wing and bonnet, we can work out where the pin switch ought to go. We don't want the switch plunger hitting a cut-out (hole) or a sloping surface, and this method means we can pinpoint a location.

12

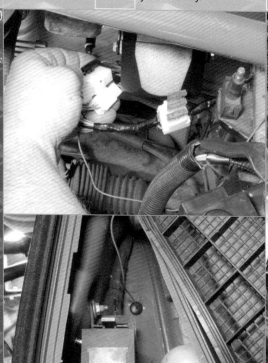
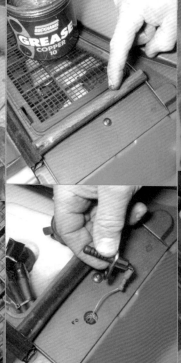
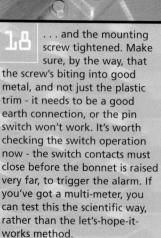

16 Notice the use of a rubber grommet, which the wire's been fed through? This isn't optional - if that pin switch wire chafes through on the sharp edges of the hole you just drilled, your alarm will be going off constantly. If the wire was a live, you'd get sparks, and maybe a fire.

17 With a new (plastic-shielded) spade terminal on our brown wire, the pin switch can be fed into its new hole . . .

18 . . . and the mounting screw tightened. Make sure, by the way, that the screw's biting into good metal, and not just the plastic trim - it needs to be a good earth connection, or the pin switch won't work. It's worth checking the switch operation now - the switch contacts must close before the bonnet is raised very far, to trigger the alarm. If you've got a multi-meter, you can test this the scientific way, rather than the let's-hope-it-works method.

13 By measuring from our copper stripe and then transferring the measurements to the wing, we can drill with confidence.

14 Open up the access panel for the washer bottle, and feel inside to make sure you're not about to drill through the washer bottle, or its supply tubing. Remember you'll actually need two holes for the pin switch - a big one for the switch body, and a smaller screw hole to mount it.

15 Would you believe it? There's no handy hole we can use to feed through our brown pin switch wire from the alarm module. Ah well, no problemo.

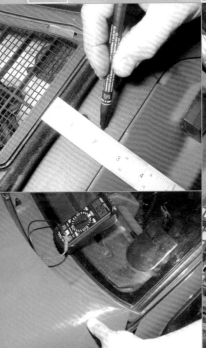

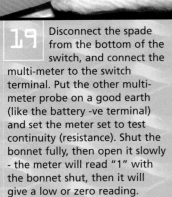
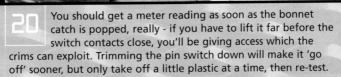
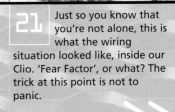

19 Disconnect the spade from the bottom of the switch, and connect the multi-meter to the switch terminal. Put the other multi-meter probe on a good earth (like the battery -ve terminal) and set the meter set to test continuity (resistance). Shut the bonnet fully, then open it slowly - the meter will read "1" with the bonnet shut, then it will give a low or zero reading.

20 You should get a meter reading as soon as the bonnet catch is popped, really - if you have to lift it far before the switch contacts close, you'll be giving access which the crims can exploit. Trimming the pin switch down will make it 'go off' sooner, but only take off a little plastic at a time, then re-test.

21 Just so you know that you're not alone, this is what the wiring situation looked like, inside our Clio. 'Fear Factor', or what? The trick at this point is not to panic.

>>

Pin switch tip 1: *Don't assume you'll automatically be able to close the bonnet fully, when you first fit your pin switch - the plunger might be so long, you'll bust the switch if you force the bonnet shut. Also, check that the switch plunger can be pushed fully down, without catching on any other vital components.*

Pin switch tip 2: *If you go too far when trimming down a pin switch, you can sometimes rescue the situation by screwing a little self-tapping screw into the top of the plunger. You can then 'adjust' the length of the plunger at will. The proper answer, though, is to buy a new switch.*

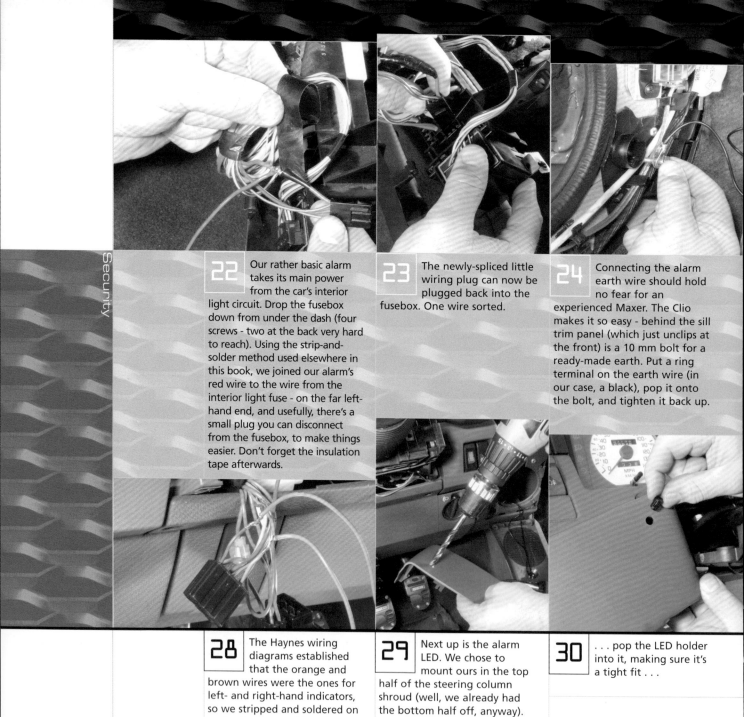

22 Our rather basic alarm takes its main power from the car's interior light circuit. Drop the fusebox down from under the dash (four screws - two at the back very hard to reach). Using the strip-and-solder method used elsewhere in this book, we joined our alarm's red wire to the wire from the interior light fuse - on the far left-hand end, and usefully, there's a small plug you can disconnect from the fusebox, to make things easier. Don't forget the insulation tape afterwards.

23 The newly-spliced little wiring plug can now be plugged back into the fusebox. One wire sorted.

24 Connecting the alarm earth wire should hold no fear for an experienced Maxer. The Clio makes it so easy - behind the sill trim panel (which just unclips at the front) is a 10 mm bolt for a ready-made earth. Put a ring terminal on the earth wire (in our case, a black), pop it onto the bolt, and tighten it back up.

28 The Haynes wiring diagrams established that the orange and brown wires were the ones for left- and right-hand indicators, so we stripped and soldered on each of our greys (doesn't matter which grey does what). All we've forgotten at this point is the insulation tape round the soldered joints - we'll speak to our mechanic about it right now...

29 Next up is the alarm LED. We chose to mount ours in the top half of the steering column shroud (well, we already had the bottom half off, anyway). Must be somewhere visible, not only for an effective deterrent to the gyppos, but so you can see what the alarm's doing, when you first test it. Drill yourself a suitable hole . . .

30 . . . pop the LED holder into it, making sure it's a tight fit . . .

25 Always a crowd-pleasing feature, the flashing indicators when the alarm goes off. On our alarm, it's two grey wires for the indicator feeds, which we've chosen to run up and across the top of the dash (along with the LED wires), to join onto the wiring from the back of the indicator stalk - you could also track them down from the fusebox. The dash top panel is secured by just five screws - one either end, and three in the windscreen vents.

26 Removing the column lower shroud isn't as easy as it first appears - see the section on white dial kits, in 'Interiors' for removal details. Taking out the indicator switch, once the shroud's off, is much simpler - undo two Torx screws . . .

27 . . . lift the switch out, and disconnect the wiring plug.

31 . . . then insert the LED itself into the holder, from below. This too should be a snug fit.

32 When you refit the top shroud (or whatever else you might have removed, to fit the LED to), make sure the LED wiring doesn't get trapped.

33 At this point, we should've been ready to just connect up our central locking wires, and test the alarm. Sadly, the Clio has what's called 'positive-pulse' central locking, so we needed the optional Microscan locking interface. Before we get to the wiring, we need a place to stash this little black box.

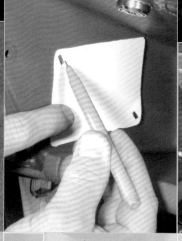

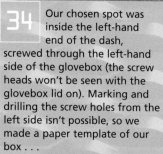

34 Our chosen spot was inside the left-hand end of the dash, screwed through the left-hand side of the glovebox (the screw heads won't be seen with the glovebox lid on). Marking and drilling the screw holes from the left side isn't possible, so we made a paper template of our box . . .

35 . . . and used it to mark the holes . . .

36 . . . for drilling through from the right. The glovebox lid's easy to remove - see how in 'Interiors'.

40 All that's left now is finding the central locking 'lock' and 'unlock' trigger wires. Two likely places to start tracking them down - driver's door loom (where it comes into the car) or behind the central locking relay, in the fusebox. This is the joker in question - let's check the wiring behind that.

41 After a little testing and probing, we found that our Clio had a white/grey 'lock' wire, and a pink 'unlock' wire. Rather than chop the fusebox wires, we stripped a little insulation off each target wire, wrapped the bared end of our new interface wire around that, and soldered the two together. This gives a permanent joint, and leaves the original wiring intact . . .

42 . . . the only thing you must remember to do is insulate the soldered connection afterwards.

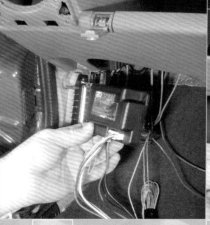

37 Our interface black box (and wiring) can now be fed into place . . .

38 . . . then screwed into position, using self-tapping screws and speed clips.

39 The black box requires its own earth (which we got from the same spot as the main alarm earth, earlier) and several live feeds (three altogether - count 'em), which we took from our auxiliary fusebox. There's also an alarm trigger wire to join to the interface - just follow the instructions in the box.

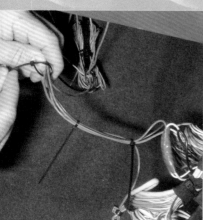

43 Also, since all that alarm interface wiring's gonna get squashed up behind the fusebox when that gets put back up, take some time tidying it up. You can loom it with tape, or use some small cable-ties, like we did.

44 So come on - does it work? Most alarms require you to "programme in" the remotes before they'll work. Test all the alarm features in turn, remembering to allow enough time for the alarm to arm itself (usually about 30 seconds). When you test it for the first time, don't forget to either shut the bonnet completely, or do like us, and hold the bonnet pin switch down. Our way, you can pull out the alarm fuses and shut it up, if something goes wrong!

45 Set the anti-shock sensitivity with a thought to where you live and park - will it be set off every night by the neighbour's cat, or by kids playing football? Finally, and most important of all - next time you park up, remember to set it!

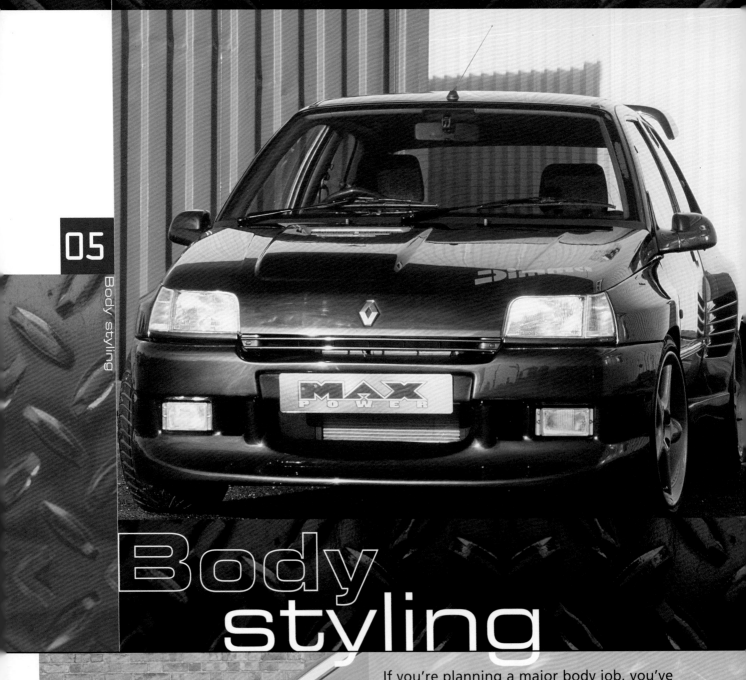

Body styling

If you're planning a major body job, you've probably already got some good ideas about how you want your Clio to look, from *"Max Power"*, *"Revs"* or *"Redline"*, or maybe from a friend's car. While it can be good to have a target car to aim for, if you're just starting out on the road towards a fully-loaded car, you probably don't want (or can't quite afford) to go 'all the way' all at once.

If you're new to the world of modifying, it's a good idea to start with smaller jobs, and work up to the full body kit gradually, as your skills increase; spending loads on a body kit is a pretty lame idea if you then make a mess of fitting it! There's plenty of small ways to improve the look of your Clio, which don't cost much, and which are simple enough to fit; start with some of these before you go too mad!

One golden rule with any body mods is to plan what you're going to do, and don't rush it. It's better that the car looks a bit stupid for a week (because you couldn't get something finished) than to rush a job and have the car look stupid forever. Do half the job properly than all of it badly. Try and think the jobs through - plan each stage. Have you got all the tools, screws or whatever before you start, or will you have to break off halfway through? If you get stuck, is there someone you can get to help, or have they gone off for the weekend? Above all, if something goes wrong - don't panic - a calm approach will prove to be a huge bonus (that job doesn't have to be done today, does it?).

If a piece of trim won't come off, don't force it. If something feels like it's going to break, it probably will - stop and consider whether to go on and break it, or try another approach. Especially on an older car, things either never come off as easily as you think, or else have already been off so many times that they either break or won't fit back on properly. While we'd all like to do a perfect job every time, working on an older car will, sooner or later, teach you the fine art of 'bodging' (finding valid alternative ways of fixing things!). Don't assume that you'll have to bodge something back on, every time - if a trim clip breaks when you take something off, it might be easier and cheaper than you think to simply go to your Renault dealer, and buy a new clip (remember, even Renault mechanics break things from time to time, so they will keep these things in stock!).

Mirror, mirror

Mirrors are another 'must have' accessory for your hot hatch. They are often quite difficult to fit, but with the right tools and our handy hints, this process should become easier! Mirrors are usually supplied in a black or carbon finish. The black-finish mirrors are obviously meant to be colour-coded to your Clio, so will need spraying at some point (usually best left 'til after you've made them fit). The carbon look will give a racing look immediately.

You can buy stick-on mirror covers which affix to the existing mirror - if the funds are tight, this is another option to give your car a new look. If you've bought 'Universal' mirrors, ensure you have some sandpaper and a sharp blade to hand, as invariably they won't fit without some manipulation! DTM and M3 style mirrors are the puppies to have this season, but if you want your Clio to stand out from this crowd, get some in a Merc-stylee, with built-in indicators and sidelights - try Auto Tint Design for these, and you won't be disappointed. Light-equipped mirrors will be easier to fit to a higher-spec Clio (RT and upwards) which already has electric mirrors and plenty of wiring in the front doors. Let's start in and mod those mirrors.

01 Inside the car, prise off the triangular trim panel to gain access to the mirror mounting plate.

02 Using yet another Torx bit (size T20) remove the two screws that hold this plate, to reveal the actual mirror mounting screws beneath. Damn cunning, yer average Frenchman.

03 Take the mirror wiring plug and disconnect it by fully depressing the catches at the sides of plug.

04 Now, before you get all carried away and start unscrewing your nuts, a word of warning. When you removed the triangular trim, a hole is left underneath. Stuff this hole with rag or tissue, to stop those nuts falling down the inside the door card; it will save a lot of effort trying to find them later! There are three mirror nuts in total, and as you can see, the third is cleverly hidden with a grommet.

Merc-style **mirrors**

05 As the last nut is being removed, ensure you are supporting the mirror, or it'll hit the deck. Carefully remove the mirror from the car, feeding the wiring plug through the hole.

06 Our rather smart M3 mirrors (which have Merc-style sidelights and side repeaters built-in) were supplied by Auto Tint Design, and are designed specifically for the Clio. Even so, we still had to trim and sand the mirror bases to get a perfect fit. Typical.

07 These must be posh mirrors, they've got wires on. Which you must feed through the mirror bases, when you're happy that they fit your Clio properly.

>>

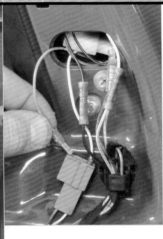

08 Now the bases get screwed onto the mirrors themselves, and they're ready to go on.

09 So what about that wiring, then? Those of you with less-posh mirrors can sit back and have a laugh while we try to sort this out. First, let's get the mirror movement wires figured out (left/right and up/down). The only way to be sure of getting this right is to try each wire from the new mirrors in the old mirror wiring plug, work the mirror switch and see if the mirror moves the right way. The results on our car:

Mirror wire colour	Car wiring colour
White	*Yellow/grey*
Red	*Pink/Grey*
Black	*Brown*

10 It's probably simpler in this case to chop off the old mirror wiring plug . . .

We didn't hang about. There's three wires to connect - a black, which we joined to a black earth wire in the door, then a white for the mirror indicators, and a blue for the sidelights. We can join the blue and white wires onto the plug pins now, using speaker terminal crimps (at this point, it doesn't matter which plug wire does what) - we'll sort that out inside the car, later.

11 . . . and bullet the old and new wires together (here, we're using double-ended joiners rather than bullets, but the idea's the same).

That was the easy bit - our mirrors need a supply from the indicators and sidelights yet, and this has to be fed into the doors. Tricky - or is it? If you can find a wire that's not actually doing anything useful, that's fed into the doors, there's no reason why you can't trace the wire back, and feed it anything you like.

12 What's this two-pin plug for, in our Clio door? It's not connected. Turns out it's for an external temperature sensor, not fitted to UK models. Just the job.

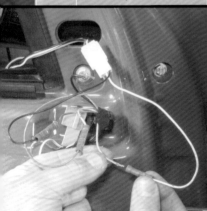

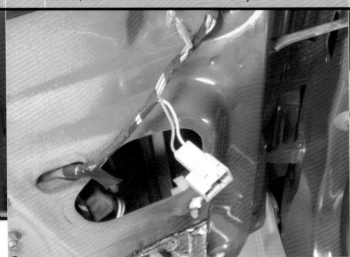

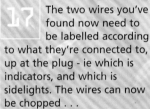

14 To improve access to the door wiring, remove it. Or at least, release the two halves of the door wiring connector from the door and pillar. To separate the plug, pull up the plastic clip fitted over the top (ours was missing). The door pillar side of the connector is held in by a Torx screw - you can then feed the wiring back into the car, and out around the dash . . .

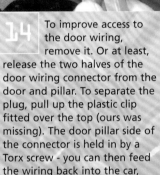

. . . and a couple of decent lengths of wire joined on straight away. The next task is to feed these wires

18 with indicators and sidelights.

15 . . . while the door half of the connector is just in a big rubber grommet - pull the wiring out of the door first, then feed it back through, and out the hole in the door panel.

The indicator bit isn't too hard. You won't be needing your side repeater lights after you've got the ones in the mirror working, so tap into the wiring for them. Having taken off the side rep itself, feed the wiring in through the wing. The new wire going to the mirror can be fed back into the engine bay (there's a big grommet next to the fusebox in the car), and joined

19 up - on our car, the indicator live was orange.

16 Renault are notorious for changing wire colours where they pass through a connector, and our Clio's no exception. To check which two wires feed up to our two-pin plug in the door, use a continuity tester between the mass of wires going in, and the two up at the plug. Eventually, you'll get a match.

If you haven't already, take down the fusebox to tap into the sidelight wiring. The fusebox is held in by four screws. On our Clio, the sidelight fuses (left and right) were 18 and 19. With the numbers as a guide, probe the wiring at the back of the fusebox - you want the sidelight wire that's fused, so it's the wire that puts the test light out when you pull its fuse out.

20 Use something better than a Scotchlok, too!

17 The two wires you've found now need to be labelled according to what they're connected to, up at the plug - ie which is indicators, and which is sidelights. The wires can now be chopped . . .

And that's it - you should now have mirrors which adjust, flash, and light up at night. Who's yer

21 daddy?

Fitting a sunstrip

The modern sunstrip, first seen as a lovely green shadeband on Cortinas and Capris back in the 70s, usually bearing imaginative slogans such as "DAVE AND SHARON". Just goes to show that some things improve with age.

There are two options to make your car look (and maybe even feel) cooler:

a The sunvisor, a screen tint band inside the screen, which is usually a graduated-tint strip. As this fits inside, there's a problem straight away - the interior mirror. The Clio mirror is bonded to the screen, and it seriously gets in the way when trying to fit a wet and sticky (nice!) strip of plastic around it. Go for a sunstrip instead.

b The sunstrip, which is opaque vinyl, colour-matched to the car, fits to the outside of the screen. Much more Sir.

A really wide sunstrip imitates the "roof chop" look seen on American hot rods, and colour-coded, they can look very effective from the front - plus, of course, you can use the space to advertise your preferred brand of ICE (no, no, NO! Not a good idea!). As it's fitted to the outside of the screen, the sunstrip has a good chance of seriously interfering with your wipers (or wiper, if you've been converted). If this happens to the point where the wipers can't clean the screen, Mr MOT might have a point if he fails your car… The wiper blades may need replacing more often, and the sunstrip itself might start peeling off - still want one? Well, you've got to, really.

Legal eagle
The rule for tinting or otherwise modifying the windscreen is that there must be no more than a 25% light reduction from standard. In theory, this means you can have a sunstrip which covers up to 25% of the screen area, but some MOT testers may see it differently. A sunstrip's got to come down the screen a fair way, to look any sense (otherwise, why bother?). You could argue that accurately measuring and calculating the windscreen area isn't actually that easy, if you get stopped, and anyway, a sunstrip also cuts out harmful glare! If you go so far down the screen that you can't see out, though - well, that's just stupid.

01 This is only stuck to the outside, so only the outside of the screen needs cleaning - excellent! Do a good job of cleaning, though - any dirt stuck under the strip will ruin the effect.

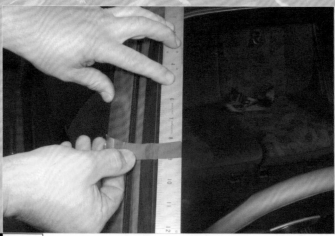

02 With the help of an assistant (if you have one handy), lay the strip onto the car, and decide how far down the screen you're going to go. Legally-speaking, you shouldn't be lower than the wiper swept area - so how much of a "badboy" are you? If you measure and mark the bottom of the strip with tape, you'll be sure to get it level, even if it's not legal.

03 Trim off the excess strip at this stage - means you'll have less flapping about when you start trying to stick it down.

04 Spray the screen with water (mixed with a drop of washing-up liquid) . . .

05 . . . then peel off the backing, spraying that as well, and wake up your assistant.

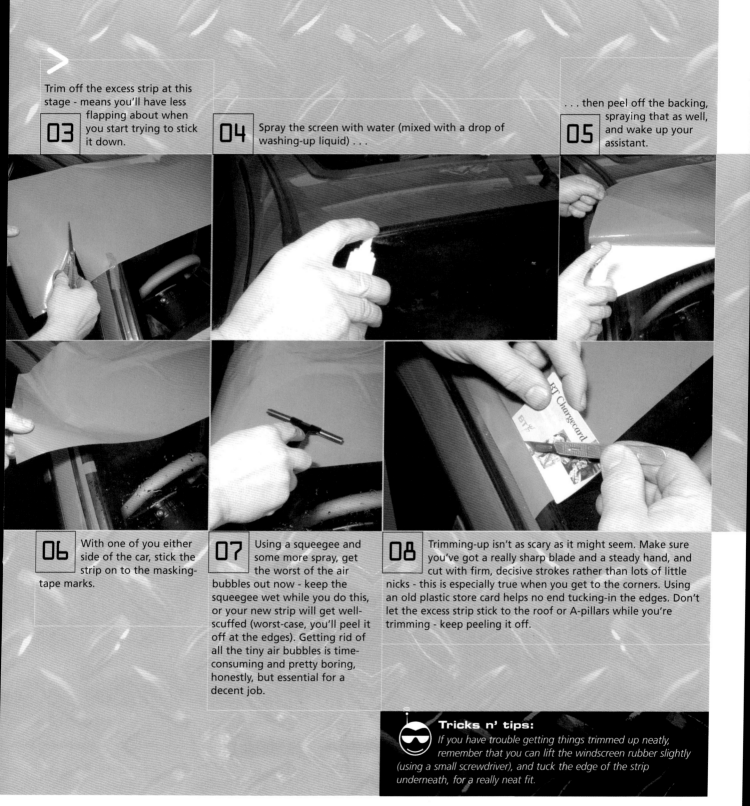

06 With one of you either side of the car, stick the strip on to the masking-tape marks.

07 Using a squeegee and some more spray, get the worst of the air bubbles out now - keep the squeegee wet while you do this, or your new strip will get well-scuffed (worst-case, you'll peel it off at the edges). Getting rid of all the tiny air bubbles is time-consuming and pretty boring, honestly, but essential for a decent job.

08 Trimming-up isn't as scary as it might seem. Make sure you've got a really sharp blade and a steady hand, and cut with firm, decisive strokes rather than lots of little nicks - this is especially true when you get to the corners. Using an old plastic store card helps no end tucking-in the edges. Don't let the excess strip stick to the roof or A-pillars while you're trimming - keep peeling it off.

Tricks n' tips:
If you have trouble getting things trimmed up neatly, remember that you can lift the windscreen rubber slightly (using a small screwdriver), and tuck the edge of the strip underneath, for a really neat fit.

Racing filler cap

Ah, the humble fuel filler cap - what you decide to do here really is a matter of taste. With most owners trying to smooth and colour-code everything they possibly can, it's a bit odd to take the already-smooth and colour-coded filler cap, and make it stand out! But for those of you who can't leave anything alone...

At least the Clio filler cap is round, unlike a few cars (Golfs, for example), so it's easier to re-create the "racing" look. If you don't want to make too much of the flap, there are stick-on/screw-on fuel cap covers available. Easy to fit, and quite effective. But, for those who really want to impress, it's got to be a complete racing conversion, which does away with the flap and the dull black filler cap below, in favour of a fully-functional alloy item to grace the Clio flanks. Trouble is, a pukka working cap will almost certainly need bodyshop assistance to fit successfully - let's see what the cheaper option looks like...

01 To make life a bit easier, you probably ought to take the cap off for most of this. Mind you, it's worth popping it back on temporarily before you stick the cover on, to check the alignment...

02 Don't overlook the importance of giving the cap a good clean, preferably with some fairly-scary solvent. If you don't get off all that silicone-based polish, any sticking activities will be very limited.

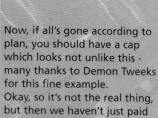

03 Time to peel off the backing . . .

04 . . . and taking your steadiest hand, line it all up, before pressing it on firmly and evenly.

05 Now, if all's gone according to plan, you should have a cap which looks not unlike this - many thanks to Demon Tweeks for this fine example. Okay, so it's not the real thing, but then we haven't just paid mega-bucks to a bodyshop for it. You decide.

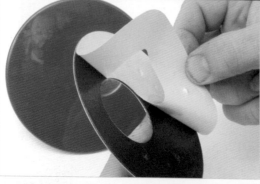

Achtung!
Fuel vapour is explosive. No smoking and no naked lights anywhere near the open fuel filler, please.

Smoothly **does it**

If you've bought a basic Clio, it's understandable that you might not want to declare this fact loudly from the rear end of your car. Badges also clutter up the otherwise clean lines. The ugly side rubbing strips (most of which give away the size of your engine, too) should at least be colour-coded, if you're at all serious about raising your game.

General bodywork smoothing (including de-seaming) takes time and skill. Your Clio will really look the business with a fully-smoothed tailgate, or even with those ugly roof gutters smoothed over. Probably best to put the pros at a bodyshop to work on this. De-stripping will require some bodywork skills, as the side strips are recessed into the doors and rear wings (plenty of filler needed). De-badging you can definitely do at home, so get to it.

The tailgate badges are also easy to dispose of, but there's a problem. Renault, in their wisdom, use pegs to locate the badges, as well as glue. Which means you're left with holes. First, soften the glue with a heatgun, remembering you're not trying to melt the badges - okay?

De-stripping and de-badging

01 Removing the side rubbing strips, whether it's just for spraying or for good, is easy. First, there's one little screw to remove . . .

02 . . . then unclip the strip, and remove it. You might break a clip or two in the process, or they might stay attached to the strip, and need transferring back (if you're refitting). One or two missing clips won't matter, as long as they're somewhere in the middle of the strip.

03 Of course you're embarrassed by that "1.2" or "RL" badge on the front of the strip. How much better would a "16V" or "Williams" badge look? No problem - removing the old badge is as easy as this.

05 Any wide-bladed tool will do to prise the badge off, but wrap the blade with some tape, to avoid wrecking your paint.

06 How satisfying is this? You're one step nearer a smoothed tailgate.

07 Unlike some other small hatches, the glue on Clio badges is easily dissolved by almost any handy solvent, as you can see. The holes are the only evidence that remains - and not for long.

47

Filling holes - DIY method 1

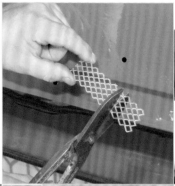

01 When it comes to car bodywork, every hole is not a goal. At least the small holes left by de-badging can be filled without stretching your talent envelope too far. For our first method, we're using a leftover piece of mesh (that's right - the stuff you do grilles with) cut to size . . .

02 . . . and "glued" into place behind the two holes with some glassfibre we mixed up earlier. Of course, you don't want the holes in the car to line up with the holes in the mesh, or we've wasted our time, so make sure you line it up half-sensibly.

03 Now we're smoothing in a first layer of filler, building up in a couple of layers or so, to get it just proud of the holes.

04 If you've got an aversion to too much sanding-down, you can always use a Stanley blade to get rid of the lumps - once the filler's dry, of course.

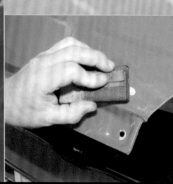

05 Wrapping the wet-and-dry paper around a flat wood block will make it easier to flush the holes. If you can still feel the holes with your finger, another light skim of filler, and another rub-down, will be needed. Skimp on this stage, and be sorry later.

06 When you've done the best you can with ordinary filler, it's time for some paint - or better still, some high-build primer, which is more useful, as it fills some of the imperfections in your filler. When you're masking, roll the tape back on itself along the edges where it meets the paint - the rounded edge on the tape means you don't get a hard edge on the new paint.

07 Always sand down the filler or primer before the top coats go on - it produces a much better finish.

08 And now the top coats - after which you'll really find out how good a fill job you did. Don't be too critical if this is your first attempt - but will your mates be as understanding?

Filling holes · DIY method 2

01 For really small holes, there is another way, you know. Our workshop manager had been dying to try this out and see whether it worked. First, cover the area around your chosen hole (two holes, in this case) with masking tape - make sure you get a decent working area around the hole.

02 Now neatly cut out your two holes in the tape.

03 Here's where we start to see the true cunning of this plan - mix up some Araldite (or similar glue for bonding metals), and apply a blob of it to a washer large enough to cover the hole, on the inside. Rich types among you may prefer to use a coin of the realm.

04 Stick the washer or coin on from inside, then stand around holding it in place while the glue dries.

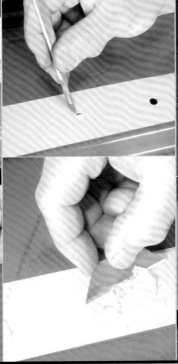

05 Mix up some filler, and apply to your hole - the masking tape prevents any getting on the paintwork. Apply more than one layer, and build the filler up evenly.

06 We found that the filler could be trimmed flat using a sharp Stanley blade, used at a very shallow angle. The filler doesn't really "take" to the masking tape, making it easier to trim away the excess.

07 Peel away the masking tape, and your hole is filled - all it needs is paint.

08 If you haven't done such a great job, remember that you can improve things by applying layer after layer of paint (wait for each one to dry). When you've built the paint up proud of the hole, T-Cut it back smooth.

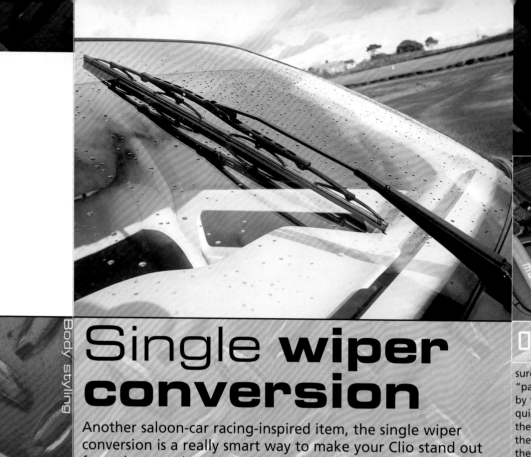

Single **wiper conversion**

Another saloon-car racing-inspired item, the single wiper conversion is a really smart way to make your Clio stand out from the crowd. Presumably, the saloon racers fit single wipers to enhance the view forward (one less wiper arm obscuring the view could make all the difference), improve the aerodynamics, and maybe even to save weight! Many Clio owners want the single wiper because it helps to remove clutter - put two Clios side by side, and the one with one less wiper looks way better. It's a fairly 'neutral' mod, too - unlike some, it works as well on a 'sport-Clio' as on a 'luxury-Clio'.

01 Unsurprisingly, the first job is to remove your old wiper arms. Make sure that the wipers are in their "parked" position, if necessary by flicking the wipers on, then quickly off. Flip up the cap at the base of each arm, unscrew the nut, and pull the arms off their splined fittings. Hopefully, yours will come off as easy as ours - easier than our tailgate wiper, anyway.

∧

When you go to lift the panels out, you'll find that they're also held in by three or four plastic clips on the back edge - these have a tendency to come off with the panel, then fall off, so watch where they go.

02 The windscreen trim panel is in two sections, joined in the middle by one Torx screw . . .

03 . . . and secured at each end by two more. There's a rubber seal at the front edge, but this doesn't seem to get in the way much.

04

05 The last thing preventing these pesky panels from parting is the washer jet tubing, which you have to pull off at various points.

06 Take out the vehicle jack, *et voilà* (as they actually do say in France) - the wiper linkage, it is revealed.

07 The linkage is held in by three bolts - this is the centre one, buried low down.

08 It's a bit of a pig getting the linkage out - there ain't a lot of room in there, and some wangling (sorry, bit of a tech term there) is required.

Now the spindles both have to be removed from the wiper frame. The driver's-side spindle can be scrapped, of course. Removing the circlips which hold the spindles in isn't hard. Finding them afterwards, when they've flown off into space, is trickier. Luckily, you only need one again - when you lose the first one, you'll be more careful next time.

With the circlip gone, the spindle's free to slide out - but notice how the various other bits are fitted. We'll be re-using those wave washers and also the little O-rings that get left behind in the wiper frame.

Just when you thought the thing was out, there's this wiring plug on the wiper motor to disconnect. Now the linkage is at your mercy.

The first things to go are the link arms from both spindles - these just prise off with the aid of a large screwdriver.

09

10

11

12

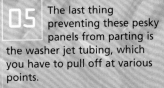

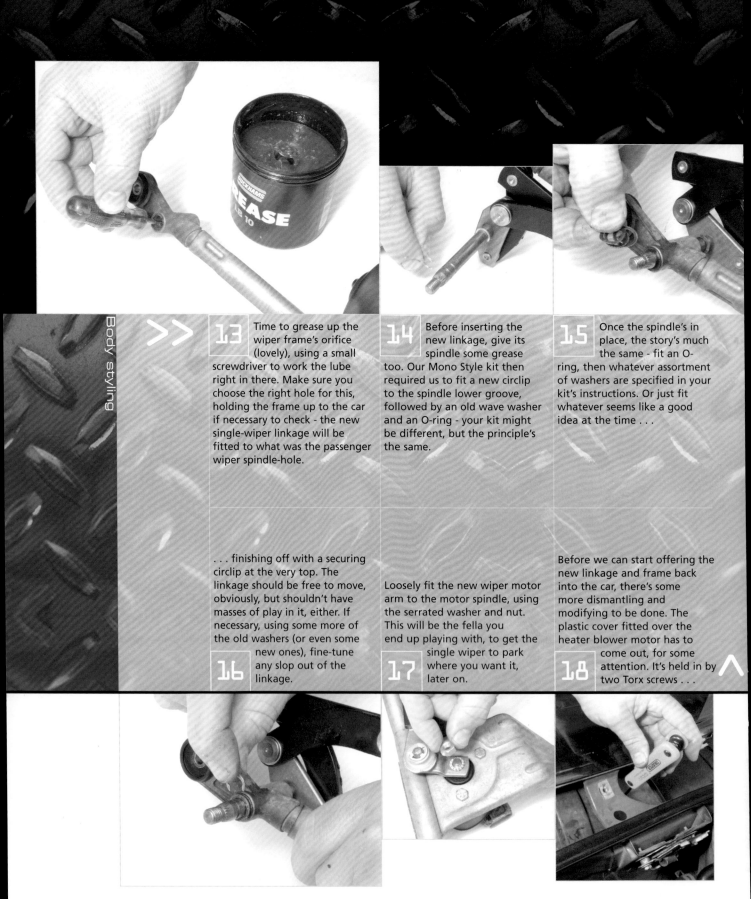

>>

13 Time to grease up the wiper frame's orifice (lovely), using a small screwdriver to work the lube right in there. Make sure you choose the right hole for this, holding the frame up to the car if necessary to check - the new single-wiper linkage will be fitted to what was the passenger wiper spindle-hole.

14 Before inserting the new linkage, give its spindle some grease too. Our Mono Style kit then required us to fit a new circlip to the spindle lower groove, followed by an old wave washer and an O-ring - your kit might be different, but the principle's the same.

15 Once the spindle's in place, the story's much the same - fit an O-ring, then whatever assortment of washers are specified in your kit's instructions. Or just fit whatever seems like a good idea at the time . . .

. . . finishing off with a securing circlip at the very top. The linkage should be free to move, obviously, but shouldn't have masses of play in it, either. If necessary, using some more of the old washers (or even some new ones), fine-tune any slop out of the linkage. **16**

Loosely fit the new wiper motor arm to the motor spindle, using the serrated washer and nut. This will be the fella you end up playing with, to get the single wiper to park where you want it, later on. **17**

Before we can start offering the new linkage and frame back into the car, there's some more dismantling and modifying to be done. The plastic cover fitted over the heater blower motor has to come out, for some attention. It's held in by two Torx screws . . . **18**

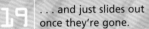

19 . . . and just slides out once they're gone.

20 The cover's raised central ridge has to be cut back quite significantly, so that the new linkage doesn't catch on it - this is a simple job with a hacksaw blade or Stanley knife.

21 With our modified cover screwed back in place, it's time for the first trial fitting - slip the linkage and frame into place (it goes back a lot easier than it came out, but don't let that fool you) . . .

22 . . . then refit the three frame mounting bolts. This is the newly-supplied (longer) centre bolt, which has to be spaced away from the car, by fitting an oversize nut and washer under the frame - if you don't, the new linkage still touches, despite chopping away the heater cover.

Bum notes

Once again, problems with a single wiper kit. Mono Style supply an oversize nut as a spacer, supposed to give the required extra clearance for the new linkage. It doesn't, and we had to add extra washers, which then meant that even the new, longer, bolt they supply still wasn't long enough, and we had to find our own. The wiper motor arm nut kept coming undone unless it was done up murder-tight. The final insult was that the new single wiper arm would not fit onto the spindle, until we enlarged the hole. Must try harder.

Tighten the bolt good 'n' proper (also see 'Bum notes'). Wouldn't

23 be a bad idea to plug the wiper motor back in at this point, either.

Now fit the wiper motor arm to the

24 motor spindle . . .

25 . . . and tighten the nut . . .

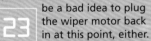

26 . . . then you find that the motor arm moves as you try to tighten the nut, so you need an open-ended spanner to hold the end of the arm still. You might just have to play with the position of this arm on the motor spindle, so don't put those tools away yet.

27 Make sure the wiper motor's in the parked position, by switching the wipers on, then quickly off again. Yes, we know there's no wiper blades fitted at this point. Fit the new wiper arm (we were trying to get ours parked in the centre) and tighten the nut enough to just hold it.

28 Do not be tempted to just switch the wiper on at this point - there's plenty still to do. Work the new linkage by hand, and see how the wiper moves. What we're trying to do first is to set the wiper blade's sweep - ie we're trying to get it to go equally across both sides of the screen. Re-position the wiper arm on the spindle until it's just right, and tighten the arm nut securely. That part is now done, and the wiper arm is set.

29 Next, we set the parked position of the motor, by undoing the motor arm nut and re-positioning the motor arm on its spindle. This can only be done by try-it-and-see - there's no logic to it that we could find! For centre parking, set the motor arm vertical, like this - if you want it off to one side, set it horizontal. You will have to play with it some, unfortunately.

30 The final act of consigning your unwanted extra wiper to the bin is to fit the blanking grommet over the driver's side spindle hole. And feel suitably chuffed, obviously.

Body styling

Travelling incognito

Window tinting is one of the best ways to disguise a naff standard interior! But surely you're not going to put up with that naff standard interior for long, are you? Of course, the other side of the coin is that tints will hide a sorted interior from thieving eyes...

As with so much in modifying, window tinting is a matter of personal taste - it can look right with the right car and colour (black is an obvious example), but it doesn't suit everybody. If you're doing your car to pose around in (and why not?) it's hard enough for people to see you in there anyway, without blacking-out the windows! On the other hand, if you're doing a full ICE install, window tinting could be one way of avoiding unwanted attention when you're not around.

There's more than a little styling element to tinting, now that you can buy "reflex film", which incorporates a layer of precious metal (which reduces UV light and reflects heat from the sun), and is available in various wild colours, to complement or contrast your car's paint job. Only downside is - it might not be legal to run it on the road, with many are advertised as "for show cars only".

Because window tinting involves sticking a layer of film to the inside of the glass, there's also an argument for saying that this might help to prevent a break-in, since your side windows won't then shatter when hit. Car security firm Toad market an adhesive film which is specifically designed to prevent break-ins in this way, and even humble window-tinting kits are claimed to offer the same effect.

Kits fall into two main groups - one where you get a roll of film, which you then cut to shape, or a pre-cut kit where the film pieces are supplied to suit your car. In theory, the second (slightly more expensive) option is better, but it leaves little margin for error - if you muck up fitting one of the supplied sections, you'll have to buy another complete kit. The roll-of-film kit may leave enough over for a few false starts... Check when buying how many windows you'll be able to do - some kits are only good for three Clio windows - how handy!. Our rolls of limo-black tint were kindly supplied by those generous lads at Autopoint in Wedmore.

The downside to tinting is that it will severely try your patience. If you're not a patient sort of person, this is one job which may well wind you up - you have been warned. Saying that, if you're calm and careful, and you follow the destructions (instructions?) to the letter, you could surprise yourself - our mechanic did, when we tried it for the first time and got a near-perfect result!

In brief, the process for tinting is to lay the film on the outside of the glass first, and cut it exactly to size. The protective layer is peeled off to expose the adhesive side, the film is transferred to the inside of the car (tricky) and then squeegeed into place (also tricky). All this must be done with scrupulous cleanliness, as any muck or stray bits of trimmed-off film will ruin the effect (tricky, if you're working outside). The other problem which won't surprise you is that getting rid of air bubbles and creases can take time. A long time. This is another test of patience, because if, as the instructions say, you've used plenty of spray, it will take a while to dry out and stick... just don't panic!

Legal eagle

The law on window tinting currently is that there must be no more than a 25% reduction in light transmission through windscreens, and a limit of 30% reduction on all other glass. Yes, yes, all very well, but how the heck do you MEASURE light reduction? Also, consider that many cars come with tinted glass as standard - so can you fit a tinting kit on top and still be legal? Hard to know what line to take, if you're stopped by Plod - try and choose a tinting kits which is EC-approved (ASK before you buy, and if you think it could be a serious issue, get a letter from the company to support the legality of the kit, to use in your defence). Some forces now take this seriously enough to have portable test equipment they can use at the roadside - if your car fails, it's an on-the-spot fine.

Tinting
windows

It's worth picking your day, and your working area, pretty carefully - on a windy day, there'll be more dust in the air, and it'll be a nightmare trying to stop the film flapping and folding onto itself while you're working.

Applying window tint is best done on a warm day (or in a warm garage - if there is such a thing), because the adhesive will begin to dry sooner. For fairly obvious reasons, don't try tinting when it's starting to get dark! It's a good idea to have a mate to help out with this job, but you might get fed up hearing "you've missed another bubble" or "you can still see that crease, y'know".

01 For the first time ever, we're going to cheat. As in, removing the glass for tinting. But it's so easy - we got the idea when we saw that our Clio has opening rear windows, which you just unbolt from the hinges. So why not try removing the front glass as well? We are the DIY dudes, after all. First, take off the door trim panel, as covered in "Interiors", and prise out the glass guide channel from the top of the door.

02 You won't believe how little holds the window glass in place - scary, really. Lower the glass down (you might have to temporarily reconnect the window switches for this) until you can get at this white plastic clip. Unbelievably, this just unhooks out of the glass, so be ready for the glass to drop - it's heavy.

03 All that's left now is a funny little clip at the back edge of the glass. Lift the glass up in the door, then give it a good tug forwards to release the clip - it should just pop out.

04 The glass is now free to be removed, so just tilt it forwards and lift it out of the door. Simple. And it makes tinting much, much easier, as we'll see.

05 Get the window being tinted clean - really clean - inside and out. Don't use anything containing ammonia or vinegar, since both will react with the film or its adhesive, and muck it up. If you didn't take out the glass - 1) clean the area around the window - it's too easy for stray dirt to attach itself to the film; 2) on door windows, wind them down slightly, to clean all of the top edge, then close them tight to fit the film.

06 Before you even unroll the film, take note - handle it carefully. If you crease it, you won't get the creases out - ever. First work out which way up the film is, by applying a small bit of really sticky tape to the front and back side - use the tape to pull the films apart, just at one corner.

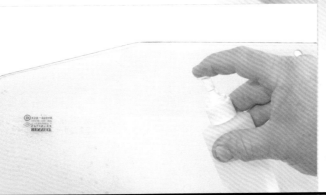

07 Lay the film onto the glass, with the clear side facing you. Unroll the film, and cut it roughly to the size of the window (on a door window, leave plenty at the bottom edge for now). Some kits have a logo on the film, which seems daft - tinting's difficult enough, without having to get a logo straight! The only benefit of a logo is to establish which layer is the tint. Make life easier - lose the logo.

08 Spray the glass with a weak soapy water solution (Folia Tec supply a small bottle of Joy fluid in their kit, but you could use a few drops of ordinary washing-up liquid). Get one of those plant sprayers you can buy cheap in any DIY store, if your kit doesn't contain a sprayer.

09 Now we're gonna see the benefit of taking the glass out. Normally, you'd stick your film to the outside of the glass, trim it up with a knife, then separate it and transfer it to the inside of the glass. We can avoid most of that - with the inside of our glass sprayed, we can peel off the clear layer, and stick our rough-trimmed film on now. So we did.

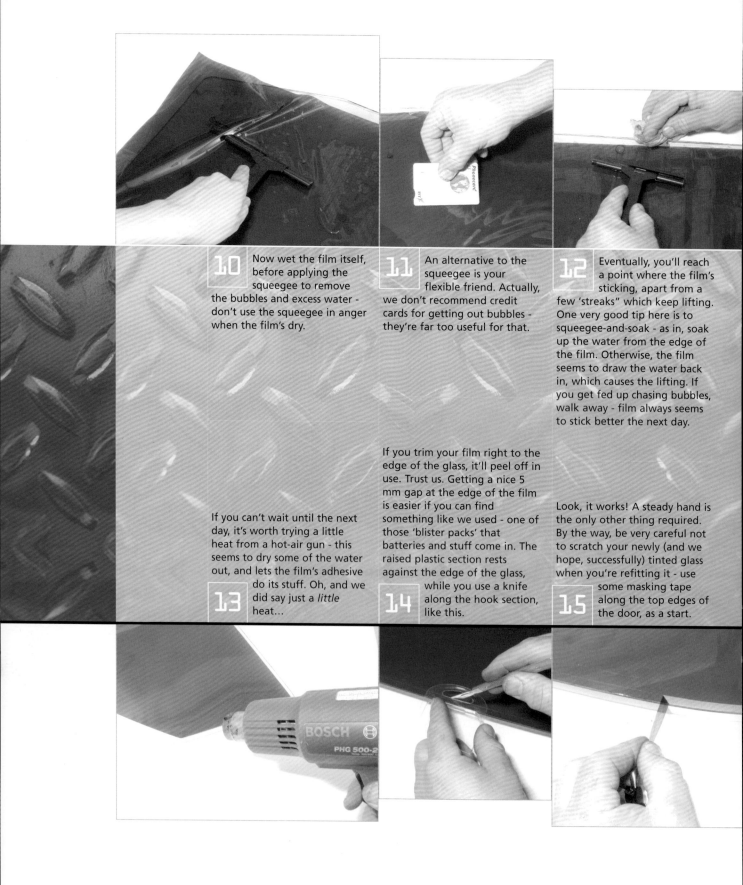

10 Now wet the film itself, before applying the squeegee to remove the bubbles and excess water - don't use the squeegee in anger when the film's dry.

11 An alternative to the squeegee is your flexible friend. Actually, we don't recommend credit cards for getting out bubbles - they're far too useful for that.

12 Eventually, you'll reach a point where the film's sticking, apart from a few 'streaks" which keep lifting. One very good tip here is to squeegee-and-soak - as in, soak up the water from the edge of the film. Otherwise, the film seems to draw the water back in, which causes the lifting. If you get fed up chasing bubbles, walk away - film always seems to stick better the next day.

If you can't wait until the next day, it's worth trying a little heat from a hot-air gun - this seems to dry some of the water out, and lets the film's adhesive do its stuff. Oh, and we **13** did say just a *little* heat...

If you trim your film right to the edge of the glass, it'll peel off in use. Trust us. Getting a nice 5 mm gap at the edge of the film is easier if you can find something like we used - one of those 'blister packs' that batteries and stuff come in. The raised plastic section rests against the edge of the glass, while you use a knife **14** along the hook section, like this.

Look, it works! A steady hand is the only other thing required. By the way, be very careful not to scratch your newly (and we hope, successfully) tinted glass when you're refitting it - use some masking tape **15** along the top edges of the door, as a start.

01 Seeing that our rear side windows could be unscrewed from the hinges was what inspired us to tint our front side windows 'glass-out'. In fact, removing the rear side windows is less easy than the fronts. You need a Torx bit for the bolt inside, and a pair of water-pump pliers outside, for the round 'nut'. And they use thread-lock at the factory, because they don't want the windows to fall off, presumably.

02 Assuming you haven't actually given up by now, in fear of cracking the glass, this is what you end up with. The grommet in the glass just clips out.

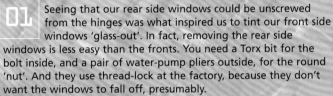

Removing rear side windows

. . . before the catch is removed on the nearest clean surface. Be warned that you'll almost certainly 'chew up' the round nuts during removal, and you'll need some black paint at least (if not some new nuts) to tidy the car up afterwards. Maybe we'll go for the 'glass-in' approach, next time. The rest of the tinting process is the same as for the fronts, besides making holes in the film for the hinge mounts, of course.

03 The rear catch is held to the pillar by two more Torx screws . . .

04 . . . then the whole window comes out, complete with the catch . . .

05

Painting by numbers

This is not the section where we tell you how to respray your entire Clio in a weekend, using only spray cans, okay? Mission Impossible, we ain't. This bit's all about how to spray up your various plasticky bits before final fitting - bits such as door mirrors, light brows, spoilers, splitters - hell, even bumpers if you like. As we've no doubt said before, with anything new, fit your unpainted bits first. Make sure everything fits properly (shape and tidy up all parts as necessary), that all holes have been drilled, and all screws etc are doing their job. Then, and only when you're totally, completely happy with the fit - take them off, and get busy with the spray cans.

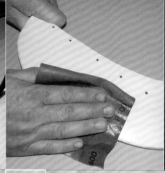

01 The first job is to mask off any areas you don't want painted. Do this right at the start, or you could be sorry; on these door mirrors, we decided to mask off just at the lip before the glass, to leave a black unpainted edge - if we hadn't masked it as the very first job, we would've roughed up all the shiny black plastic next, and wrecked the edge finish.

02 Remove any unwanted "seams" in the plastic, using fine sandpaper or wet-and-dry. Some of these seams look pretty cool, others don't - you decide. Also worth tidying up any other areas you're not happy with, fit-wise, while you're at it.

03 Especially with "shiny" plastic, you must rough-up the surface before spray will "bite" to it, or - it'll flippin' flake off. Just take off the shine, no more. You can use fine wet-and-dry for this (used dry), but we prefer Scotchbrite. This stuff, which looks much like a scouring pad, is available from motor factors and bodyshops, in several grades - we used ultra-fine, which is grey. One advantage of Scotchbrite is that it's a bit easier to work into awkward corners than paper.

04 Once the surface has been nicely "roughened", clean up the surface using a suitable degreaser ("suitable" means a type which won't dissolve plastic!). Generally, it's ok to use methylated spirit or cellulose thinners (just don't inhale!), but test it on a not-so-visible bit first, so you don't have a disaster.

05 Before you start spraying (if it's something smaller than a bumper) it's a good idea to try a work a screw into one of the mounting holes, to use as a "handle", so you can turn the item to spray all sides.

06 Another good trick is to use the screw to hang the item up on a piece of string or wire - then you can spin the item round to get the spray into awkward areas.

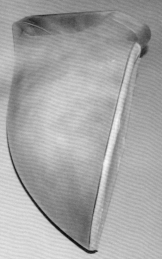
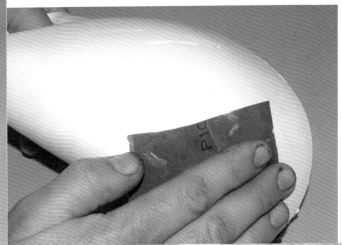

07 If you like a bit of wildlife in your paint, you can't beat the great outdoors. If it's at all windy, you'll end up with a really awful finish and overspray on everything (which can be a real bitch to get off). Even indoors, if it's damp weather, you'll have real problems trying to get a shine - some kind of heater is essential if it's cold and wet (but not one with a fan - stirring up the dust is the last thing you want).

08 If you're a bit new at spraying, or if you simply don't want to mess it up, practice your technique first (steady!). Working left-right, then right-left, press the nozzle so you start spraying just before you pass the item, and follow through just past it the other side. Keep the nozzle a constant distance from the item - not in a curved arc. Don't blast the paint on too thick, or you'll have a nasty case of the runs - hold the can about 6 inches away - you're not trying to paint the whole thing in one sweep.

09 Once you've got a patchy "mist coat" on (which might not even cover the whole thing) - stop, and let it dry (primer dries pretty quickly). Continue building up thin coats until you've got full coverage, then let it dry for half an hour or more.

10 Using 1000- or 1200-grade wet-and-dry paper (used wet), very lightly sand the whole primered surface, to take out any minor imperfections (blobs, where the nozzle was spitting) in the primer. Try not to go through the primer to the plastic, but this doesn't matter too much in small areas.

11 Rinse off thoroughly, then dry the surfaces - let it stand for a while to make sure it's *completely* dry, before starting on the top coat.

12 Make sure once again that the surfaces are clean, with no bits left behind from the drying operations. As with the primer, work up from an initial thin mist coat, allowing time for each pass to dry. As you spray, you'll soon learn how to build a nice shine without runs - any "dry" (dull) patches are usually due to overspray landing on still-wet shiny paint. Don't worry if you can't eliminate all of these - a light cutting polish will sort it out once the paint's hardened (after several hours).

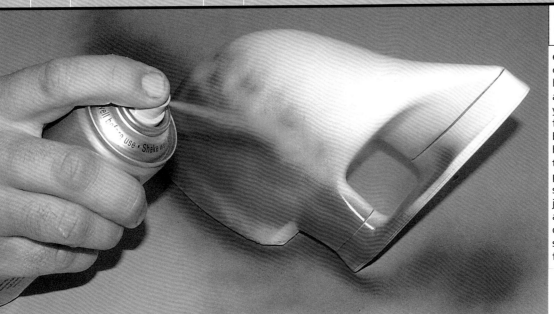

13 Especially with a colour like red (which is notorious for fading easily), it's a good idea to blow on a coat or two of clear lacquer over the top - this will also give you your shine, if you're stuck with a very "dry" finish. It's best to apply lacquer before the final top coat is fully hardened. The spraying technique is identical, although pro sprayers say that lacquer should be applied pretty thick - just watch those runs! Lacquer also takes a good long while to dry - pick up your item too soon, for that unique fingerprint effect!

De-locking

One very popular way to tidy up the Clio lines is to do away with the door locks, and even the door handles - but be careful.

Removing the rear door handles (on 5-door models) is okay, legally/MOT-speaking, but removing the front door handles will land you in trouble, come MOT time. There's something in the Construction & Use regs which requires an independent mechanical means of door opening from outside, probably so fire-fighters can get you out, if you stick your Nicole-mobile on its roof, or in a ditch… So - don't spend loads of time (or money, at a bodyshop) having cool and trendy mods done, which you then have to spend more money undoing!

Removing door lock barrels

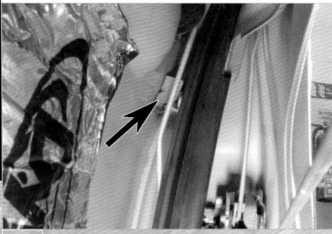

01 First, the door trim panel has to come off - but you knew that already. Look in "Interiors" for door trim panel removal. Trying to get a shot of the clip which holds the lock barrel in place was not easy, so don't all write in and complain. The good news is, it's a lot easier to remove it, once you've found it . . .

. . . you probably don't even need the pliers we've got in this picture, it's so easy. **02**

Equally non-brain-taxing is removing the lock barrel, once you've deprived it of its retaining clip - it literally falls out of the door, with only the operating rod needing to be unhooked from it. **03**

Reach back inside the door panel, and clip the lock barrel rod out of its spring clip. You can do this by feel - I'm not trying to get the camera in there again. Phase 1 of the de-locking process is now complete. **04**

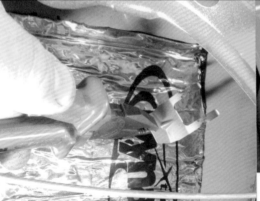

Removing door handles

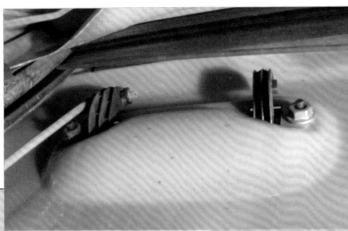

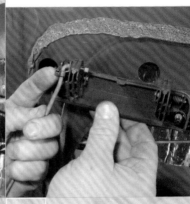

01 As we've already said, it's not a good idea to remove and flush your handles, unless you've got a very understanding, very unobservant, or very easily-bribed, MOT tester. The only reason we're showing you how to remove your handles is to colour-code them, okay? With the door trim panel off, peer inside and you'll see that the handles are held on by a nut either end.

02 So take your trusty spanner and best feeling hand, and remove the two nuts. But how does that handle operating rod come off? Of course, what we really mean is, how does it come off without busting it?

03 With the handle out of the door, it's easier to show you. The end of the rod's located in a plastic clip, which you release by swinging the rod towards you . . .

04 . . . and then out to the side. Once you've got your handle out, have a practice so you can refit it with confidence.

05 Colour-coding is the same procedure as for any other plastic spraying - give the handle a good rough-up with some Scotchbrite first . . .

06 . . . then start spraying (plastic primer first). This rather stylish method of suspending the handle for spraying works very well. After the colour base coat, treat those handles to a seriously-shiny coat of lacquer (and then don't touch for 24 hours!).

07 And the finished result. De-locked as well, it's the perfect way to clean up those elegant, understated Clio lines.

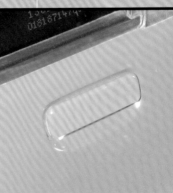

Removing the evidence

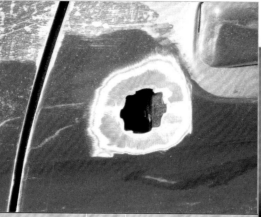

01 This looks like another job for - welding-boy! Better get the edges of the hole ready for some welding action. Filler alone, by the way, is not an option here.

02 One piece of card inside the door, one pen. One cardboard template, to make a metal "plug" from.

03 No-one ever sees welding-boy - he's so fast, you can only see him by where he's been.

04 Now a little rub-down, possibly with the grinder to start . . .

05 . . . and the filler can come out for a brief walk-on part. Now all we need is some paint. The same method will, of course, be put to good use on our de-repeatered front wings, too.

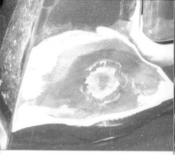

Remote locking

So you can lock and unlock your freshly de-locked doors, you'll need to buy and fit a remote central locking kit, which you can get from several Max Power-advertised suppliers (our Microscan kit, supplied by Performance Products Ltd of Chester, is really an extension kit for our chosen alarm, but is pretty typical of what you'll get). If your Clio already has central locking, you're in luck - buy yourself a cheap car alarm, and a central locking interface.

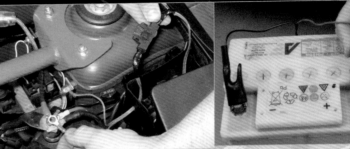

Tricks 'n' tips
If your battery goes flat, you'll be locked out. We ran two thin wires from the battery terminals (with a 10-amp fuse in the live, and the ends insulated), and tucked them away for access from below in an emergency. By connecting a slave battery to these wires (do not try jump-starting), you'll put enough juice into the system to operate the locks, saving you a red face. Think it over.

To wire up your alarm interface, the best advice is to follow the instructions with the kit - it's impossible to second-guess detailed instructions like this. For what it's worth, though, one piece of advice to bear in mind when tracking down the locking trigger wires is not to disconnect the wiring plugs inside the driver's door, for testing - the locking system won't work at all if you do, and you won't learn anything! On our Clio, the lock and unlock trigger wires were white/grey (lock) and pink (unlock), with a black earth wire, and a red/yellow live feed - all found behind the central locking relay in the fusebox (below the passenger-side dash).

When you come to test the operation, first make sure at least one window's open, in the unlikely event you lock yourself out. Also check that the doors are locked when the alarm's armed, and not the other way round!

Central locking kit

If your Clio doesn't have central locking as standard, don't despair - there's several kits out there to help you towards your goal.

Our project Clio already had central locking, so regrettably there are no Clio-specific photos to show you, but hopefully, the details below, together with your kit's instructions, will help you out.

Before you start fitting your new lock solenoids, it makes sense to test them. Connect them all together as described in your kit's instructions - with power connected to all the solenoids, pull up on the operating plunger of one, and all the rest should pop up too - clever, eh?

Decide where you're going to mount the lock control unit, then identify the various looms, and feed them out to the doors.

The new lock solenoids must be mounted so they work in the same *plane* as the door lock buttons. It's no good having the lock solenoid plungers moving horizontally, to work a button which operates vertically! Make up the mounting brackets from the metal bits provided in the kit, and fit the solenoids loosely in place.

The kit contains several items which look uncannily like bike spokes - these are your new lock operating rods, which have to be cut to length, then joined onto the old rods using screw clamps. It's best to join the old and new rods at a straight piece of the old rod, so feed the new rod in, and mark it for cutting.

Cut the new rod to the marked length, fit the cut rod to the solenoid, then slip the clamp onto it. Fit the solenoid onto its bracket, and offer the rod into place, to connect to the old rod. Join the new rod and old rod together, and fasten the clamp screws tight. If the clamp screws come loose, you're basically going to be locked out.

Now you can connect up the wires - the easy bit is joining up inside the door. Hopefully, your kit's instructions should be sufficient, but if not, you'll have to resort to the Haynes manual wiring diagrams.

Bumpers 'n' bodykits

The Mk 1 Clio is a well-established (if slightly rare) vehicle in the world of modding - and the good news is, there's a fair choice in bodykits.

Admittedly not much Jap-style stuff, or anything out-of-this-world radical, but some nice old-school kits. Most popular are the various wide-arch kits, usually known as the Clio "Maxi" or "F2", whoever you choose to buy yours from. Wide-arch is the way to go (for obvious reasons) if you're after big alloys; you can get 17s on a standard 16V Clio for one very good reason - the flared arches. With a decent wide-arch kit and a well-briefed bodyshop, 18s are quite possible. Then there's the Joker, Terminator and Alien kits, all offering plenty of extra foglight action at the front end, with a deep bumper and splitter.

Our kit is a proper French one, from French France - a company called AS Design (don't worry, at least one of them over there speaks English), and they turn out a pretty decent kit, which fits very well. Apart from the spraying, we did all the fitting ourselves - and so could you. This one bonds onto the existing bumpers - you chop off the bottom half, and attach the new bits with a combination of self-tappers and mastic.

Rear bumper

01 Get the rear of the car in the air, and both rear wheels off - do the job properly, as we tell you in "Wheels & tyres" . The first items to go are the rear wheel arch liners (which may have gone already, in the 17-inch rim fitting process). If not, you just undo one nut inside the arch . . .

02 . . . and one screw (two on the left-hand side) at the base of the bumper . . .

03 . . . and the offending plastic can be removed for good.

04 There's not a lot holding the bumper itself on, to be honest - just two nuts at the back edge, underneath (one in a recess) . . .

05 . . . then one bolt each side, inside the wheelarch . . .

06 . . . and off she pops. Pull out the end of the bumper to release the retaining peg inside . . .

07 . . . then lower away, and disconnect the plugs from the number plate lights.

08 As far as fitting the bodykit goes, it's much the same story we had for the front bumper. Put the new section on, eye it up . . .

09 . . . then chop off the bit you don't need any more, and drill, screw, mastic it on.

10 Ah, but it's never quite as easy as that. The rear bumper's a bit of a pig, as you can't easily get a screw in the bumper ends. To get over this, buy a pack of small shelving brackets from a DIY store (the little right-angled ones), and trim to size.

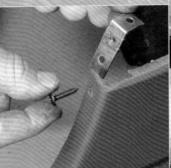

11 The trimmed bracket can then be drilled through and screwed to the end of the old bumper . . .

12 . . . to give an excellent mounting point for a small bolt. Sorted.

Front bumper

We took off our front bumper as part of the Morette headlight fitting process, just in case you think we're cheating here. Our Clio RT came with standard front fogs, which is gonna make fitting the new kit's lights a whole lot easier, later. But right now, they're in the way - luckily it's only two screws . . .

01

. . . and they're off (you'll already have disconnected the wiring, to get the bumper off).

02

Plonk the new 'lower bumper' onto the old one, and notice how well it fits. Very well, that is. The main cut line will already be pretty obvious, even from this pic, but mark up the central grille too, so you can trim that out.

03

It's a long job, cutting off the bottom half of your bumpers - flimsy plastic it ain't. If you have to use a hacksaw blade, get more than one, and wrap one end with masking tape, to save your hands. We'd like to tell you that this is really how we did it . . .

04

08 We're such perfectionists. Some sandpaper wrapped round a block of wood really gets those cut edges flat.

09 When you're happy with the fit (and you could do a trial fitting on the car, just to make absolutely sure), it's time to line it all up precisely, and drill some holes. You don't need to go mad with holes - with the mastic as well, six or eight screws will be plenty, but make sure you get one in each bumper end.

10 Before the mastic gun comes out, it's a good plan to roughen-up any shiny painted bits with some 'paper or Scotchbrite, to help it stick better.

11 You don't have to make pretty patterns with your mastic, just get a good covering on. This black stuff's well-messy to use - try getting it off your hands afterwards! The wisdom, therefore, is don't put too much on, as it'll ooze out when you do the screws up, and you'll be wiping it off forever.

05 . . . but we can't lie to you. We already had a workshop airline, so we borrowed an air hacksaw from our local bodyshop, and it flew through it - definitely the tool of choice, but fortunately not essential.

06 So how did we do? Offer on the new section, and check the fit.

07 You'll probably find there's a bit of trimming-up to do - the flatter you can get the join between the two pieces, the better the final fit will be. Don't rely too heavily on mastic to make good the rough edges.

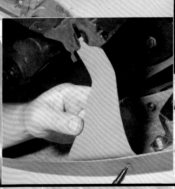

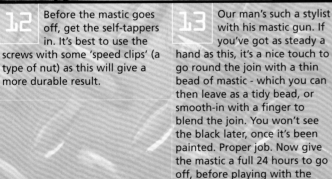

12 Before the mastic goes off, get the self-tappers in. It's best to use the screws with some 'speed clips' (a type of nut) as this will give a more durable result.

13 Our man's such a stylist with his mastic gun. If you've got as steady a hand as this, it's a nice touch to go round the join with a thin bead of mastic - which you can then leave as a tidy bead, or smooth-in with a finger to blend the join. You won't see the black later, once it's been painted. Proper job. Now give the mastic a full 24 hours to go off, before playing with the bumper any further.

14 Full marks to AS Design - they don't want their new bumper to be flimsy in any way. They provide these funny-shaped glassfibre 'plates', to brace the bumper to the old bumper brackets under the front end. Offer the plates in place, and mark them and the bumper edge for drilling . . . . . . then fix 'em in position.

15 Suppose it is important your new fogs/spots don't wobble about. There - that wasn't hard, was it? A pukka DIY bodykit.

Meshing a bumper

Don't mesh with me, boy

A meshed grille or bumper is just one way to demonstrate who's the daddy of the cruise, and it does a great job of dicing any small insects or rodents foolish enough to wander into the path of your motor. So if you're sick of scrubbing off insect entrails from your paint, and fancy getting even, read on…

Which style of mesh to choose? Classic diamond-shape, or round-hole? In our humble opinion, the round-hole mesh works best on modern roundy-shaped cars (like say, the Corsa) - for everything else, we'll settle for the original and best. But wait - the choice doesn't end with what shape you want. Mesh can now be had in various anodised colours too, to match or contrast with the rest of your chosen paint scheme.

01 Anyone can mesh a hole. Ab-so-lutely anyone - it's dead easy. First, measure your hole, then cut out a roughly-sized piece of mesh, leaving some over the sides to bend around the edges of your hole.

02 Having chopped the bottom off our old front bumper, we were left with these little stumps of the previous front bumper 'grille'. We decided to use these stumps as a marker point for bending down our new section of mesh, so out came the marker pen.

. . . then decide how you're going to pin it in place. This is the top edge of our mesh, and we're drilling through into the old bumper, to put in some self-tappers. Notice we've now done away with the 'stumps' we had earlier (we were worried they'd be visible).

03 Getting a straight line is tricky when bending mesh, but not if you bend it round something else. We're sure we won't be alone in having a few MDF offcuts lying about.

04 Trim off any excess mesh . . .

05

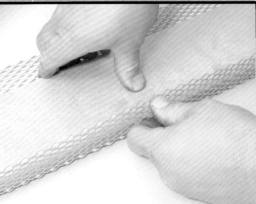

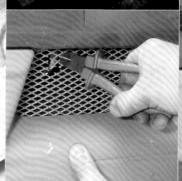

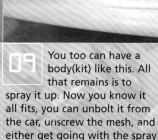

06 Self-tapping screws really are the best way to secure mesh . . .

07 . . . especially when your bodykit manufacturer provides ready-made holes for fixing it to. Nice.

08 The only remaining problem was that our newly-meshed bumper wouldn't fit back on when we tried it. The reason? We'd forgotten about the front towing eye. Now you could just cut this off - it's not essential - but it'd be a long job with a hacksaw. Better to keep it, and demonstrate your prowess with the side-cutters instead, to trim neatly round it.

09 You too can have a body(kit) like this. All that remains is to spray it up. Now you know it all fits, you can unbolt it from the car, unscrew the mesh, and either get going with the spray cans or hand it to a bodyshop.

. . . and smoothing it in by hand to make sure it's stuck. This man's wearing gloves - he's had mastic on his hands before, obviously (it's virtually impossible to get off). Wait for the mastic to dry before cutting any holes in it, for exhausts or towing eyes. Using the mastic method, it shouldn't take more than about 10 minutes to mesh your average hole - so what are you waiting for?

It won't always be possible to use the self-tapper method to secure your mesh - but don't panic. Mesh can also be secured using glassfibre (very sticky stuff, and chances are, your bodykit's made of it - so it's bound to work). Wear gloves.

Another common way to approach the mesh-application problem is to use the same stuff we bonded the kit on with - mastic. Very easy to apply. Here, we've got a bonnet vent hole being meshed, and the first job is to bend the edges of the mesh over . . .

. . . before pinning them with a thick bead of the black stuff . . .

10

11

12

13

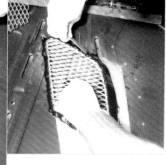

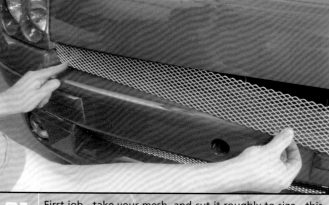

Meshing the front grille

The Clio's hardly got a front grille, really - blink and you'd miss it. But - rip out the plastic excuse for a grille and replace with mesh, and you've got yourself a kicking exterior feature, suddenly. Our old 'grille' came out while we were fitting our Morette lights, in case you're still wondering what we're talking about.

01 First job - take your mesh, and cut it roughly to size - this bit we do with the bonnet on.

02 Now the bad news - to do a decent job, the bonnet must come off. But - this isn't difficult on a Clio, providing you've got an able-bodied mate handy. With one of you on each side, undo the two nuts on each bonnet hinge, and it lifts away. Make sure you don't lose the metal packing plates fitted between the hinge and bonnet.

03 Once you're over the shock of how easy it is to remove a Clio bonnet, you can start making up some mesh mounting brackets. These we're adapting from some small shelf brackets from the local DIY store - you could fit just one in the centre, but we chose two. The outer ends of the mesh can be secured using the old headlight mounting screw holes (left over when we fitted our Morettes).

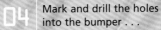

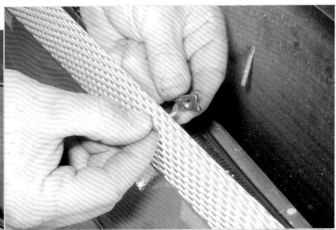

04 Mark and drill the holes into the bumper . . .

05 . . . and screw the brackets in place. If you go for fairly fine-pattern mesh, you really don't see the brackets behind unless you look closely - especially if you choose bright-finish brackets.

06 To make your mesh mounting as discreet as possible, you need some small self-tappers, and some 'speed clips' or 'cage nuts' clipped to your brackets, for them to screw into.

07 Moving out to the edges of our mesh, we come to the bonnet hinges. Might be nice if you could still open the bonnet after meshing the grille, so get trimming with the side-cutters . . .

08 . . . and check that the hinges are free to move. You don't really want to find out you got it wrong, after you put the bonnet back on.

09 At the ends, we used several washers behind the mesh, to bring it forward, which meant using a longer self-tapper than we really anticipated. The only long ones we had were black, which looked a bit obvious against the mesh. So we sprayed them silver - simple.

10 This really is one heavily-modded Clio front end, and the mesh grille looks great with the de-badged bonnet. Don't worry - the two brackets don't show up as much as this in real life (and you could always get away with just one in the centre, if you prefer). And no, we don't know what the hole in the front bumper's for, either. Starting handle? At least the number plate will cover it.

Side skirts

Side skirts can act as an "artificial" way of visually lowering the car, making it seem lower to the ground than it really is, and they also help to "tie together" the front and rear sections of a full bodykit. But where did skirts really come from?

As with so much else in modifying, it's a racing-inspired thing traceable back to the famous Lotus "ground-effect" F1 cars, which blew the opposition away.

So will fitting skirts to your Clio give you race-car levels of downforce, greatly increasing your overtaking opportunities at the next roundabout? You already know the answer, I'm afraid...

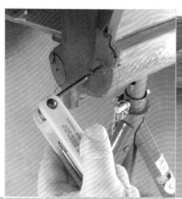

01 If the skirts you've got are of decent quality, fitting is a piece of - very easy indeed. With the help of a willing accomplice, offer one on, making sure you've got it the right way round. Does it fit any sense? Now's the time to exercise your right to send it back, if it don't. Otherwise, some minor adjustments with a Stanley knife may be the best solution. At the front end, we figured we'd re-use this screw, which holds the wheel arch liner in place . . .

02 . . . now we offer up the skirt, and try to mark where the hole needs to be in it, to line up with the one in the car. We're talking best-guess territory here . . .

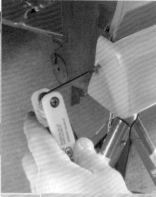

03 . . . but fortunately, we're spot-on. Okay, so those wheel arch liners might have to go when we try our 17s on, but the hole will still be there, so our skirts will still fit.

04 At the back end, there's no ready-made hole for us to pillage, so we'll have to make our own. There's not much room for error with the drill . . .

05 . . . but there's just enough room for a self-tapper, with a speed clip behind.

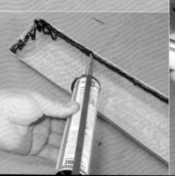

06 Okay, so you're sure the skirt's a good fit, and you've done all the trimming and general fettling. Get brave - get out the mastic gun, and bond it on for good. Or maybe you should spray it first? Your choice. Anyway, when you're finally ready, get a good thick bead of the black on there . . .

07 . . . and, like we did for the bumpers, run another fine bead along the join to the body. Nothing to it, really.

Tailgate **smoothing**

Achieving the complete "smooth-tailgate" look isn't too involved a procedure, providing you know someone who can weld, and are handy with filler and spray. Completely smoothing the tailgate is a logical extension of de-badging - the first thing to go is the rear wiper. Rear wipers are undoubtedly useful, and were put there for a good reason, but hey - that's just boring. Remove the rear wiper and the lock button, and fill over the holes - easy, eh?. Well, yes, except that most of the holes are too big to just filler over, and will probably need glassfibre matting or welding. At least you don't have to relocate the number plate on a Clio.

If you're going to de-lock the tailgate, you'll need to devise a means of opening the thing afterwards, if only so your mates can admire your ICE install. Options range from attaching a cable to the lock itself, feeding it through for manual operation, or fitting a solenoid kit and wiring it up to a convenient switch.

Tailgate lower trim

01 Only fitted to the Phase 2 Clios, this inoffensive piece of plastic is supposed to 'link' the smoked rear lights together. Gee whizz. At least removing is easy - with the inner trim panel prised off, remove the screws at each end . . .

02 . . . and the ones almost-cunningly hidden in the middle . . .

03 . . . and the smokey strip is no more. You could always spray it body-colour and refit, but we never seem to take the easy option!

Rear wiper

01 Lift the cover from the tailgate wiper arm, and unscrew the nut underneath.

02 Hopefully your wiper arm will come off without resorting to such drastic means as this little puller. Our wiper arm just wasn't coming off any other way. If you have to resort to extreme violence, try not to damage the surrounding tailgate, or you'll be making even more work for the bodyshop.

03 Going inside, prise down the tailgate trim panel. If you really need to see this, it's in the previous section. For more advanced users, the next job is unplugging the wiper motor.

04 Now it's just three little bolts . . .

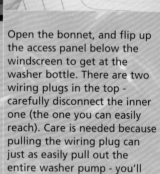

05 . . . and the wiper motor can be consigned to the bin. If enough people start doing it, the council will have to set up wiper motor recycling points - we've got quite a collection by now.

06 There's the small matter of the rear washer to deal with next. Getting rid of it's easy - pull off the washer tube . . .

07 . . . and unclip the washer jet (which is actually the 'surround' for the wiper arm mounting) from the tailgate. So far, so good. But what happens if you accidentally squirt the washers? You get a boot full of water, that's what. Luckily, sorting this problem isn't too tricky either - had your choice of French hatch been a Saxo, you'd be in for a ton of work about now.

08 Open the bonnet, and flip up the access panel below the windscreen to get at the washer bottle. There are two wiring plugs in the top - carefully disconnect the inner one (the one you can easily reach). Care is needed because pulling the wiring plug can just as easily pull out the entire washer pump - you'll then have a small flood to deal with. Tape up the plug once you've disconnected it.

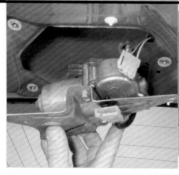

Tailgate button

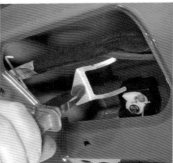

01 If you haven't already, prise down the tailgate trim panel. Here we are in mid-prise.

02 Before you can get to the lock button any sense, you have to lose the wiper motor as well - luckily, ours disappeared very recently (this job's covered on the previous page). Pull the lock button operating rod out of the little red clip . . .

03 . . . then, with that out of the way, use a pair of pliers to slide off the lock button's metal retaining clip.

04 The lock button should now fall out of the tailgate. If not, the reason why is the lock operating rod's still clipped into it - you can just see the end of the rod inside the hole here. We'll be needing that later, for our lock solenoid.

Tailgate smoothing

01 When you've got big holes in your tailgate to fill, the filler doesn't come out 'til much later. For a proper job, you cut out a piece of metal, stick it inside your hole, and weld it in.

02 No matter how good a welder you are, you'll always need a grinder.

03 Now the filler comes out to play, to hide the evidence - soon, no-one will suspect a thing.

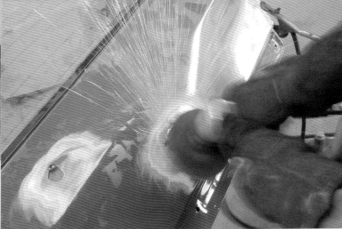

>>

04 After much professional sanding-down, this is how your tailgate should look. You'll never achieve a totally-smooth finish with just one layer of filler - a few light skims after the initial one will eventually give you perfection. For filling-in the tiny air holes which appear when you rub down, use cellulose putty, which is 'thinner' than normal filler. To get a flat surface, always use a flat piece of wood to wrap your wet-and-dry around. Take your time - if it's not quite right now, it'll look worse sprayed.

05 Filler's all very well, but you can't use it to hide everything. The smoked plastic strip on our tailgate went ages ago, but we can't put a great lump of filler at the base of the tailgate, to hide where it used to be - it'd fall off the first time you slam it shut! Tony at Sedna's has made up a strip of metal with a narrow flange at the top edge, which we first try for size . . .

06 . . . before welding it in place. We'll only be needing a light skim of filler now.

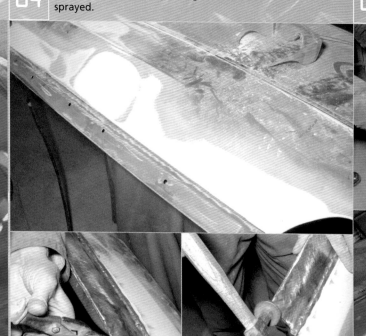

07 Once it's cooled, the ends can be trimmed. Rather than trim off all the metal, the idea is to leave enough that we can bend over a narrow edge.

08 This is where your bodyshop man earns his money - you or I start attacking our cars with hammers to delicately shape something like this, and the end result's a warzone. The metal edge that's been folded over can be tacked in place . . .

09 . . . before the filler comes out once more. Now it looks like a smoothed tailgate - all it need now is paint.

10 The professional touch - always ends up looking better, and if it doesn't, you've got someone else to blame!

Tailgate removal

01 It's all very well for us to say 'take your tailgate to a bodyshop to have the holes filled-in' - how does it come off, then? It's actually quite a bit of work, mostly in removing wiring. There's quite a major harness to disconnect in there, held on by clips like this, which can be prised apart.

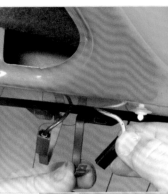

02 There's wires for the heated rear window . . .

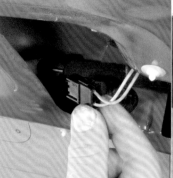

03 . . . and the tailgate lock (if you've got central locking). We assume if you're going this far that you've already unplugged your rear wiper motor.

04 Feeding all this wire out will be easier if you remove the right-hand corner trim, held on by a Torx screw - just lets you get your hand inside.

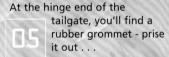

At the hinge end of the tailgate, you'll find a rubber grommet - prise it out . . .

05

. . . then, making sure all the wires are disconnected, pull the harness through.

06

The two tailgate support struts are released by prising out the metal spring clips. Don't pull the struts off their balljoint fittings until you've been joined by an able-bodied volunteer from the audience.

07

The two tailgate hinge nuts are hidden above two oval-shaped panels at the back of the headlining. Only undo these once your assistant has arrived, and is supporting at least one half of the tailgate's weight. Pop off the support struts, and the tailgate is away.

08

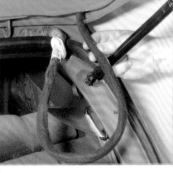

Tailgate
remote
release

It might be a good idea if you could still open your flushed tailgate, don't you think? How are you meant to put the shopping in - er... I mean how are you meant to show off that wicked boot install, if you can't open the boot?

01 Our Clio already had central locking, and it's quite a common fitment across the range. We managed to rig up a remote release, using just the standard components - if your Clio is a manual-locking pauper model, you could always raid the scrapyard for the Clio bits you need. With the tailgate trim panel off, disconnect the actuator wiring plug, and remove the single Torx mounting screw . . .

02 . . . then the motor's just located on a single push-in peg, and it just slides out. Also unclip the actuator's operating rod - we'll be recycling that, too.

03 The actuator must now be mounted vertically inside the tailgate, because the tailgate lock rod moves in a vertical plane. We used a metal strip approx 175 mm long to screw the motor to, but there's lots of trial-and-error involved getting it shaped to mount on the tailgate.

04 The actuator operating rod we salvaged earlier can now be clipped into the eye on the actuator pushrod. It's not easy to see, but we secured the end of the rod with a small split-pin.

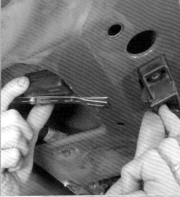

05 This is the tailgate lock, secured by two large Torx screws. Normally, the lock operating rod is free to move in a large slot on the lock operating lever - we found we needed a bolt through one end of the slot (which you can see here) to reduce the range of movement available.

06 Now all these bits have to be assembled and trial-fitted to the tailgate, to see if any of our cunning plans are going to work. First in is the actuator, with its operating rod attached . . .

07 . . . then we can hook the rod onto the lock lever . . .

08 . . . before finally getting our first inkling of whether we're anywhere close. Remember - that actuator has to be mounted so it'll work in a straight, vertical line. Since the actuator's skewed on the metal bracket, the bracket will have to sit at an angle on the tailgate.

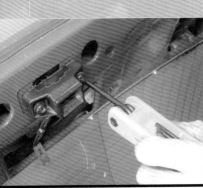

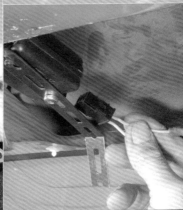

09 Let's screw the tailgate lock in place now - that can only go in one position.

10 Obviously, if we're re-using the old boot central locking actuator, we'd better have its wiring plug - chop it off with plenty of wire attached.

11 From the Haynes manual wiring diagrams, we established that the beige wire was earth. With a ring terminal fitted to it, we'll be able to use one of the mounting bracket screws later on as an earth point. The purple wire (obviously the live) got the bullet.

12 Doctored wiring plug gets re-united with actuator. Ahh.

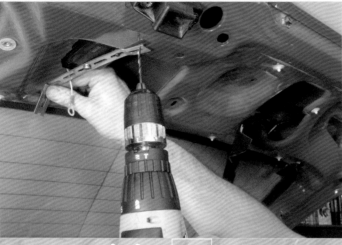

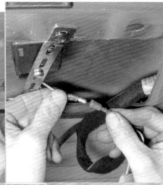

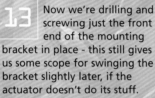

13 Now we're drilling and screwing just the front end of the mounting bracket in place - this still gives us some scope for swinging the bracket slightly later, if the actuator doesn't do its stuff.

14 So where are we going to get a decent switched live supply from, to work the actuator? We don't want to mess about running new wires into the tailgate - what if there was something in the tailgate, no longer needed, with its own dashboard switch, which we could re-assign? Like the rear wiper, perhaps? Turns out it's the grey wire we want, so it got chopped . . .

15 . . . then bulleted and connected to the doctored actuator wiring plug. So to work the tailgate, all you have to do is flick the rear wiper switch on, then off. Don't leave the switch in the on position, or the tailgate won't shut, as the lock's being held open by the actuator (yes, it's the voice of bitter experience talking here).

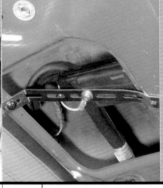

16 All that's left are the details. We fitted our earth wire using the actuator mounting screw, in the end - but we could've used one of the mounting bracket screws instead. Don't be tempted to use the black earth wire from the wiper motor plug - it's not a good enough earth to rely on.

17 Our actuator worked better with the mounting bracket moved further over than expected . . .

18 . . . but when we were happy, out came the drill, and the bracket was nailed. If you're using self-tappers, it's good practice to also use 'speed clips' behind, to give the screws something to bite into (helps stop the screws coming loose).

19 The finished article's so neat, it's almost a shame to refit the tailgate trim panel.

Rear spoilers

No Clio can claim to be fully-kitted without a rear spoiler - even if it's just standard rear window type from a 16V or RSi, fitted to a basic model. But we don't want to give you that.

The Clio roof slopes down quite a bit towards the rear, and so is in dire need of something pert to perk up its rear end. Going all discreet really isn't an option, so most Clio owners (and most bodykit manufacturers) favour something along the lines of a DTM style flipped-up spoiler, to give the rear a lift. Get hold of one of these, flush your tailgate, and you're well on the way to toning up your rear end. So to speak.

01 It's not absolutely essential, but getting a mate to help when you're first eyeing-up a rear spoiler for fitting is a big plus. And it gives you someone else to blame. Stick on two big patches of masking tape, roughly where the spoiler mountings will be, and while your assistant holds it straight and central, mark round the spoiler 'legs'.

02 Just in case you thought that's all there was to it, you really should now open the tailgate, and check that you'll still be able to open it, with the new plastic/fibreglass in place. Make new marks as necessary.

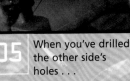

03 Now you have to mark the spoiler mounting holes, inside your newly-drawn outlines (ours had four holes altogether). Turn the spoiler upside-down, and measure the hole-centre distances from the front of the spoiler 'legs'. By measuring the same distances on your masking tape outline, you can accurately mark where the holes need to be.

04 This is brave stuff - there's no going back now. Don't use brute strength when drilling through this close to the tailgate glass - need we say more about what could happen? Also, don't expect to drill right through to the inside - the Clio tailgate is multi-skinned, as we're about to prove. Stop drilling when you're through the first 'layer'.

05 When you've drilled the other side's holes . . .

06 . . . it's time-out for a quick trial fitting. Our spoiler, like most universal types, has threaded holes, so you can fit bolts up from inside the tailgate to secure it in place . . .

>>

07 . . . but what you can also do is get some studs (bolts without heads) or threaded bar the right size, and screw these into the threaded holes, to take nuts.

08 With the studs fitted, we can see if those holes are in the right place. Does the spoiler sit right, or are adjustments needed? You can adjust the fit of the spoiler at this stage by filing-out the drilled holes - but only do this a little at a time, and re-check the fit often.

09 The fun part on Clio spoiler fitting comes when you realise they really weren't meant to have a tailgate spoiler at all. Meaning you have to make two stuffin' great holes in the tailgate, to give you any chance of tightening the mounting nuts/bolts. Establish where your tailgate access holes need to be, and mark them out neatly, for drilling . . .

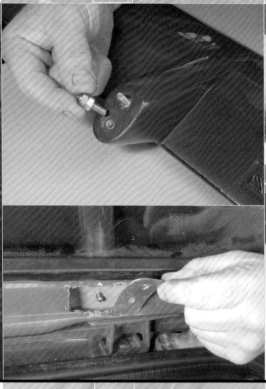

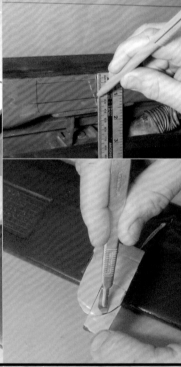

14 Because our mechanic wasn't happy about chopping away so much metal, he wanted to put some strength back into the tailgate by making up two small plates, roughly the same size as the two 'footprints' of the spoiler 'legs'. With two holes drilled through for the studs, these get bolted up inside the tailgate, and should mean there's less strain around the mounting holes.

15 Another cause for concern was that, while the bottoms of the spoiler 'legs' are flat, the Clio tailgate is curved. Not only does this look naff, it means there's potential for the spoiler to wobble about more than would be cool. The answer? Well, you could spend ages with a grinder, profiling the legs to the tailgate... Or you stick on some thick double-sided tape . . .

16 . . . and trim it to shape with a sharp knife. This will compress nicely when the mountings are tightened up, and being sticky also helps to pin the spoiler in place. Another winner.

10 . . . lots and lots of drilling. In the absence of a special tailgate-hole-making tool, I'm afraid we had to resort to the drill-lots-of-holes method . . .

11 . . . then bash along the drilled line of holes with a small chisel, remembering all the time that's glass over your head . . .

12 . . . until you have something that looks like a reject from the shuriken factory in your hand. And yes, there's another skin of metal behind the red stuff, so keep going.

13 If you've made your hole big enough (and in the right place), you'll be able to fit your stud-equipped spoiler in place, and secure it inside using nuts and washers. The washers are especially important if a great deal of filing 'adjustments' had to be made.

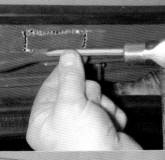

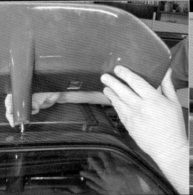
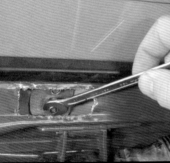

17 So it's peel off the backing tape, slot her in position . . .

18 . . . fit your bracing plates inside, with washers and (Nyloc, please, we don't want them coming undone) nuts, and tighten it all up. No 1.4 litre Clio ever had so much rear downforce - what a racer!

19 Hang on, our mechanic's not happy yet. Not wanting the world to see the extent of the butchery that's been inflicted on this innocent Clio tailgate, he fabricates two neat metal plates . . .

20 . . . and screws them in place over the unsightly holes, with two self-tappers. Pride in the job, we calls it - bit of red over those plates, and no-one would suspect a thing. Except anyone reading this, of course.

Wheelarch mods

Your new 17s will doubtless catch on the front edge of the bumper, but this depends on what bodykit you may have fitted. Our bonded-on kit certainly had problems, as did the stock front bumper before that. The best way to deal with the problem of catching is to get busy with the chopping tools, and trim off the

01 inside edge of the bumper. One problem sorted.

The law states that not one smidgeon of rubber shall protrude from outside your wheelarches, and the MOT crew will not be impressed if your new rubber's rubbing, either. This presents something of a problem, if you're fitting wide 17s, especially to a car that's also having a radical drop job. If you've exhausted all possibilities with spacers (or wheels with a more friendly offset - see "Wheels & tyres"), those arches are gonna have to be trimmed.

Our wheelarch mods were done at a bodyshop - but if you're brave and reasonably talented, there's nothing to stop you having a go yourself. The only trouble we had with our 17s was on the front - we couldn't get any steering lock at all, at first. On the rear, the wheels were tight, admittedly, but there's not much of an arch lip to roll, so you wouldn't really gain much by doing that. If you have problems on the back, you can always bring the rear end up a little, on the torsion bars - see 'Suspension'.

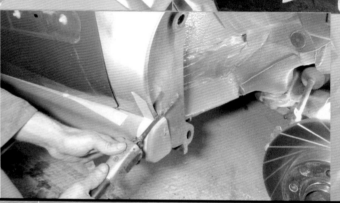

02 We really should've known better when we fitted those side skirts. By slipping the front edge of the skirt over the wheelarch liner, we've made a real problem for ourselves - don't make the same mistake. Now we've got to trim down the skirt before we can even think about taking the arch liner out, which is essential.

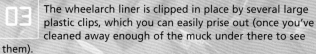

03 The wheelarch liner is clipped in place by several large plastic clips, which you can easily prise out (once you've cleaned away enough of the muck under there to see them).

04 This is a major piece of plastic, and it's not hard to see why it might cause problems for oversize rims.

With the plastic removed, we can see what we're dealing with. Most of the metal edges you can see here are surplus to requirements, and can be trimmed back. The best way to go about this is to pop your 17-incher on, and turn the steering little by little, to see what the tyre hits next, and trim it away. Remember to allow about half an **05** inch of movement room.

This is the finished result on our Clio, with a little glassfibre used to make good the butchery inflicted on the front of the skirt. Now we can get **06** full lock in either direction.

The only problem left is that there's not much vertical travel left, with the wheel on lock, before the top of the tyre fouls the top of the arch - our car had a 55 mm drop on the front, and we **07** wouldn't advise going any more than this (maybe go for slightly less, for road use).

Bonnet vents

Once you've got your bodykit on, it's only natural you'll want a bonnet vent, isn't it? Respect. But this is one SCARY job to tackle yourself, unless you're really that good, or that brave. Leave it in the hands of the professionals, is our advice. Plenty of options - you can get little louvres stamped in as well, to complement your Evo, Impreza, Integrale or Celica GT4 main vent. A more recent trend is the F50 vent, but this is often a tad large for the Clio's weeny bonnet. There's even been a feature car with a bonnet scoop from a (sensible) Kia Sedona people carrier! Truly, anything goes.

If you're not one of the 16V-owning brigade, you can at least pretend by fitting the 16V's bonnet bulge (there's nothing like having an impressive bulge, or two). You could even buy a complete 16V bonnet - might not cost as much as you'd think, especially for a pattern item. Perhaps because the Mk 1 Clio's a bit old-school in the styling department, an equally well-used bonnet vent like the Evo seems to work very well. But the choice, as always, is yours. Be brave - be original.

Respraying

01 Here's one we didn't mask up earlier. Pro bodyshops even have special hoods to fit over your wheels.

02 There's nothing like being prepared. The tailgate's hung up, the bonnet's on a stand, and the rear spoiler's... er... sitting on a plank?

Not happy with your Clio's "pensioner blue" paint? Fancy something just a tad more head-turning than stomach-churning? There's really only one answer - and it's time to call in the pros. DIY is what we're all about, but we're not going to pretend this is something we'd undertake lightly ourselves - there's no such thing as a simple respray (not one that'll look good afterwards, at any rate).

Our Clio didn't have a full respray, but by the time we'd smoothed the tailgate, bonded-on a bodykit, de-badged the bonnet and removed the side repeaters, it wasn't very far off.

03 This chap knows what he's doing. This must've been the first part of the job - how do we know this? Because you can still see him.

04 Is this what's known as the 'red mist'? Now you see why he's wearing the attractive breathing apparatus - and this is just the red base coat. Lacquer's even more evil stuff to breathe in.

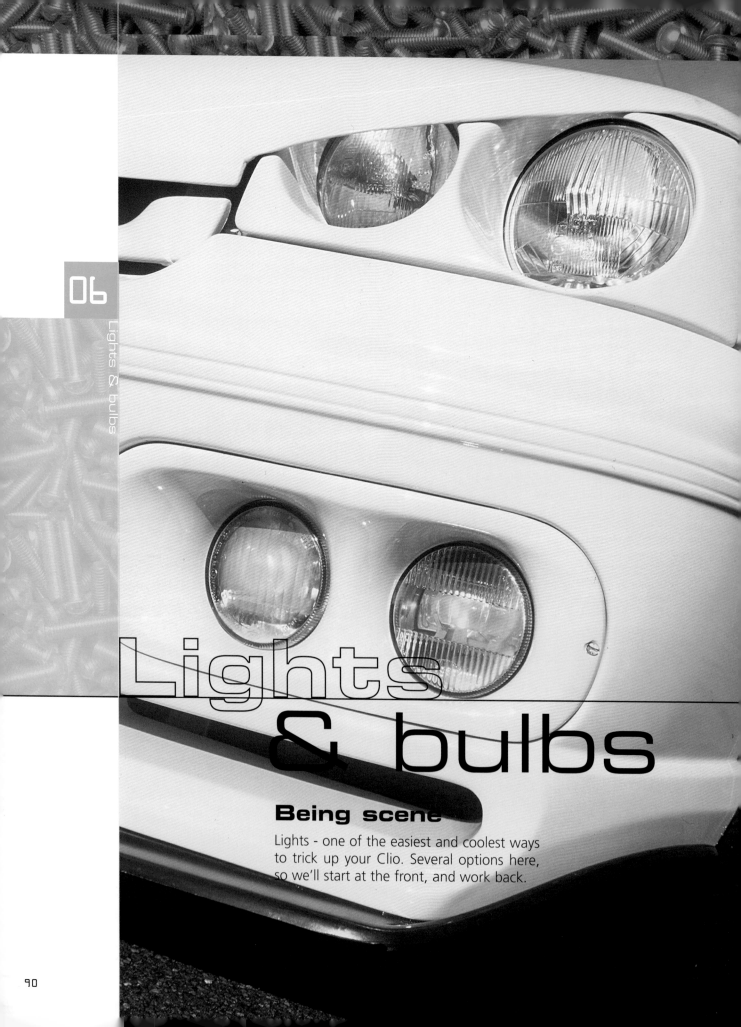

Lights
& bulbs

Being scene

Lights - one of the easiest and coolest ways
to trick up your Clio. Several options here,
so we'll start at the front, and work back.

Headlights

Almost nothing influences the look of your Clio more than the front end, so the headlights play a crucial role.

If you took our advice at the start of the book, and didn't buy a Phase 3 Clio, you're in luck - there's much more choice in lights for Phase 1 and 2 models. Shame really, 'cos the Phase 3 models are the ones most in dire need of a headlight makeover. There just ain't no justice.

What's available?

For most people, there's several popular routes to modding the Clio headlights - some cheap, and… well… some rather less cheap (but more effective).

The popular cheap option is stick-on headlight "brows", which do admittedly give the rather bland Clio front end a tougher look. The brows are best sprayed to match the car, before fitting - some have sticky pads, others can be fitted using mastic. Street-cred on the cheap, and (if you want) a cheap alternative to a proper "badboy" bonnet.

Another cheap option is again stick-on - this time, it's stick-on covers which give the twin-headlight look. This is basically a sheet of vinyl (shaped to the headlights, and colour-matched to your car) with two holes cut in it. Dead easy to fit, but dare we say, a bit tacky? Just our opinion. A cheap and simple way to get close to the Morette look.

If you want tinted headlights, you could try spray-tinting them, but go easy on the spray. Turning your headlights from clear glass to non-see-through is plain daft, even if it's done in the name of style. A light tint is quite effective, and gives you the chance to colour-match to your Clio. Unlike newer cars, there don't seem to be any companies offering ready-made tinted replacement lights for the Clio. At least, not yet. With tinted headlights, you'd be wise to tint those clear front indicators too, of course, so you'll be looking to fit some orange bulbs too.

Getting more expensive, we're looking at complete replacement lights - "proper" twin-headlights, available as a kit from the French company Morette (ours came from those good-natured fellas at Auto Tint Design). Typically around £300 a set at time of writing, these are for lads who're seriously into their cars - maximum cred, and no-one's gonna accuse you of owning a "boring" Clio ever again! The light surrounds have to be sprayed to match your car, and fitting is not without some difficulties, but the finished result is SO worth it.

Another "headlight" option often featured on Clios actually belongs in the bodywork section - it's the "badboy" bonnet. By cunningly welding-in a couple of triangular plates to your standard

Clio bonnet, a bodyshop (or handy DIY-er) can create a really mean look, using just the standard lights. Excellent.

Finally, there's one more adventurous option for those who really want their car to look something different. Definitely one for the bodyshop, but you won't beat it for effect - try fitting standard headlights from another car altogether. A popular choice is the Mk 1 Laguna, but there's no limit if you use your imagination.

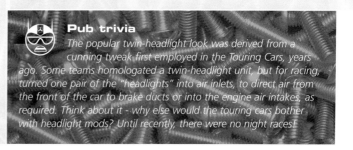

Pub trivia
The popular twin-headlight look was derived from a cunning tweak first employed in the Touring Cars, years ago. Some teams homologated a twin-headlight unit, but for racing, turned one pair of the "headlights" into air inlets, to direct air from the front of the car to brake ducts or into the engine air intakes, as required. Think about it - why else would the touring cars bother with headlight mods? Until recently, there were no night races!

Morette
twin headlights

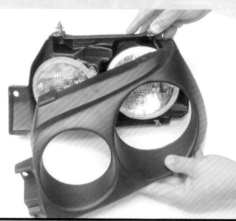

01 You can, of course, choose when you're going to colour-code your Morette headlight surrounds. We decided to do ours as the first step, rather than fit them and take them off again (the surround screws aren't easy to get at, in place). Just four screws hold each surround on.

02 Even though these are far too new to have suffered from silicone, it's still a good idea to clean, rough-up and clean again before spraying.

03 Now it's plastic primer (not ordinary primer yet - it's not 'elastic') . . .

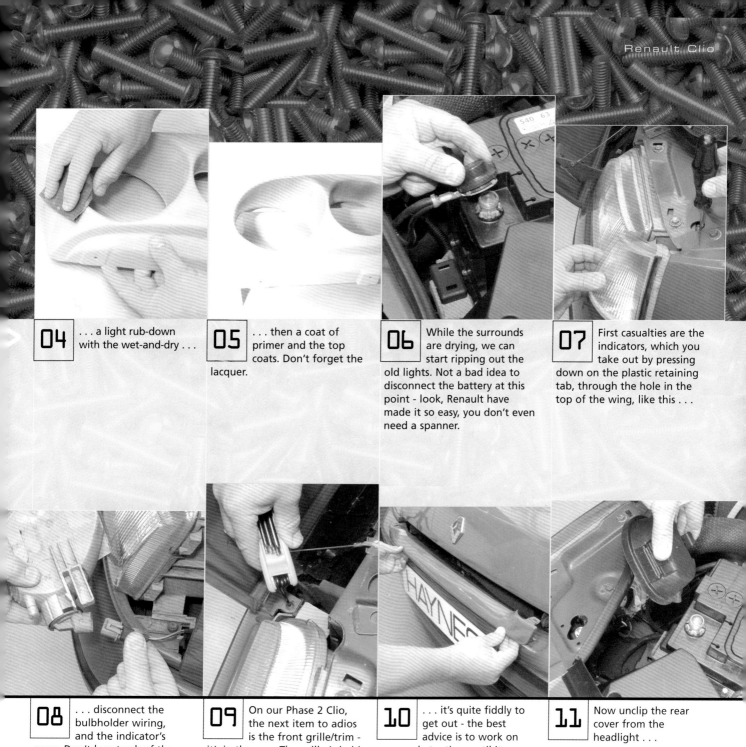

04 . . . a light rub-down with the wet-and-dry . . .

05 . . . then a coat of primer and the top coats. Don't forget the lacquer.

06 While the surrounds are drying, we can start ripping out the old lights. Not a bad idea to disconnect the battery at this point - look, Renault have made it so easy, you don't even need a spanner.

07 First casualties are the indicators, which you take out by pressing down on the plastic retaining tab, through the hole in the top of the wing, like this . . .

08 . . . disconnect the bulbholder wiring, and the indicator's gone. Don't lose track of the indicator wiring - you'll be needing that again later.

09 On our Phase 2 Clio, the next item to adios is the front grille/trim - it's in the way. The grille is held by a Torx screw at each end, and there's a clip in the middle . . .

10 . . . it's quite fiddly to get out - the best advice is to work on one end at a time until it unclips.

11 Now unclip the rear cover from the headlight . . .

12 . . . and pull off the wiring plugs (main/dipped beam and sidelight) from the bulbs. Worth noting which plug does what, as this will reduce the confusion later when wiring-in the new lights.

13 The headlight levelling adjuster is easy enough to disconnect, but tricky to show you. To make things clearer, we shot it with the headlight out - first, there's a lever which you press in to detach the balljoint fitting . . .

14 . . . and the cable outer fitting is a bayonet fitting on the light, so twist and pull to remove it. The adjuster cable's a bit redundant on your new lights, but don't cut it off unless you're sure the car will never be put back to standard.

15 Meanwhile, your headlight isn't out yet. There's three bolts holding it on top . . .

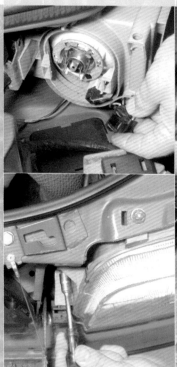
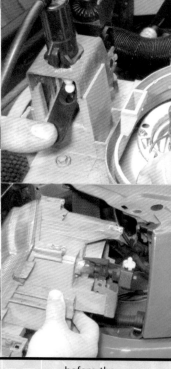
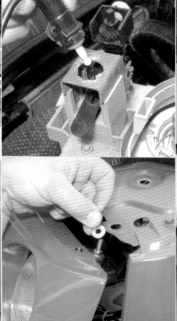

16 . . . and one removed from in front . . .

17 . . . before the headlight finally slides out. It's a lot easier on a Fiesta, we can tell you.

18 You can pretty much fit your new Morettes right away - complete with colour-coded shells, of course. Put a washer on each stud, before it goes in . . .

19 . . . and one on each before you fit the mounting nuts.

20 Hmm. Before and after. Now tell me these lights ain't worth the money. Cheers to Auto Tint Design, for helping us to transform the front of our Clio.

21 They might look sweet, but they don't work yet. To make more room for wiring up the left-hand light, you could take out the battery completely, but there's not much chance of improving things on the right-hand side. With well-designed lights like these, getting it all working is pretty easy - the main headlight bulb plug goes straight on the outer light . . .

22 . . . while these two little spade connectors push into the old sidelight wiring plug. Simple so far, or what?

23 Getting a wee bit more technical now, we need to identify the old wire for main beam - according to our Haynes wiring diagram, it's a white wire. Using the Scotch-lok connector supplied, join the yellow wire from the Morettes to the white wire - crush the connector with pliers to do a decent job. Incidentally, if your main beam ever stops working, that connector could be your prime suspect…

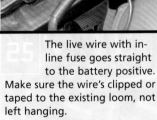
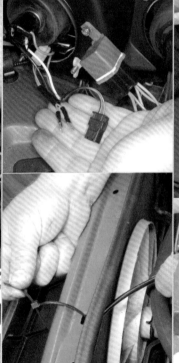
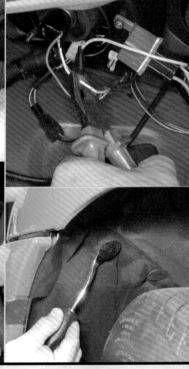

24 Now we need a good earth for the grey wire with the ring terminal. You're close enough to the battery that you could run one straight from the negative connection, but we found a nice bolt on the gearbox mounting, just crying out to be used. Do it back up tight.

25 The live wire with in-line fuse goes straight to the battery positive. Make sure the wire's clipped or taped to the existing loom, not left hanging.

26 All that remains is to run the wiring harness from the left-hand light to the right, and plug that in too. Nothing to it. Again, make sure the lighting wires get fed across the engine neatly - there's a radiator in the picture, for starters, which gets hot enough to melt things. Cable-tie the wiring up to the engine front panel, using the holes Renault have thoughtfully provided, and you'll have no probs.

27 You'll have noticed by now there's a slight lack of indicators. Morette provide you with two new lights, to fit to the front bumper, but this means the bumper's got to come off, as you'll be cutting holes. First to go are these two push-in plastic clips, holding the wheel arch liners (if you're already on 17s, these may have disappeared long ago).

28 There's now a small screw (Torx, obviously - it's French) at the bottom edge of the bumper . . .

29 . . . and a nut underneath . . .

30 . . . before the wheel arch liner comes right out (together with all the er, muck, that it's been saving your arches from). As you can see, we haven't got our 17s on. Yet.

31 All that's left holding the bumper on is a bolt inside the wheel arch . . .

32 . . . and one more, in the 'starting handle' hole at the front. Never heard of starting handles? Ask Granddad.

33 The ends of the bumper are pegged into the front wings, either side - flex the bumper outwards slightly to disengage the ends, then lower it on the floor.

34 If your Clio's got front fogs already, might be an idea to disconnect the wiring to 'em, if you're planning on moving the bumper very far. Just a thought.

35 When it comes to marking out holes, always measure from a reference point, to make sure you get the holes equally spaced. Indicators can't be too close together (500 mm apart, minimum), and mustn't be too close to the headlights (allow at least 40 mm).

36 We marked up a hole for the indicators Morette supply, then we decided to fit something smaller, for reasons you'll see in a minute. In case we needed to go back to the Morette plan, though, we drilled our new hole in the top corner of the one we'd already marked out. Clever, eh? So - drill first . . .

37 . . . then use a hacksaw blade to shape the (smaller) hole.

We're substituting some tasty (and above all, small) side repeaters for the indicators. Before we go further, this is actually not legal, as side reps only have 5-watt bulbs in, and front indicators need to have 21 watts. Problem. But stick around for a still-sexy and legal solution. To run side reps in the front, we need bulbs. Our Merc-style mirrors have side reps in, so we won't be

38 needing our old bulbholders - you could blag some from your local scrappy.

39 So here's our new (illegal) side rep going in, wired-up and ready to connect to . . .

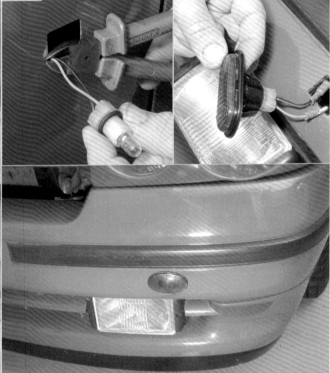

40 . . . the old indicator wiring, once its plug's been chopped, and the wires bulleted-up.

41 How gacky are those Morette indicators? They're bigger (and uglier) than some standard lights!

42 Back to our legal issue again. Not wanting to encourage you to break the law, we searched for a legal set of small indicators - and found some. Try a motorbike accessory supplier (like MPS - www.thefastone.co.uk) for some fairing indicators. These are sweet-looking, inexpensive, and come with road-legal bulbs - and here's one we fitted earlier. You don't even have to chop your old side rep bulbholders off, for these. Bonus.

Headlight **bulbs**

Make your Clio look like an Audi or a Beemer, the easy way. Currently very popular, the new bad-weather and "blue" headlight bulbs are an excellent way to boost headlight performance, and are perfect with blue LED washer jets. The blue bulbs you buy in most accessory shops will be legal, 60W/55 bulbs, and are no problem. Don't be tempted to buy the mega-powerful bulbs you can get from rallying suppliers (any over 60W/55 are in fact illegal for use in this country) - as with all other non-standard lights, the boys in blue will love pulling you over for a word about this, so ask before you buy.

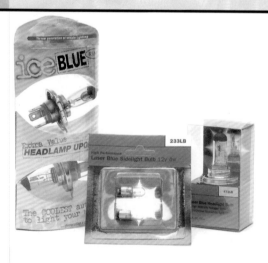

Even if you're not bothered about the legality of over-powerful bulbs (and you might well argue that being more powerful is the whole point of fitting), there's other problems with monster bulbs. First, they give off masses of heat, and loads of people have melted their headlights before they found this out. Don't believe us? Try fitting some 100W/90s and put your hand in front of the light, close to the glass. Hot, isn't it? The excess heat these bulbs generate will damage the headlights eventually, either by warping the lens, burning off the reflective coating, or melting the bulbholders. Maybe all three.

The increased current required to work big bulbs has also been known to melt wiring (this could lead to a fire) and will almost certainly burn out your light switch. There's no headlight relay fitted as standard, so the wiring and switch were designed to cope only with the current drawn by standard-wattage bulbs; if you're going for high power, a relay must be fitted (much as you'd have to, to fit foglights or spots).

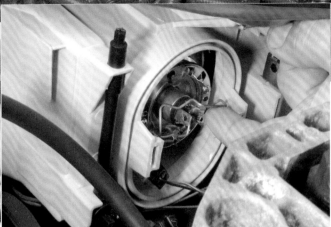

01 At the back of the headlight, pull off this plastic cover . . .

02 . . . then whip off the headlight wiring plug (it's the big one).

03 You'll now find a wire clip with two prongs on it, which you squeeze together, and hinge down . . .

Blue headlight **bulbs**

04 . . . and now the bulb falls out - if it hasn't already. If you've any plans to re-use it or sell it, hold it only by the metal bits, not the glass.

05 Now to fit our blue bulbs (H4 type, of course). Some bulb packaging makes it very easy to pull the bulb out by the glass, which will instantly ruin it - if you touch the bulb glass, wipe it clean with a little meths (methylated spirit - colour purple, not white spirit - colour white). Otherwise, your new bulb will suffer premature death. Secure with the wire clip, plug in, cover on. Simple.

Tips 'n' tricks
Put the old bulbs in the glovebox - carrying spare bulbs is a good way to get a let-off from Plod, if they stop you for having a bulb gone. Be smart. Carry spares.

Front fog/spotlights

Extra lights are a must on the Clio, if only to give some features to the rather bland front end (most bodykits have the facility for one or more pairs of lights, so it's gotta be done, really). On our Clio, we had it easy - our RT already had front fogs, so wiring-in the new lights which came with our bodykit was no effort. The lights just bolted in place, then the old wiring plugs were chopped and new spades crimped on. But suppose your Clio's a little more billy-basic than ours - read on.

If you're fitting fogs, they must be wired in to work on dipped-beam only, so they must go off on main beam. The opposite is true for spotlights. Pop out the main light switch (or pull down the fusebox) and check for a wire which is live ONLY when the dipped beams are on. The Haynes wiring diagrams will help here - on our Clio, it was a brown wire we needed.

Once you've traced your wire, this is used as the live (+ve) feed for your foglight relay. Did we mention you'll need a relay? You'll need a relay. A four-pin one will do nicely. Splice a new wire onto the feed you've found, and feed it through to the engine (there's a huge bulkhead grommet inside the passenger footwell). Decide where you'll mount the relay (next to the battery seems obvious) and connect the new wire onto terminal 86.

For your other relay connections, you'll need an earth to terminal 85 (plenty of good earth spots around the battery). You also need a fused live supply (buy a single fuseholder, and a 15 or 20 amp fuse should be enough) and take a new feed straight off the battery positive connection - this goes to terminal 30 on your relay.

Terminal 87 on your relay is the live output to the fogs - split this into two wires, and feed it out to where the lights will go. Each foglight will also need an earth - either pick a point on the body next to each light, or run a pair of wires back to the earth point you used earlier for your relay. Simple, innit?

With the wiring sorted, now you'd best fit the lights. Over to you. Most decent foglights come with some form of mounting brackets.

To look their best, hopefully your new lights can slot into pre-cut holes in your new front bumper/bodykit.

To connect the wiring to the lights, you'll probably need to splice on your wires from terminal 87 to the new wiring plugs which came with the lights - not too difficult. Plug it all together, and test - you should now have some rather funky fogs!

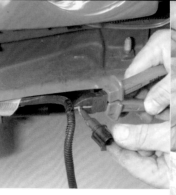

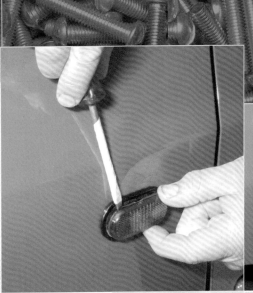

Side repeaters

There's a range of "standard" colours that side reps come in (clear, red, smoked, green and blue). If you're going for the same colour rear clusters, try to buy your lights from the same manufacturer, for greater chance of getting the same shade. Clear lenses can be coloured using special paint, if the particular shade you want isn't one of the standard ones, but the paint must be applied evenly to the lens, or this will invite an easily-avoided MOT failure. Bodyshops can colour clear lenses to the exact shade of your car, by mixing a small amount of paint with loads of lacquer - looks quite trick when it's done.

01 Fitting new side repeaters, in theory, is dead easy - getting the old ones out is a bit of a pain. You might not be too worried about busting your old side reps, but scratching your paintwork won't make your day. Whatever type of screwdriver you use to prise the light out with, wrap some masking tape around it first.

02 The light unit is actually in two pieces - the orange lens and a black surround. You'll be needing the surround again, more than likely, if you're not fitting different-shape lights. The bulbholder is a twist-and-pull bayonet fitting . . .

Side repeaters must still show an orange light, and must be sufficiently bright (not easy to judge this point, and no two coppers have the same eyesight!). The stock bulbs are white, so to get an orange light from your new lights, you'll have to change the bulbs too, to orange ones. Unfortunately, on clear lenses, you can then see the orange bulbs through the lenses, leading to what's known as the "fried egg" effect. To get round this, there are special bulbs available which provide the orange light without being as obviously orange from outside. Or get LED side repeaters, like we did on our Fiesta project car.

Besides the various colour effects, side repeaters are available in many different shapes. Any shape other than standard goes, really - one popular choice at the moment are the Focus-style triangular lights.

Or how about ditching the repeaters altogether, and get some tasty Merc-style mirrors, with side reps built-in? You could smooth your front wings, then...

03 . . . while that nasty clear bulb just pulls out, to make way for a smart new orange one. The future's bright.

04 Fit the smoked lens to the old surround, plug in the bulbholder, and there we have it - a sexy smoked side rep, in a Clio stylee.

Our Merc-style mirrors had side repeaters built-in. For details on fitting and wiring-up the mirrors (and their lights), refer to the section in 'Body and Exterior'.

Rear **lights**

The most popular choices for tweaking the Clio rear lights seem to be light brows, covers, or afterburner-style replacement units - not much available in coloured or clear clusters, though you could always spray-tint your standards to match your motor. Afterburners aren't to everyone's taste, but done well, they can look really lush (thanks to Auto Tint Design for supplying our set). Such style comes at a price, but it's not excessive, considering the finished effect. Up to you.

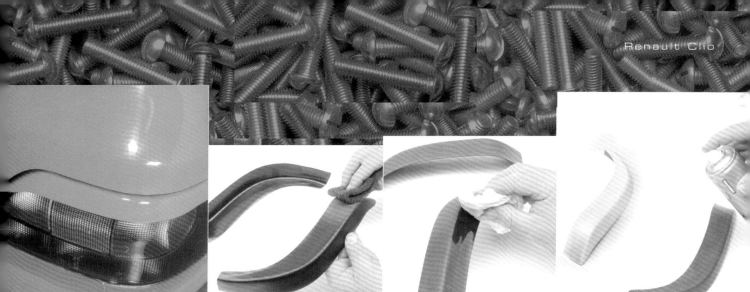

Rear light brows

As a cheap first option to trick up your Clio back end, there's no beating light brows (ours came from top brow supplier RGM). Easy to fit, they're even easy to remove at MOT-time, if your tester is less-than-understanding about modding.

01 So here we are - two shapely black bits of plastic (which are surprisingly easy to get mixed up, we found). That's black plastic. Unless you're fortunate enough to own a black Clio, you'll be missing the point slightly if you don't treat the brows to some paint before fitting. The first job is to rough-up the plastic surface with some wet-and-dry, or a bit of Scotchbrite (a scouring-pad-type material, available from motor factors).

02 With the plastic lightly roughed-up (this gives a better 'key' for the paint, in case you were wondering), give the brows a wipe down with solvent (such as panel-wipe, also available from motor factors) and let them dry.

03 Now a light coat of plastic primer - it must be proper 'plastic' primer, or it won't be flexible, and you could be doing this job all over again when the paint starts cracking and flaking off. Don't say we didn't warn you.

. . . and press firmly onto the light. Worth making sure that the light itself is silicone-free as well, by giving it a good clean first. Now, should you ever feel the need to take the brows off, the Velcro will stay stuck to the light, in the right places to let you put them back on later. Of course, this means that light brows ain't exactly thief-proof, but there's hardly a black market for stolen brows, so don't worry too much.

So how do we fix the brows to the lights? Glue? Screws? Er, no - it's Velcro, actually. Cut the complete Velcro strip (ie both halves - don't separate them yet) into handy short lengths, and stick to the brows. When you're ready, peel off the second backing from the Velcro . . .

04 A light rub-down with some fine-grade wet-and-dry . . .

05 . . . and we're ready for the top coats - not forgetting the lacquer after the base colour coat, of course.

06

07

Afterburner rear lights

When buying any rear light clusters, it's not a good idea to go for the cheapest you can find, because you'll be buying trouble.

Cheap rear light clusters don't have rear foglights or rear reflectors, so aren't really legal. Mr. Plod is well-informed on this point, and those sexy rear lights are way too big a come-on for him to ignore.

You can buy stick-on reflectors, but these are about as sexy as NHS specs (you'd have to be pretty unlucky to get pulled just for having no rear reflectors, but don't say we didn't warn you). And what happens if your car gets crunched, parked at night with no reflectors fitted? Will your insurance try and refuse to pay out? You betcha.

Like the Morettes, these lights are made for spraying, but save yourself some masking-up work by dismantling as much as you can first. Only the innermost lights don't come out. Make a very careful note of which bit goes where (stick some tape-labels on), as this will avoid most of the head-scratching later, when putting it all back together.

The rear foglight problem could perhaps be solved by spraying the clear bulb itself red, but it won't fool every MOT man.

The best solution? Only buy UK-legal lights, like these very tasty 'afterburners' from Auto Tint Design. Any questions on light legality? Why not check out the ABC Design website tech tips page, at www.abcdesignltd.com - if you've any questions after that, you can E-mail them. We're so good to you.

01 Removing and refitting the rear light clusters shouldn't tax your brain too much. First, open the tailgate and unscrew the funny little black plastic 'nut'.

02 Yes, that really is all there is to it - the light should just come away. Now unplug the main wiring connector for the rear lights . . .

03 . . . and the smaller one, which runs the number plate lights, and the standard clusters are off to the car boot sale. What d'you reckon? A tenner each?

04 Before we get the cans out, let's try the new lights for fit. Oh dear - we have a problem. The new mounting bolt just isn't long enough (short by about 25 mm), and we need a replacement. If you can't get a longer bolt, buy some M6 threaded bar from a DIY store, with a few nuts.

05 Fortunately, replacing the mounting bolt is easy, and soon, we're ready to try again.

06

07 Not another problem? Now the bolt is in the wrong place - as in, it doesn't line up with the hole in the car (25 mm too far to the left). Yes, we did check it was the same with the original bolt, too.

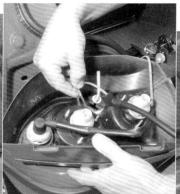
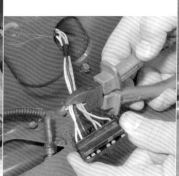
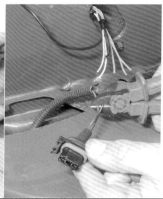

08 Don't try this at home! We thought if we drilled a new hole in the right place, all would be sorted. Well, it didn't work - it pulled the light in at the wrong angle. So - all we could do was bend the new bolt we'd made (dead easy, in a vice), to line up with the old hole, and this worked a treat.

09 So now we know that the lights will actually fit, let's get 'em working. The wires supplied with the afterburners look a lot like HT leads, but they only contain two thin wires - one with a red stripe, which you should connect to the centre terminal on the back of each bulb in the light cluster.

10 Time for some butchery. Chop off the old multi-plug for the rear lights (but leave enough wire attached to the plug so's you could re-connect it, if the car gets put back to standard later) . . .

11 . . . and do the same job on the smaller plug, for the number plate lights.

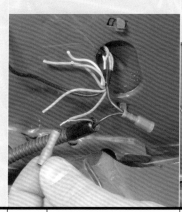

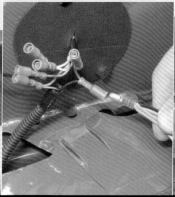

12 Match up the wire colours between the number plate and rear light (in our case, a blue and a black wire) and join each pair into one female bullet. The black wires are earths, and there'll be four more to join into this bullet, so better make it a blue one at least, like we did.

13 Fit (female) bullet connectors to all the remaining wires from the rear light. Before we go any further, in case you wondered what the black stick-on circle is for - it's for sealing the hole in the body where the wires pass through. You'll notice we've also used some stylish red gaffer tape to seal the other redundant holes. Water in your boot is something you can live without.

14 Now to wire up. First, let's deal with those earths, as they're very easy. See if you can get all four earth wires (the ones without the red stripe) into one blue male bullet, and join into the one you fitted earlier. Shortly after we took this shot, we found that the earth wire from the afterburner LEDs is BROWN, not black - don't you make the same mistake.

15 Bullet up the remaining wires on the afterburners (with males). Now have an assistant work each of the lights in turn (switch on the lights, press the brake pedal, that kind of thing), while you dab a bullet onto the rear light wiring, to see what comes on. Not perhaps the most scientific way to do it, but it's simple and it works.

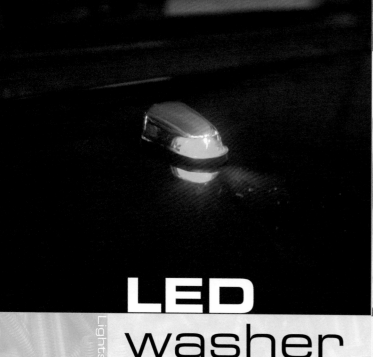

LED
washer
jets

Now we're talkin'! Very popular at cruises, these are a very easy-to-fit and effective way to make your Clio stand out.

Shame they don't seem to be available in many colours yet, but blue works well in any case, and the chrome finish even manages to look good in daylight. Just remember they're not strictly legal - Plod will tell you that you're only meant to be showing white light to the front. But you'd have to say you'd be having a bad night if he pulled you for two little blue lights...

01 Your first task is to prise off the washer tubes from the old jets, from under the bonnet. Not too difficult.

02 The tricky part is not losing the washer tubes, once you've disconnected them - you'll be needing them again, remember. This is just one solution - you can poke anything you like up there.

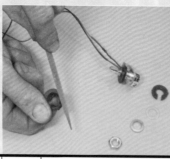

03 Before you can fit your new jets into the bonnet, you need to select the right plastic spacer from the ones provided. The spacer is meant to lock the jet into place, and stop it from being turned. None of our spacers fitted exactly, so here we're filing one down.

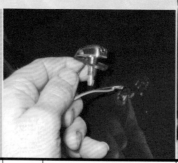

04 Pop the jet into the bonnet . . .

05 . . . then fit the spacer in from underneath. We used a blob of grease to hold the spacer in position.

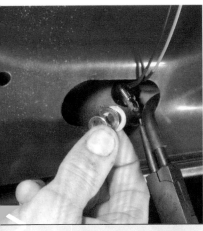

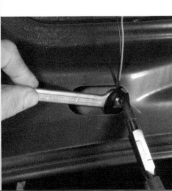

Next, it's on with the washer and nut, which is where things all get a bit fiddly.

Tighten up the nut . . .

. . . then refit the washer tube.

Now we need to start sorting the wiring out. First, the wires have to be fed through the bonnet - this is much easier if you tape the wires to a thicker piece of wire, and poke it through. We chose to feed the wiring for each jet down opposite sides of the car, but you could join them together at this point.

10 Cable-tie the wiring to the bonnet hinge, and make sure it can't get trapped, or stretched, or rubbed through. Okay, we're not talking about huge current here, but if they stop working, it won't make your night, will it?

11 Since the LEDs will only really show up at night, it makes sense to have them come on with the sidelights (which stay on once the headlights are on, by the way). Twist and pull the sidelight bulbholder from the back of the headlight, then cut into the grey/red live wire.

12 Connect the LED red wire to the sidelight live, twisting the two together into one bullet connector.

13 The LED black wire is the earth, and will need a ring terminal on, before it can be connected to a convenient earth point. Here's one we used earlier, just behind the headlight.

Wheels & tyres

Your most important decision ever?

This is where it's at - alloy wheels are the most important styling decision you'll ever make. No matter how good the rest of your car is, choose the wrong rims and your car will never look right. Choose a good set and you're already well on the way to creating a sorted motor. Take your time and pick wisely - wheel fashions change like the weather, and you don't want to spend shedloads on a set of uncool alloys.

None of the standard alloys cut it (with the possible exception of the Williams goldies - but only on a Monaco-blue machine, please), and should very quickly be dumped. Advice on which particular wheels to buy would be a waste of space, since the choice is so huge, and everyone will have their own favourites - for what it's worth, though, we reckon anything in a five-spoke or multi-spoke design seems to look best on a Clio, but go for something a little more original by all means. Beyond those words of dubious wisdom, you're on your own - car colour and your own chosen other mods will dictate what will look right on your car.

Fitting 17s or 18s will be a great deal less stressful if you get wheels with exactly the right offset - otherwise, your arches won't just have to be "trimmed" - they'll be BUTCHERED! Fitting wheels with the wrong offset may also do unpleasant things to the handling. The correct offset for all Mk 1 Clios is 42.

Lead us not into temptation

Before we go any further into which wheels are right for you, a word about insurance and security. Fitting tasty alloys to your Clio is one of the first and best ways to make it look cool. It follows, therefore, that someone with dubious morals might very well want to unbolt them from your car while you're not around, and make

their own car look cool instead (or simply sell them, to buy spot cream and drugs).

Since fitting a set of top alloys is one of the easiest bolt-on ways to trick up any car, it's no surprise that the market in stolen alloys is as alive and kicking as it currently is - your wheels will also look very nice on any number of other cars, and the owners of those cars would love to own them at a fraction of the price you paid... It's not unknown for a set of wheels to go missing just for the tyres - if you've just splashed out on a set of fat Yokohamas, your wheels look even more tempting, especially if you've got a common-size tyre.

Tell your insurance company what you're fitting. What will probably happen is that they'll ask for the exact details, and possibly a photo of the car with the wheels on. Provided you're happy to then accept that they won't cover the extra cost of the wheels if they get nicked (or if the whole car goes), you may find you're not charged a penny more, especially if you've responsibly fitted some locking wheel bolts. Not all companies are the same, though - some charge an admin fee, and yes, some will start loading your premium. If you want the rims covered, it's best to talk to a company specialising in modified cars, or you could be asked to pay out the wheel cost again in premiums. The daftest thing you can do is say nothing, and hope they don't find out - we don't want to go on about this, but there are plenty of documented cases where insurance companies have refused to pay out altogether, purely on the basis of undeclared alloy wheels.

How cheap are YOU?

Hopefully, you'll be deciding which wheels to go for based on how they look, not how much they cost, but inevitably (for most ordinary people at least), price does become a factor. Surely buying a cheaper wheel must have its pitfalls? Well, yes - and some of them may not be so obvious.

Inevitably, cheaper wheels = lower quality, but how does this manifest itself? Cheap wheels are often made from alloys which are more "porous" (a bit like a sponge, they contain microscopic holes and pockets of air). Being porous has two main disadvantages for a wheel, the main one being that it won't be able to retain air in the tyres. The days of tyres with inner tubes are long gone (and it's illegal to fit tubes to low-profile tyres), so the only thing keeping the air in are the three "walls" of the tyre, with the fourth "wall" being the inside of the wheel itself. If you like keeping fit by pumping up your tyres every morning, go ahead - the rest of us will rightly regard this as a pain, and potentially dangerous (running tyres at low pressure will also scrub them out very effectively - what was that about saving money?).

Porous wheels also have difficulty in retaining their paint or lacquer finish, with flaking a known problem, sometimes after only a few months. This problem is made worse by the fact that porous wheels are much harder to clean (brake dust seems to get ingrained into the wheels more easily) - and the more you scrub, the more the lacquer comes off.

The final nail in the coffin for cheap wheels is that they tend to corrode (or "fizz") more. This not only looks terrible if visible from outside, but if you get corrosion between the wheel and the hub, you won't even be able to take the things off! Yes seriously, grown men with all the specialist tools in the world at their disposal will be scratching their heads when faced with wheels which simply **will not** come off.

Tricks 'n' tips

Whenever you have your wheels off, clean off any hub corrosion with wet-and-dry paper, then coat the hub mating surfaces with copper (brake) grease. There's no way you'll suffer stuck-on wheels again. "Proper" alloys come with a plastic collar which fits inside the wheel - an essential item, it centres the wheel properly and reduces wheel-to-hub corrosion. Do not chuck out.

Buying an established, popular make of wheel has another hidden benefit, too. Choosing a popular wheel will mean more suppliers will stock it, and the manufacturers themselves will make plenty of them. And if you're unlucky enough to have an accident (maybe a slide on a frosty road) which results in non-repairable damage to one wheel, you're going to need a replacement. If you've chosen the rarest wheels on the planet, you could be faced with having to replace a complete set of four, to get them all matching… A popular wheel, even if it's a few years old, might be easier to source, even second-hand.

The Sunday morning ritual

It's a small point maybe, but you'll obviously want your wheels to look as smart as possible, as often as possible - so how easy are they going to be to clean?

The real multi-spokers and BBS-style "wires" are hell to clean - a fiddly toothbrush job - do you really want that much aggro every week? The simpler the design, the easier time you'll have. For those who like nothing better than counting their spokes, though, there are several really good products out there to make your life less of a cleaning nightmare.

Tricks 'n' tips

It's worth applying a bit of car polish to the wheels - provided it's good stuff, and you can be sure of getting the residue out of the corners and edges, a polished wheel will always be easier to clean off than an unpolished one. You can also buy waxes which are tailor-made for the job.

Bolt from the blues

Don't forget about locking wheel bolts (see "Hold on to your wheels" further on) - bargain these into a wheel/tyre package if you're buying new.

A word of warning about re-using your existing wheel bolts, should you be upgrading from steel wheels. Most steel-wheel bolts are not suitable for use with alloy wheels (and vice-versa, incidentally). Make sure you ask about this when buying new wheels, and if necessary, bargain a set of bolts into the price. Most bolts for use with alloys will have a washer fitted, for two very good reasons - 1) the bolt will pull through the wheel hole without it, and 2) to protect the wheel finish.

Another point to watch for is that the new wheel bolts are the correct length for your fitment, taking into account whether you've fitted spacers or not. Bolts that are too short are obviously dangerous, and ones that are too long can foul on drum brakes, and generally get in the way of any turning activities. If in doubt ask the retailer for advice. Always check that the wheels turn freely once they've been put on, and investigate any strange noises before you go off for a pose.

Tricks 'n' tips

If you're keeping a steel wheel as your spare (or even if you're keeping an original alloy), keep a set of your original wheel bolts in a bag inside the spare wheel. Locking bolts especially might be too long when fitted to a thin steel wheel, and might jam up your brakes!

Other options

If you're on a really tight budget, and perhaps own a real "basic" model Clio, don't overlook the possibility of fitting a discarded set of standard alloys, possibly from another Renault entirely - check that the stud pattern's the same, obviously. Getting the right wheel bolts also applies here, not just with aftermarket wheels.

If the Renault range of wheels is too limiting, don't be too quick buying (for instance) alloys suitable for other makes altogether. For instance, some Rover, Vauxhall and VW alloys have the same stud pattern (PCD), so they'll go on alright, but the offset is more than a bit different (like, 49 for Vauxhall, where it should be 42 - have fun). In the case of some alloys (Ford, for example), the stud pattern may be only fractionally different, but if you put these on, the strain on the bolts is too great, and they can fracture or work themselves loose…

Size **matters**

For us Brits, biggest is best - there are Clios out there with 18s and up. And yes, the mags all say you can't be seen with anything less than 17-inchers. In Europe, meanwhile, they're mad for the small-wheel look, still with seriously dropped suspension of course.

On many small cars (the Clio included), 15-inch rims are the biggest you can sensibly fit before you really have to start looking at sorting the arches, but they'll still improve the handling (unlike 17s, which often have the exact opposite effect!). Keep the wheel width to 6.5J as well, if you can - 7J rims will lead to headaches. Going bigger than 15s, we wouldn't rule out the possibility of some arch massaging even on 16s, especially if they're 7Jx16s and you're determined to slam the car down. Don't get too suckered into the whole 17-inch rims thing - if you slam the car down, modern 15s and 16s look nearly as good, and are much less work.

The only standard Clios that'll take 17s easily are the 16V and Williams, thanks to their flared arches. Lucky there's so many wide-arch bodykits for lesser Clios, then, innit?

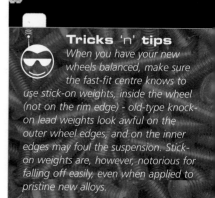

Tricks 'n' tips

When you have your new wheels balanced, make sure the fast-fit centre knows to use stick-on weights, inside the wheel (not on the rim edge) - old-type knock-on lead weights look awful on the outer wheel edges, and on the inner edges may foul the suspension. Stick-on weights are, however, notorious for falling off easily, even when applied to pristine new alloys.

We're going for 17s on our non-wide-arch Clio because we're brave, and we've got a decent bodyshop on the case if it all goes Pete Tong.

Clios without flared arches will only really have problems on the front, running 17s. Even with the car lowered, the wheels will go straight on, but the operative word here is 'straight' - start turning the steering, and the tyres will catch quite badly. Luckily, sorting the areas which catch isn't too bad a job, even if you don't have a tame bodyshop at your disposal - see 'Wheelarch mods' in the Bodywork section. We had no major problems on the rear with 17s - if they rub, you can file down the small arch lip yourself, which should cure the problem.

We like a challenge

To be honest, successfully fitting big wheels in combination with lowered suspension is one of the major challenges to the modifier.

At least the Clio has reasonably roomy front arches (or they can be made to be easily, by taking out the plastic wheelarch liners). As much as anything, tyre WIDTH is what ultimately leads to problems, not so much the increased wheel diameter.

If the tyres are simply too wide (or with wheels the wrong offset), they will first of all rub on the suspension strut (ie on the inside edge of the tyre). Also, the inside edges may rub on the arches on full steering lock - check left and right. Rubbing on the inside edges can be cured by fitting offsets or spacers between the wheel and hub, which effectively pull the wheel outwards, "spacing" it away from its normal position (this also has the effect of widening the car's track, which may improve the on-limit handling - or not). Fitting large offsets must be done using special longer wheel studs, as the standard ones may only engage the bolts by a few threads, which is highly dangerous.

Rubbing on the outside edges is a simple case of wheelarch lip fouling, which must be cured by rolling out the wheelarch return edge, and other mods. If you've gone for REALLY wide tyres, or have already had to fit offsets, the outer edge of the tyre will probably be visible outside the wheelarch, and this is a no-no (it's illegal, and you must cover it up!).

The other trick with fitting big alloys is of course to avoid the "Clio 4x4 off-road" look, which you will achieve remarkably easily just by popping on a set of 17s with standard suspension. The massive increase in ground clearance is fine for Farmer Palmer, but won't win much admiration on cruises - guilty of having "fistable" arches, M'lud! Send him down! Overcoming this problem by lowering can be a matter almost of inspired guesswork, as much as anything (see "Suspension").

Speedo error? Or not?

One side-effect of fitting large wheels is that your car will go slower. Yes, really - or at least - it will appear to go slower, due to the effects of the mechanically-driven speedometer.

As the wheel diameter increases, so does its circumference (distance around the outside) - this means that, to travel say one mile, a large wheel will turn less than a smaller wheel. Because the speedometer is driven from the gearbox final drive, the apparent vehicle speed is actually based on the number of complete revolutions of the wheel. Therefore, for a given actual speed, since a larger-diameter wheel will be turning at a slower rate than a smaller wheel, and the method for measuring speed is the rate of wheel rotation, a car with larger wheels will produce a lower speedo reading than one with smaller wheels - but it's NOT actually going any slower in reality. So don't worry if you

think you've reduced your Clio's performance somehow with the monster rims, 'cos you 'aven't.

With the ever-increasing number of those lovely grey/yellow boxes with a nasty surprise inside, spare a thought to what this speedo error could mean in the real world. If (like most people) you tend to drive a wee bit over the posted 30s and 40s, your real speed on 17s or 18s could be a bit more than the bit more you thought you were doing already, and you could get an unexpected flash to ruin your day. What we're saying is, don't drive any faster, to compensate for the lower speedo reading. Actually, the speedo error effect on 17s and 18s really is tiny at around-town speeds, and only becomes a factor over 70. But then, Officer, you couldn't possibly have been going over 70, could you? Officer?

Jargon explained

Rolling radius - the distance from the wheel centre to the outer edge of the tyre, or effectively, half the overall diameter. The rolling radius obviously increases with wheel size, but up to a point, the effects are masked by fitting low-profile tyres, with "shorter" sidewalls. Above 16-inch rims, however, even low-profiles can't compensate, and the rolling radius keeps going up.

PCD - this isn't a banned substance, it's your Pitch Circle Diameter, which relates to the spacing of your wheel holes, or "stud pattern". It is expressed by the diameter of a notional circle which passes through the centre of your wheel studs, and the number of studs/bolts. Unlike the offset, the PCD often isn't stamped onto the wheels, so assessing it is really a matter of eyeing-up and trying them on the studs - the wheel should go on easily, without binding, if the stud pattern is correct. On a Mk 1 Clio, the PCD is 100 mm with four studs, which is given as 100/4, or 4 x 100.

Offset - this is determined by the distance from the wheel mounting face in relation to its centre-line. The offset figure is denoted by ET (no, I mustn't), which stands for einpress tiefe in German, or pressed-in depth (now I KNOW you're asleep). The lower the offset, the more the wheels will stick out. Fitting wheels with the wrong offset might bring the wheel into too-close contact with the brake and suspension bits, or with the arches. Very specialised area - seek advice from the wheel manufacturers if you're going for a very radical size (or even if you're not). The correct offset for Clios of all sizes is ET 42.

Hold on to your wheels

The minute you bang on your wicked alloys, your car becomes a target.
People see the big wheels, and automatically assume you've also got a
major stereo, seats and other goodies - all very tempting, but that
involves breaking in, and you could have an alarm. Pinching the wheels
themselves, now that's a doddle - a few tools, some bricks or a couple of
well-built mates to lift the car, and it's easy money

The trouble with fitting big wheels is that they're only screwed on, and are just as easily screwed off, if you don't make life difficult for 'em. If you're unlucky enough to have to park outside at night (ie no garage), you could wake up one morning to a car that's *literally* been slammed on the deck! Add to this the fact that your car isn't going anywhere without wheels, plus the damage which will be done to exhaust, fuel and brake pipes from dropping on its belly, and it's suddenly a lot worse than losing a grand's worth of wheels and tyres…

The market and demand for stolen alloys is huge, but since most people don't bother having them security-marked in any way, once a set of wheels disappears, they're almost impossible to trace. Thieves avoid security-marked (or "tattooed") wheels (or at least it's a

pretty good deterrent) - and it needn't look hideous!

When choosing that car alarm, try and get one with an "anti-jacking" feature, because thieves hate it. This is sometimes now called "anti-tilt", to avoid confusion with anti-hijacking. Imagine a metal saucer, with a metal ball sitting on a small magnet in the centre. If the saucer tilts in any direction, the ball rolls off the magnet, and sets off the alarm. Highly sensitive, and death to anyone trying to lift your car up for the purpose of removing the wheels - as we said, the crims are not fond of this feature at all. Simply having an alarm with anti-shock is probably not good enough, because a careful villain will probably be able to work so as not to create a strong enough vibration to trigger it - mind you, it's a whole lot better than nothing, especially if set to maximum sensitivity.

Locking nuts/bolts

Locking wheel bolts will be effective as a deterrent to the inexpert thief (kids, in other words), but will probably only slow down the pro.

Thieves want to work quickly, and will use large amounts of cunning and violence to deprive you of your stuff. If you fit a cheap set of locking bolts, they'll use a hammer and thin chisel to crack off the locking bolt heads. Some bolts can easily be defeated by hammering a socket onto the bolt head, and undoing the locking bolt as normal, while some of the key-operated bolts are so pathetic they can be beaten using a small screwdriver. So - choose the best bolts you can, but don't assume they'll prevent your wheels from disappearing. Insurance companies seem to like 'em - perhaps it shows a responsible attitude, or something...

There seems to be some debate as to whether it's okay to fit more than one set of locking bolts to a car - some people we know value their wheels so highly that they've fitted four or five sets of bolts - in other words, they've completely replaced all the standard bolts! The feeling against doing this is that the replacement locking bolts may not be made to the same standard as factory originals, and while it's okay to fit one set on security grounds, fitting more than that is dangerous on safety grounds (bolt could fail, wheel falls off, car in ditch, owner in hospital...).

Obviously, you must carry the special key or tool which came with your bolts with you at all times, in case of a puncture, or if you're having any other work done, such as new brakes or tyres. The best thing to do is rig this onto your keyring, so that it's with you, but not left in the car. The number of people who fit locking bolts and then leave the key to them cunningly "hidden" in the glovebox or the boot... incredible stupidity... if only the low-lifes out there were as daft! You don't leave a spare set of car keys in your glovebox as well, do you?

How to change a set of wheels

You might think you know all about this, but do you really?

Okay, so you know you need a jack and wheelbrace (or socket and ratchet), but where are the jacking points? If you want to take more than one wheel off at a time, have you got any axle stands, and where do they go? If you've only ever had wheels and tyres fitted by a garage, chances are you're actually a beginner at this. It's surprising just how much damage you can do to your car, and to yourself, if you don't know what you're doing - and the worst thing here is to think you know, when you don't...

What to use

If you don't already have one, invest in a decent hydraulic (trolley) jack. This is way more use than the standard car jack, which is really only for emergencies, and which isn't really stable enough to rely on. Lifting and lowering the car is so much easier with a trolley jack, and you'll even look professional. Trolley jacks have a valve, usually at the rear, which must be fully tightened (using the end of the jack handle) before raising the jack, and which is carefully loosened to lower the car down - if it's opened fully, the car will not so much sink as plummet!

Axle stands are placed under the car, once it's been lifted using the jack. Stands are an important accessory to a trolley jack, because once they're in place, there's no way the car can come down on you - remember that even a brand new trolley jack could creep down (if you haven't tightened the valve), or could even fail completely under load (if it's a cheap one, or knackered, or both).

Under NO circumstances use bricks, wooden blocks or anything else which you have to pile up, to support the car - this is just plain stupid. A Clio weighs plenty for a "small" car - if you want to find out just how solidly it's built, try crawling under it when it's resting on a few poxy bricks.

Where to use it

Only ever jack the car up on a solid, level surface (ideally, a concrete or tarmac driveway, or quiet car park). If there's even a slight slope, the car's likely to move (maybe even roll away) as the wheels are lifted off the ground. Jacking up on a rough or gravelled surface is not recommended, as the jack could slip at an awkward moment - such as when you've just got underneath...

How to use it - jacking up the front

Before jacking up the front of the car, pull the handbrake on firmly (you can also chock the rear wheels, if you don't trust your handbrake).

If you're taking the wheels off, loosen the wheel bolts BEFORE you start jacking up the car. It's easily forgotten, but you'll look pretty silly trying to undo the wheel bolts with the front wheels spinning in mid-air. Standard alloys have a prise-off cover fitted over the bolts - well, at least they tried.

We'll assume you've got a trolley jack. The next question is - where to stick it? Up front, there's a sturdy-looking square-ish subframe under the engine, which will do nicely, but use a section away from the holes, and put a nice flat offcut of wood on your jack head first, to spread the load. You can jack on the sill jacking points (which are marked by little notches on the sill edges), but it's better to leave those for your axle stands.

Once you've got the car up, pop an axle stand or two under the front sill jacking points. These points are shown by having a narrow slot cut in the flange (to locate the standard jack into), and this is the only part of the sill it's safe to jack under or rest the car on. On the RSi, 16V and Williams, you'll have to unclip a cover for access to the sill jacking points, and even then, access to them might not be all you'd like. With the stands in place, you can lower the jack so the car's weight rests on the stands. For maximum safety, spread the car's weight between the stands and the jack - don't lower the jack completely unless it's needed elsewhere.

I'm sure we don't need to tell you guys this, but don't jack up the car, or stick stands under the car, anywhere other than kosher jacking and support points. This means - not the floorpan or the sump (you'll cave it in), not the suspension bits (not stable), and not under the brake/fuel pipes (ohmigawd).

How to use it - jacking up the rear

When jacking up the rear of the car, place wooden chocks in front of the front wheels to stop it rolling forwards, and engage first gear.

If you're taking the wheels off, you don't have to loosen the wheel bolts before lifting the car, but you'll be relying on your handbrake to hold the wheels while you wrestle with the bolts. Much cooler (and safer) to loosen the rear wheel bolts on the ground too.

Jacking and supporting the rear end is a little trickier. You have the choice of jacking under the rear suspension arm (right at the end, under the shock absorber lower mounting), or under the rear "axle" itself. The axle option's safer, as it won't move as much when you start jacking, and won't load the rear suspension. There's also a strengthened section in front of the rear "axle" at each end, but you'll need a piece of wood (also avoid the exhaust on one side, and the fuel tank on the other). The axle stand can go under the sill jacking point at the rear, again indicated by a slot in the sill edge.

Remember not to put your axle stands under any pipes, the spare wheel, or the fuel tank, and you should live to see another Christmas.

Finally...

As far as possible, don't leave the car unattended once it has been lifted, particularly if kids are playing nearby - football goes under your car, they go under to get it, knock the jack, car falls... it would almost certainly be your fault.

01 No, no, no - this has nothing to do with long-haired interior designers. Changing wheels is a serious business, so pay attention. Before fitting your new wheels, there's stuff to check - first, have you got a nice ally/plastic ring inside the hub? Make sure it's there, as it acts to centre the wheel properly, and may help to stop the wheel rusting on. Ever had a rusted-on wheel? Your local fast-fit centre will have, and they'll tell you it ain't funny...

02 Even with the ring of plastic confidence, the metal bits can still corrode on. Equip yourself with some copper brake grease, and smear some on the wheel boss, inside.

03 Speaking of corrosion - how rusty are those wheel hubs? Quite to very, we suspect. Take a wire brush, and use it wisely - the less rust and muck there is to start with, the better the wheels will centre-up, too, when you offer 'em on.

Changing wheels

This is one set of wheels no fast-fit centre will have trouble shifting - just don't get any on the brake disc pad surfaces. You'll be doing yourself a favour if some of the same copper grease finds its way onto the wheel bolt threads, though. **04**

Pop the wheel onto the studs, then on with the nicely-greased bolts (oo-er), and tighten up as far as possible by hand. You have got some locking bolts, haven't you? Keep your locking wheel bolt tool somewhere safe, but not obvious. The glovebox is convenient, but way too obvious! **05**

Always tighten the wheel bolts securely (ideally, to the correct torque - 90 Nm). This can only be done properly with the wheel back on the ground. Don't over-tighten the bolts, or you'll never get them undone at the roadside, should you have a flat! D'oh! **06**

If your wheels have a centre cap of some kind, fit it. Not only does it look better, but some wheel centre caps cover the wheel bolts - might be all the theft-deterrent you need, to stop an opportunist... **07**

Always nice to see a good brand of tyre on a decent alloy. How cool do cheap tyres look?

Tyres

To some people, tyres are just round and black - oh, and they're nearly all expensive, and don't last long enough. When you're buying a new set of wheels, most centres will quote prices with different tyres - this is convenient, and usually quite good value, too, but look carefully at what you're buying.

Some people try and save money by fitting "remould" or "re-manufactured" tyres. These aren't always the bargain they appear to be - experience says there's no such thing as a good cheap tyre, with wheel balancing problems a well-known downside, for starters.

Without wanting to sound like an old advert, choosing a known brand of tyre will prove to be one of your better decisions. Tyres are the only thing keeping you on the road, as in steering, braking and helping you round corners - what's the point of trying to improve the handling by sorting the suspension if you're going to throw the gains away by fitting naff tyres? Why beef up the brakes if the tyres won't bite? The combination of stiff suspension and cheap tyres is inherently dangerous - because the front end dives less with reduced suspension travel, the front tyres are far more likely to lock and skid under heavy braking.

Cheap tyres also equals more wheelspin - might be fun to be sat at the lights in a cloud of tyre smoke, but wouldn't you rather be disappearing up the road? Another problem with really wide tyres is aquaplaning - hit a big puddle at speed, and the tyre skates over

Tricks 'n' tips

When buying tyres, look out for ones which feature a rubbing strip on the sidewall - these extend over the edge of the wheel rims, and the idea is that they protect the rim edges from damage by "kerbing". Any decent tyre has them - discreet and very practical, and much better than a chewed-up rim.

the water without gripping - this is seriously scary when it first happens. Fitting good tyres won't prevent it, but it might increase your chances of staying in control. The sexiest modern low-profile tyres have a V-tread pattern, designed specifically to aid water dispersal, which is exactly what you need to prevent aquaplaning - try some, and feel the difference!

Finally, cheap tyres ruin your Clio's appearance - a no-name brand emblazoned in big letters on your tyre sidewalls - how's that going to look? If you're spending big dosh on wheels, you've gotta kit 'em out with some tasty V-tread tyres, or lose major points for style. Listen to friends and fellow modifiers - real-world opinions count for a lot when choosing tyres (how well do they grip, wet or dry? How many miles can you get out of them?) Just make sure, before you splash your cash on decent tyres, that you've cured all your rubbing and scrubbing issues, as nothing will rip your new tyres out faster.

Marks on your sidewalls

Tyre sizes are expressed in a strange mixture of metric and imperial specs - we'll take a typical tyre size as an example:

205/40 R 17 V

for a 7-inch wide 17-inch rim

205 width of tyre in millimetres

40 this is the "aspect ratio" (or "profile") of the tyre, or the sidewall height in relation to tyre width, expressed as a percentage, in this case 40%. So - 40% of 205 mm = 82 mm, or the height of the tyre sidewall from the edge of the locating bead to the top of the tread.

R Radial.

17 Wheel diameter in inches.

V Speed rating (in this case, suitable for use up to 150 mph).

Pressure situation

Don't forget, when you're having your new tyres fitted, to ask what the recommended pressures should be, front and rear - it's unlikely that the Renault specs for this will be relevant to your new low-low profiles, but it's somewhere to start from. If the grease-monkey fitting your tyres is no help on this point, contact the tyre manufacturer - the big ones might even have a half-useful website! Running the tyres at the wrong pressures is particularly stupid (you'll wear them out much faster) and can be very dangerous (too soft - tyre rolls off the rim, too hard - tyre slides, no grip).

Speed ratings

Besides the tyre size, tyres are marked with a maximum speed rating, expressed as a letter code:

T   up to 190 km/h (118 mph)

U   up to 200 km/h (124 mph)

H   up to 210 km/h (130 mph)

V   inside tyre size markings (225/50 VR 16) over 210 km/h (130 mph)

V   outside tyre size markings (185/55 R 15 V) up to 240 km/h (150 mph)

Z   inside tyre size markings (255/40 ZR 17) over 240 km/h (150 mph)

If you've got marks on your sidewalls like this, you're in trouble - this has almost certainly been caused by "kerbing".

08 Suspension

If your Clio's still sitting on standard suspension, it's probably safe to say it doesn't cut it - yet. If you've decided you couldn't wait to fit your big alloys, the chances are your Clio is now doing a passable impression of a tractor. An essential fitment, then - so how low do you go, and what nasty side-effects will lowering have?

The main reason for lowering is of course, to make your car look cool. Standard suspension is always set too soft and too high - a nicely lowered motor really stands out instantly. Lowering your car should also improve the handling. Dropping the car on its suspension brings the car's centre of gravity closer to its roll and pitch centres, which helps to pin it to the road in corners and under braking - combined with stiffer springs and shocks, this reduces body roll and increases the tyre contact patch on the road. But - if improving the handling is really important to you, choose your new suspension carefully. If you go the cheap route, or want extreme lowering, then you could end up with a car which don't handle at all…

How low to go?

Assuming you want to slam your suspension so that your arches just clear the tops of your wicked new rims, there's another small problem - it takes some inspired guesswork (or hours of careful measuring and head-scratching) to assess the required drop accurately, and avoid any nasty rubbing

As for what to buy, there are basically three main options when it comes to lowering, arranged in order of ascending cost below:

1 *Pair of front lowering springs.*

2 *Matched pair of front lowering springs and shock absorbers, and a pair of rear shocks.*

3 *Pair of front 'coilovers' (and rear shocks)*

sounds and the smell of burning rubber. Lowering springs and suspension kits will only produce a fixed amount of drop - this can range from 20 mm to a more extreme drop of anything up to 80 mm. Take as many measurements as possible, and ask around your mates - suppliers and manufacturers may be your best source of help in special cases. We dropped our Clio by 55 mm on the front, which was just right for our 17s, but it didn't leave much wheel travel - 35 or 40 mm might have been more sensible for road use. Coilovers have a range of adjustment possible, which is far more satisfactory - at a price.

Bar-brawls - best avoided

Think you're a good mechanic? Here's where you get to prove it - or maybe not. If this is your first outing with the spanners, lowering the rear of your Clio properly might be better left to a professional. The reason for this is the manufacturer's choice of rear suspension - the Clio is fitted with a torsion-bar rear axle (a favourite choice with the Frenchies).

For the uninitiated amongst you, torsion-bar rear suspension doesn't use coil springs, but instead uses hefty steel bars. The steel bars are splined at each end, and link each trailing arm to the centre of the axle crossmember. These steel bars twist as the suspension moves up and down throughout its travel, and it's the bars' resistance to this twisting (or torsional force) which provides the rear suspension springing.

Resetting the rear ride height is an involved procedure - not especially difficult or dangerous, but it can be damn fiddly (remember, anything sounds easy enough after a few pints, so trust us on this one). If you muck it up, you can lose the preload on the bars, which means the back will be lower, but floppy as well. You'll need an unusual tool called a slide hammer, or else make up a susbstitute. On an older car, you could also be facing the possibility of rusted-in bits, and a really big slide-hammer is the only answer if you get into that. Even if you have the job done by a garage, you'll be doing everyone a favour if you give the torsion bars a blast with some WD-40, a week or two before. The positive side though, is that you can lower the rear ride height without purchasing any new springs - the only cost involved is the labour. It's worth treating the newly-lowered rear to some nice Spax or Koni dampers, though.

Lowering springs

The cheapest option by far, but with the most pitfalls and some unpleasant side-effects. Lowering springs are, effectively, shorter versions of the standard items fitted to your Clio at the factory. However, not only are they shorter (lower), they are also uprated (stiffer) - if lowering springs were simply shorter than standard and the same stiffness (the same 'rate'), you'd be hitting the bump-stops over every set of catseyes. With lowering springs, you just fit the new springs and keep the original shock absorbers ('dampers') - even if the originals aren't completely knackered, you're creating a problem caused by mis-matched components. The original dampers were carefully chosen to work in harmony with the original-rate springs - by increasing the spring rate without changing the dampers, you end up with a situation where the dampers will not be in full and effective control of the spring motion. What this usually does before long is wreck the dampers, because they simply can't cope with the new springs, so you really don't save any money in the end.

The mis-matched springs and dampers will have other entertaining side-effects, too. How would you like a Clio which rides like a brick, and which falls over itself at the first sign of a corner taken above walking pace? A very choppy ride and strange-feeling steering (much lighter, or much heavier, depending on your luck) are well-documented problems associated with taking the cheap option, and it doesn't even take much less time to fit, compared to a proper solution. Even if you're a hard man, who doesn't object to a hard ride if his car looks cool, think on this - how many corners do you know that are completely flat (ie without any bumps)? On dodgy lowering springs, you hit a mid-corner bump at speed, and it's anyone's guess where you'll end up.

If cost is a major consideration, and lowering springs the only option for now, at least try to buy branded items of decent quality - some cheap sets of springs will eat their way through several sets of dampers before you realise the springs themselves have lost the plot. Needless to say, if riding around on mis-matched springs and shocks is a bit iffy anyway, it's downright dangerous when they've worn out (some inside 18 months!).

Springs are generally only available in a very few sizes, expressed by the amount of drop they'll produce - most people go for 60 mm or so, but there's usually 35 to 40 mm springs too if you're less brave (or if you've simply got massive rims).

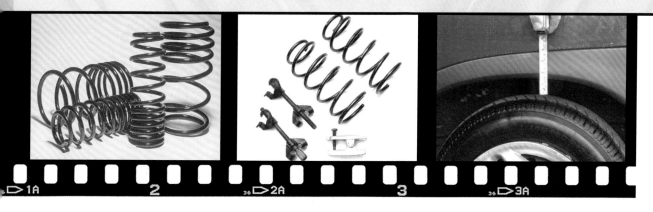

Suspension **kit**

A far better choice, Sir - matched springs and dampers are a genuine 'upgrade', and respect is due. There are several branded kits available, and Renault specialists may do their own. With a properly-sorted conversion, your Clio will handle even better, and you'll still be able to negotiate a set of roadworks without the risk of dental work afterwards. Actually, you may well be amazed how well the Clio will still ride, even though the springs are clearly lower and stiffer - the secret is in the damping.

Some of the kits are billed as 'adjustable', but this only applies to the damper rates, which can often be set to your own taste by a few minutes' work (don't mistake them for cheap coilovers). This Playstation feature can be quite a good fun thing to play around with, even if it is slightly less relevant to road use than for hillclimbs and sprints - but be careful you don't get carried away and set it too stiff, or you'll end up with an evil-handling car and a CD player that skips over every white line on the road!

Unfortunately, although you will undoubtedly end up with a fine-handling car at the end, there are problems with suspension kits, too. They too are guilty of causing changes to steering geometry (have it reset) and once again, you're into guesswork territory when it comes to assessing your required drop for big wheels. Generally, most suspension kits are only available with a fairly modest drop (typically, 35 to 60 mm).

Before you order your suspension kit, arm yourself with one vital statistic. With one of the front wheels off, measure how far apart the two bolts are, that hold the bottom of the strut to the wheel hub - and we're looking for the distance between the bolt centres here. Is it 52 mm or 54 mm? Take your time finding out, and if you're not sure which bolts we mean, look ahead to the kit fitting sequence later on. The 54 mm hubs are supposed to be fitted to Clios of 1.4 litres and up, but our 1.4 RT had the 52 mm hubs. Blummin' marvellous.

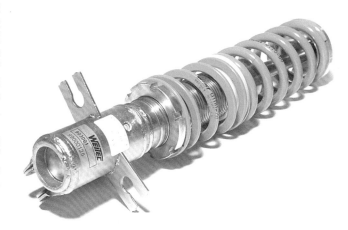

Our 1.4 Clio had a 55 mm lowering kit fitted, which hunkers the car down nicely on 17s, but we wouldn't advise going any lower. If you regularly carry passengers, a more modest 35 or 40 mm drop would be better for use with 17s, to give you some wheel-movement room when the car's on any lock.

Coilovers

If you've chosen coilovers, well done again. This is the most expensive option, and it offers one vital feature that the other two can't - true adjustability of ride height, meaning that you can make the finest of tweaks to hunker down on your new rims (coilovers are an almost-essential choice if you're trying for 18s). Coilovers give you more scope to fit those big rims now, lower it down as far as poss, then wait 'til next month before you have the arches rolled, and drop it down to the deck. Coilovers are a variation on the suspension kit theme, in that they are a set of matched variable-rate springs (some have separate 'helper' springs too) and shocks, but they achieve their adjustability in a way which might not guarantee as good a ride/handling mix as a normal kit.

A coilover set replaces each spring and shock with a combined unit where the coil spring fits over the shocker (hence 'coil' 'over') - nothing too unusual in this, because so far, it's similar to a normal front strut. The difference lies in the adjustable spring lower seat, which can lower the spring to any desired height (within limits).

Unfortunately, making a car go super-low is not going to be good for the ride or the handling. Coilover systems necessarily have very short, stiff springs, and this can lead to similar problems to those found with cheap lowering springs alone. If you go too far with coilovers, you can end up with a choppy ride, heavy steering and generally unpleasant handling. Combine a coilover-slammed car with big alloys, and while the visual effect may be stunning, the driving experience might well be very disappointing. At least a proper coilover kit will come with shock absorbers (dampers) which are matched to the springs, unlike a 'conversion' kit.

Coilover conversion

A better-value option is the 'coilover conversion'. If you really must have the lowest, baddest machine out there, and don't care what the ride will be like, these could be the answer. Offering as much potential for lowering as genuine coilovers (and at far less cost), these items could be described as a cross between coilovers and lowering springs, because the standard dampers are retained (this is one reason why the ride suffers). What you get is a new spring assembly, with adjustable top and bottom mounts - the whole thing slips over your standard damper. Two problems with this solution (how important these are is up to you):

1 Your standard dampers will not be able to cope with the uprated springs, so the car will almost certainly ride (and possibly handle) like a pig if you go for a really serious drop - and okay, why else would you be doing it?

2 The standard dampers are effectively being compressed, the lower you go. There is a limit to how far they will compress before being completely solid (and this could be the limit for your lowering activities). Needless to say, even a partly-compressed damper won't be able to do much actual damping - the results of this could be… interesting…

Front Suspension

Tricks 'n' tips

Don't start this job without coil spring compressors, or you'll be sorry! A torque wrench is also pretty important, and you'll be needing one or two new bits from a dealer, depending on which Clio you've got.

01 Clio front struts are just a p-of-p to get off - bonus! First, loosen the wheel bolts, jack up the corner of the car you're working on, and take off the wheel. Get an axle stand under the car, too - see 'Wheels & tyres' for more info. Undo the two big nuts 'n' bolts holding the bottom of the strut to the wheel hub - notice that the nuts are at the back. Get two new nuts each side, and do it now.

02 Separate the strut base 'clamp' from the hub (shouldn't be hard, but rust could be a factor, so we couldn't rule out the need for some persuasion with heavy objects), and we're more than halfway there already…

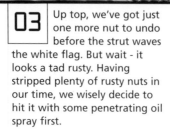

03 Up top, we've got just one more nut to undo before the strut waves the white flag. But wait - it looks a tad rusty. Having stripped plenty of rusty nuts in our time, we wisely decide to hit it with some penetrating oil spray first.

04 Now armed with a 21 mm spanner and a 6 mm Allen key (on our car), the nut gives up the fight. Don't undo it all the way, or your foot will find out how heavy Clio struts are.

05 When you're ready, undo the top nut the last few turns, and lower the strut out in an orderly and controlled fashion (much less painful).

Respect

For the next bit, you MUST use coil spring compressors ('spring clamps'). Medical attention will be required if you don't. Do we have to draw you a diagram? The spring's under tension on the strut, even off the car - what do you think's gonna happen if you just undo it? The spring-embedded-in-the-forehead look is really OVER, too.

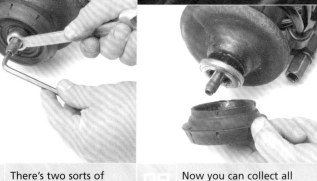

06 You might be needing these bits again, so don't lose them. If your top plates are like ours, and have a built-in strut top nut, sort yourself out two new plates from a Renault dealer. Never re-use old nuts with a plastic insert (Nyloc nuts) as there's a risk they won't stay done up properly. Self-dismantling suspension you can live without.

07 There are two clamps, each with two hooks, which sit over one of the spring coils. You won't get the hooks over the top and bottom coils, but try the next nearest. Fit the two clamps opposite each other, then tighten the big bolt up the middle of each to compress one side of the spring - this must be done evenly, one side after the other, or the un-clamped side might fly off. Respect is due here - this is scary stuff.

08 There's two sorts of Clio front suspension strut. Ours was held together by a nut on top, which you undo while holding the centre rod still with your trusty 6 mm Allen key (again). Bigger-engined Clios have a tiny round spring clip which locates in a groove - lever it out with a screwdriver, but watch where it goes, as it's a bit lively, and you might need it again!

09 Now you can collect all those bits you'll be needing again - like the top rubber mount, which has a small spacer on top, and the bigger bearing underneath . . .

10 . . . the spring top plate . . .

11 . . . and the bump stop.

12 What we won't need again is that soggy old spring - but take care slackening off the spring clamps (like, each one a bit at a time) if you don't fancy finding out just how springy it actually is!

13 Says it all really. Lowering... springs. It's a bit of a shame they make them look so good, too, considering they're stuffed under the wheelarches (and will soon be covered in stuff).

>>

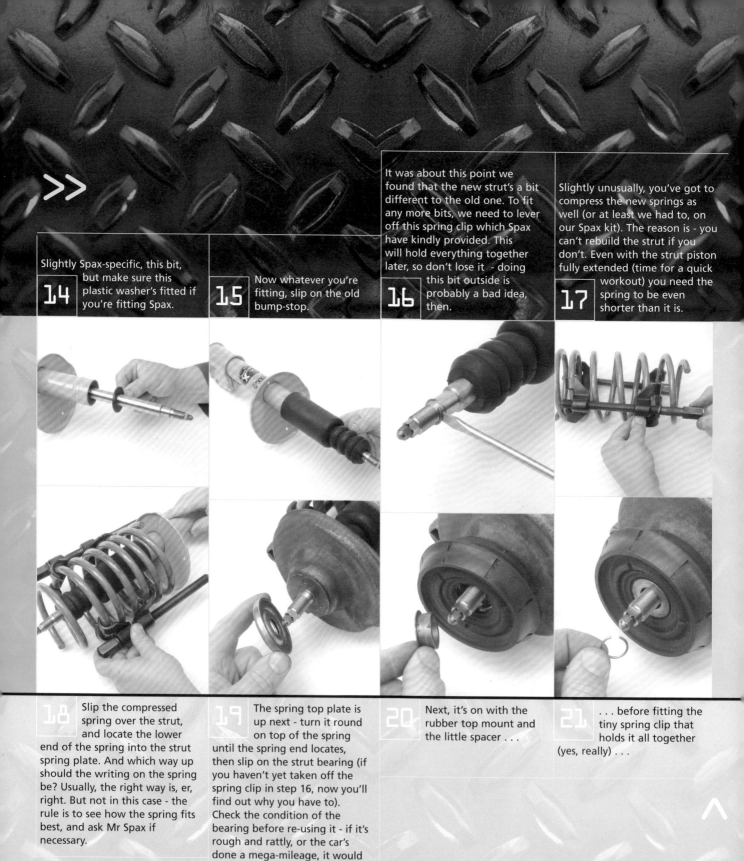

14 Slightly Spax-specific, this bit, but make sure this plastic washer's fitted if you're fitting Spax.

15 Now whatever you're fitting, slip on the old bump-stop.

16 It was about this point we found that the new strut's a bit different to the old one. To fit any more bits, we need to lever off this spring clip which Spax have kindly provided. This will hold everything together later, so don't lose it - doing this bit outside is probably a bad idea, then.

17 Slightly unusually, you've got to compress the new springs as well (or at least we had to, on our Spax kit). The reason is - you can't rebuild the strut if you don't. Even with the strut piston fully extended (time for a quick workout) you need the spring to be even shorter than it is.

18 Slip the compressed spring over the strut, and locate the lower end of the spring into the strut spring plate. And which way up should the writing on the spring be? Usually, the right way is, er, right. But not in this case - the rule is to see how the spring fits best, and ask Mr Spax if necessary.

19 The spring top plate is up next - turn it round on top of the spring until the spring end locates, then slip on the strut bearing (if you haven't yet taken off the spring clip in step 16, now you'll find out why you have to). Check the condition of the bearing before re-using it - if it's rough and rattly, or the car's done a mega-mileage, it would be better to fit new. Both sides.

20 Next, it's on with the rubber top mount and the little spacer . . .

21 . . . before fitting the tiny spring clip that holds it all together (yes, really) . . .

22 ... make sure the clip is properly located in the groove, using a screwdriver if you need to.

23 Now you can (slowly and evenly) unwind the spring clamps. Notice that we didn't entirely trust our little spring clip to stop everything flying apart, and (very wisely) fitted the strut top nut temporarily. But we needn't have worried.

24 Feed the new strut in under the arch, and (if you like) hold it in position by loosely tightening the strut top nut/top plate.

25 You might need to 'persuade' the strut-to-hub bolts through, like we did. But is your difficulty caused by an excess of yellow paint, or is it something else? Have you got the wrong-size kit for your hubs? Read the words of wisdom in the intro pages.

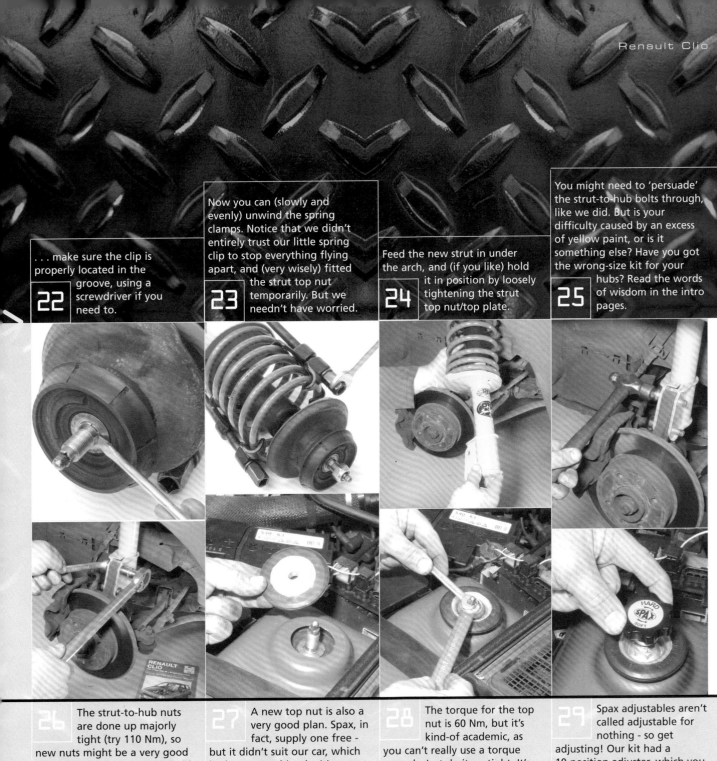

26 The strut-to-hub nuts are done up majorly tight (try 110 Nm), so new nuts might be a very good idea. If these come loose (as old, re-used nuts have a tendency to), the consequences will range from strange to serious. Your choice.

27 A new top nut is also a very good plan. Spax, in fact, supply one free - but it didn't suit our car, which had a nut combined with a strut top plate. D'oh! The same thinking still applies though, and we had to source a new top plate each side from Renault.

28 The torque for the top nut is 60 Nm, but it's kind-of academic, as you can't really use a torque wrench. Just do it up tight. It's worth jacking up under the front hub before you start tightening, then wade in with your 21 mm spanner (and a smaller one, to hold the flats on top of the strut piston). And that's all there is to it.

29 Spax adjustables aren't called adjustable for nothing - so get adjusting! Our kit had a 10-position adjuster, which you start by setting at position 5 (five clicks). Follow the instructions with your kit, and don't be shy of ringing the company concerned for setting advice if you're not happy with the handling or ride.

Rear
Suspension

01 The first stage should really take place weeks before you actually want your Clio lowered - pop this plastic cap off your torsion bar (you can do this with the wheel on, and the car on the ground) . . .

The adjustment procedure involves removing the torsion bars with a slide hammer, setting both trailing arms to the correct height, then re-inserting the bars, ensuring their splines are correctly engaged. Sounds easy when you say it quickly, but believe us, it might not be when you try it. Here's what happened when we did our 1.4 Clio.

02 . . . and spray in some WD-40. It's not unheard-of for the torsion bar splines to rust onto the suspension arms. This will very quickly put a stop to any lowering activities you had in mind - so the magic spray saves the day.

03 Before we get to the lowering itself, we really need to unbolt those tired old rear shocks. You were going to fit some uprated ones anyway, weren't you? Weren't you? If you're lowering the front, it'll end up stiffer - lowering the rear on the torsion bars won't stiffen it up, so some decent shocks will be needed to do the job. You'll need to reach up behind and hold the large nut (19 mm) as the top bolt (16 mm) is undone . . .

04 . . . but the shock's lower bolt (18 mm) isn't such a problem (it's got a 'captive' nut), and the old unit's soon history.

05 With the shock out of the picture, we can do our first bit of measuring. Pick two handy points, one on the suspension arm and one on the inside of the wheelarch, and with the arm hanging free, measure the distance between. Pick two points which you can duplicate on the other side of the car, to make sure you get it level when you get to that side.

06 Now we'll be needing that slide hammer, and here's what the bits look like. Basically, it's a piece of threaded rod (M10 size, available from motor factors and DIY stores), with two big nuts locked together on the end. The handle slides along the rod, and has to be heavy and solid to have any effect. Reckon you can make one? If not, any good tool hire shop should trust you with one for a morning.

07 Taking our slide hammer, we first screw the threaded rod into the end of the torsion bar (yes, Mr Renault's provided you a nice hole). Screw the rod in properly, or you'll wreck the thread when you smack it. Now the trick is to jerk the handle outwards from the car, to hit the nuts and give the torsion bar a shock. I'm sure there's a bad-taste joke in there somewhere.

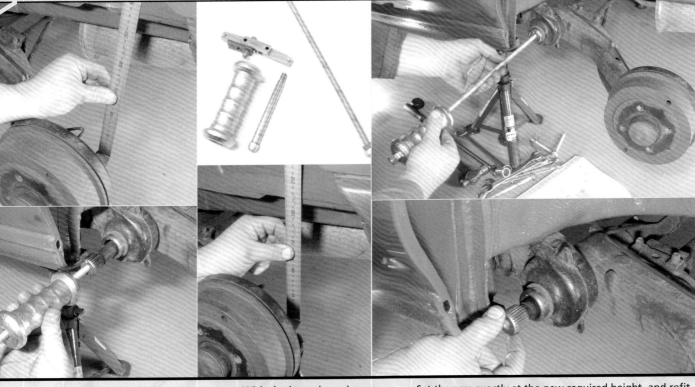

08 Do this enough times, and it'll bring tears to your eyes. No, actually, if you're doing it right, you should see the torsion bar's splined end gradually emerge from the arm, as you bang it out with the hammer. As we said previously, the bar's also splined into another fitting in the middle of the car (you just can't see it, on our lowly 1.4 Clio).

09 With the bar released, you're over the worst. Now pop a jack under the suspension arm, and get ready to measure again. Using the same two measuring points as before, raise the arm until it's set at your required drop. Our front Spax setup lowered the front by 55 mm, so we wanted the same at the back. Here's our calculations (your figures might be different):

*1st measurement (arm hanging) - 285 mm.
Required drop - 55 mm.
2nd measurement = 230 mm.*

10 Set the arm exactly at the new required height, and refit the torsion bar. If it won't go in, turn it by one spline and try again - it should eventually slide in quite smoothly. Don't tap it fully home until you've checked how the car's sitting, but we got ours spot-on both sides, first go. And this is the first Clio we'd lowered. Smug mode.

11 Once the other side's been lowered too, it's time to put the wheels back on, and see how you did. At this point, there's no rear shocks, so the back end will be very floppy indeed - don't drive it like this! All you're really doing is checking that the car's level, so take a measurement from the base of the bumper each side, and make sure they're near-enough identical. If not, you've mucked something up, and the torsion bars will have to be reset (Steps 8 to 10).

12 With the suspension successfully lowered, all we need is our new shock. Jack up, wheels off, and cue the other "half" of Mr Spax's PSX kit. The mounting bolt bushes provided aren't just for show - fit one half of each bush either side of the shock's top mount.

13 It's the same trick for the lower mounting bolt as well. Both shock mounting bolts were done up tight before, and should be again - here's the torque specs.

Rear drum brake Clio:
Top bolt - 80 Nm,
bottom bolt - 60 Nm
Rear disc brake Clio:
Top bolt - 115 Nm,
bottom bolt - 85 Nm

Spot the difference - Clios with rear disc brakes

Sportier Clios (RSi, 16V and Williams) have a rear axle which is totally open - the torsion bars and anti-roll bars are completely naked under there! You'll see that there are four bars altogether, with a little joining link in between - don't touch the anti-roll bars, which are the ones nearest the back of the car. The torsion bars, therefore, are the ones towards the front. Have we made this clear enough? We hope so. The process for lowering is much the same as for our more basic Clio (in fact, it's a bit easier, as you can see better what's going on with the bars).

14 Before putting the wheels back on, there's one last job. If, that is, you've got adjustable shocks like our Spax ones. You can adjust them later when the wheels are on the car, but it makes sense to put them to their basic recommended setting now. Refer to the instructions supplied if you're not sure where to set them. For safety, at least set both rears the same. These have twenty-flippin-eight possible settings - count 'em!

Nasty side-effects

Camber angle and tracking

With any lowering 'solution', it's likely that your suspension and steering geometry will be severely affected - this will be more of a problem the lower you go. This will manifest itself in steering which either becomes lighter or (more usually) heavier, and in tyres which scrub out their inner or outer edges in very short order - not funny, if you're running expensive low-profiles! Sometimes, even the rear tyres can be affected in this way, but that's usually only after some serious slammage. Whenever you've fitted a set of springs (and this applies to all types), have the geometry checked ASAP afterwards.

If you've dropped the car by 60 mm or more, chances are your camber angle will need adjusting. This is one reason why you might find the edges of your fat low-profiles wearing faster than you'd like (the other is your tracking being out). The camber angle is the angle the tyre makes with the road, seen from directly in front. Race cars have the front wheels tilted in at the top, out at the bottom - this is extreme negative camber, and it helps to give more grip and stability in extreme cornering (but if your car was set this hard-core, you'd kill the front tyres very quickly!). Virtually all road cars have a touch of negative camber on the front, and it's important when lowering to keep as near to the factory setting as possible, to preserve the proper tyre contact patch on the road. Trouble is, there's not usually much scope for camber adjustment on standard suspension, which is why (for some cars) you can buy camber-adjustable top plates which fit to the strut tops. Setting the camber accurately is a job for a garage with experience of modified cars - so probably not your local fast-fit centre, then.

Rear brake pressure regulator

Clios of the RSi, 16-valve or Williams persuasion (ones with rear discs) have a rear brake pressure-limiting valve fitted, which is linked to the rear suspension. The idea is that, when the car's lightly loaded over the rear wheels, the braking effort to the rear is limited, to prevent the wheels locking up. With the boot full of luggage, the back end sinks down, and the valve lets full braking pressure through to the rear. When you slam the suspension down, the valve is fooled into thinking the car's loaded up, and you might find the rear brakes locking up unexpectedly - could be a nasty surprise on a wet roundabout! The Clio's valve is fairly easy to adjust - the best idea would be to get underneath and see how it looks when unloaded (on standard suspension), and try to re-create the same condition once the car's been dropped.

On the Clio, the brake pressure regulator is under the car, in front of the spare wheel. The regulator linkage consists of a threaded rod and locknut, and does offer a limited amount of ride-height-related adjustability. The rod should be set so that, with the car resting on its wheels, any slack in the linkage has just been taken up. Chances are, if your Clio's been dropped by much more than 35 to 40 mm, there won't be enough adjustment, and further mods will be necessary, probably to lengthen the threaded rod.

Smile - a brace that's cool

Another item inspired by saloon racing, the strut brace is another underbonnet accessory you shouldn't be without. Some of them might even do something useful, like brace your struts...

The idea of the strut brace is that, once you've stiffened up your front suspension to the max, the car's 'flimsy' body shell (to which the front suspension struts are bolted) may not be able to cope with the 'immense' cornering forces being put through it, and will flex, leading to unsatisfactory handling. The strut brace (in theory) does exactly what it says on the tin, by providing support between the strut tops, taking the load off the bodyshell.

Where this falls down slightly (at least, for road use) is that 1) no-one's going to have a road car set that stiff, 2) no-one's going to drive that hard, and 3) the Clio shell isn't exactly made out of tin foil. The strut brace may indeed have a slight effect, but the real reason to fit one is for SHOW - and why not? Strut braces can be chromed, painted or anodised, and can be fitted with matching chromed/coloured strut top plates - a very tasty way to complement a detailed engine bay.

People also fit strut braces to the rear suspension mounts, usually on cars where the rear seats have been junked. Again, nice for show, but don't expect it to actually DO very much.

Front strut brace

01 The first thing to do is put the brace in its place! Our Momo brace came from the Momo-masters at Brown & Geeson. Lay it onto the strut tops, and see how much other stuff it interferes with. On our Clio, it was obvious immediately that the ignition coil on the passenger wing, and the MAP sensor on the driver's side, would need modifying. One other small problem - once the brace is on, you can't change the standard air filter. So... fit an induction kit!

02 The MAP sensor's easy - it just needs moving inwards slightly. Unbolt it, and with the brace in position, mark up a new hole.

03 Drill yourself a new hole, then re-mount the sensor.

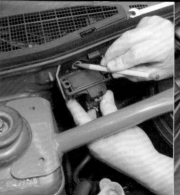

04 The coil needs to be lowered about 100 mm. Unplug the HT king lead and the other wiring plugs, and unbolt it from the inner wing. Our method was to bolt on two metal strips, the same length as the required 'drop', with holes drilled either end . . .

05 . . . note that the suppressor (the little black thingy with the wire) must still be earthed on one of the strip mounting bolts.

06 With the strips in place, mount the coil securely back onto the wing studs. The coil's a bit too important to be flapping about (don't expect it to work for long unless it's properly fixed in).

07 Okay - with the obstacles eliminated, we can get on with fitting the brace itself. First job is to mark up the holes - and this brace is such an accurate fit, there's not much room for movement. Or for error.

Once you've drilled one hole, it pays to fit a temporary bolt straight away, to pin the brace. Most of the braces we've seen don't come with their own mounting bolts and washers, so you'll need to grab some from a DIY centre - we used M8 bolts, which we cut down to 25 mm long later.

Whether you fit the bolts down from above, or up from below (like us), you'll need to get your hand inside the strut towers from below at some point. Hmm… tricky - there's a spring in there. Undo the strut top mounting plate, then raise the car just a little - with the pressure off the spring, it will move enough to let your hand in.

The effectiveness of your new brace depends a lot on how well it's fixed. Don't be shy about tightening the bolts/nuts. When you're happy it's not moving, let the car down and re-tighten the strut top plates, using the info in the front suspension fitting section earlier. All you need to do now is convince yourself you CAN feel a difference, round your favourite bend…

To make sure the holes go where we want, using a centre-punch seemed like a good plan.

08

09

10

11

09 Brakes

Remember the middle pedal?

It's the one next to the throttle - some people don't use it much. Uprating the brakes is actually a very easy bolt-on upgrade, but there are some points to consider.

One of the strangest, given that improving the brakes should in theory also improve your chances of avoiding an accident, is that insurance companies do not like performance brakes. You should still tell them, but be prepared for bad news. To them, it seems that fitting sporty brakes must automatically make you drive like Colin McRae - the clear implication is that if you need better brakes, you've either also uprated the engine (and not told them?), or you simply drive on the limit everywhere. Shame. We just like to know our cars will stop quickly. That, actually, might be another reason why they don't like better brakes - you stop better, but does the old dodderer behind you? Crunch.

Uprating the brakes will be a complete waste of time if you're a cheapskate on tyres. Cheap, no-name tyres or remoulds won't be able to translate extra braking power into actual vehicle-stopping power - they'll give up their grip on the tarmac and skid everywhere. Something like 90% of braking is done by the front wheels - ie the ones you steer with. If you consider that locked-up wheels also don't tend to steer very well, you'll begin to get an idea why good brakes and bad tyres are a well-dodgy mixture.

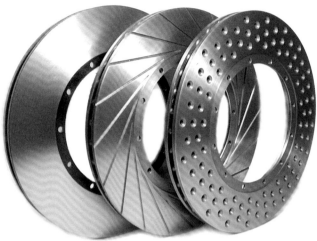

Groovy discs

Besides the various brands of performance brake pads that go with them, the main brake upgrade is to fit performance front brake discs and pads. Discs are available in two main types - grooved and cross-drilled (and combinations of both).

Grooved discs (which can be had with varying numbers of grooves) serve a dual purpose - the grooves provide a "channel" to help the heat escape, and they also help to de-glaze the pad surface, cleaning up the pads every time they're used. Some of the discs are made from higher-friction metal than normal discs, too, and the fact that they seriously improve braking performance is well-documented.

Cross-drilled discs offer another route to heat dissipation, but one which can present some problems. Owners report that cross-drilled discs really eat brake pads, more so than the grooved types, but more serious is the fact that some of these discs can crack around the drilled holes, after serious use. The trouble is that the heat "migrates" to the drilled holes (as was intended), but the heat build-up can be extreme, and the constant heating/cooling cycle can stress the metal to the point where it will crack. Discs which have been damaged in this way are extremely dangerous to drive on, as they could break up completely at any time. Only fit discs of

this type from established manufacturers offering a useful guarantee of quality, and check the discs regularly.

Performance discs also have a reputation for warping (nasty vibrations felt through the pedal). Now this may be so, but of course, the harder you use your brakes (and ones you've uprated may well get serious abuse), the greater the heat you'll generate. Okay, so these wicked discs are meant to be able to cope with this heat, but you can't expect miracles. Cheap discs, or ones which have had a hard time over mega-thousands of miles, will warp. So buy quality, and don't get over-heroic on the brakes.

Performance pads can be fitted to any brake discs, including the standard ones, but are of course designed to work best with heat-dissipating discs. Unless your Clio's got a tuned Williams lump under the bonnet, don't be tempted to go much further than "fast road" pads - anything more competition-orientated may take too long to come up to temperature on the road. Old dears always step off the pavement when your brakes are cold, remember!

Lastly, fitting all the performance brake bits in the world is no use if your calipers have seized up. If, when you strip out your old pads, you find that one pad's worn more than the other, or that both pads have worn more on the left wheel than the right, your caliper pistons are sticking. Sometimes you can free them off by pushing them back into the caliper, but this could be a garage job to fix. If you drive around with sticking calipers, you'll eat pads and discs. You choose.

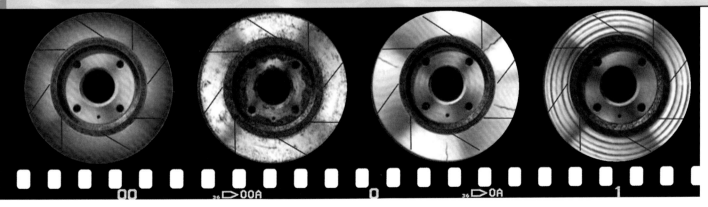

Brake
discs
and pads

Loosen the wheel bolts, jack up the corner of the car you're working on, and take off the wheel. Make sure you've got an axle stand under a solid part of the car in case the jack gives out. Have a look in "Wheels & tyres" for more info on jacking up. First job is to pull out the tiny wire clip holding the pad retaining plate in place - on our car, someone had **01** bodged in a split pin instead of the real thing. It happens.

Now pliers can be put to **02** good use removing the pad retaining plate . . .

RED·DOT

07 It's also not a bad plan to smear on (or even, brush on) some copper grease. This also helps the new disc to take up the correct position, and if you ever want to take your new discs off again, you'll be glad you did. While the disc's off, wouldn't this be a great chance to paint the calipers? Are you that organised?

08 Like the hubs, the new discs must be clean before fitting. Most discs are coated with a sticky or oily substance, to stop them rusting in the box - any decent brake-cleaning solvent will shift it. You might also think your new discs are identical. Chances are, they're not, and they should only be fitted with the grooves facing a certain way (this is the left front). Check your paperwork - our new multi-grooved discs were supplied by Red Dot Racing Ltd, with matching pads. Cheers, chaps!

09 Those two screws you had such fun removing must now be refitted to hold the new disc on. Or did you mangle up the screw heads, getting them off? New screws it is, then. Whichever way you go, the screws don't need to be hugely tight.

... before removing the pads themselves. As always, we seem to be removing perfectly-good pads yet again! Yours for a fiver. If they haven't already been chopped, disconnect the pad wear warning sensor wires. To set the caliper in the right position for new pads, lever between the back of the outer pad and the caliper, to **03** pull the caliper outwards (and push the piston in).

The discs are reassuringly held on by two Torx screws. But now you want them to come undone, and they just might not. Shock tactics, like tapping the area around the screw head to disturb the rust, combined with a dose of WD-40, should see them give up. Make sure you use the right-size Torx bit - a chewed-up screw **04** head is something you don't need.

Remember!
It's a good idea to have your brake mods MOT-tested once you've fitted new discs and pads, and you might even be able to "blag" a free brake check at your local fast-fit centre if you're crafty! Brakes are a serious safety issue, and unless you're 100% confident that all is well, demo-ing your car's awesome new-found stopping ability could find you in the ditch...

Not only perfectly-good pads, but a recently-renewed brake disc as well. Are **05** we mad?

The rust that was giving us a hard time getting the disc off now has to go, along with any other crud. If the wheel hub isn't totally pristine, the new disc won't sit on quite straight, and will eat its way through the new pads in no time. All for the sake of a few **06** minutes with a wire brush.

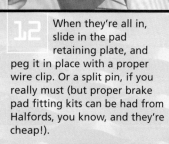

10 The little bullet-shaped thingies with wires are your pad wear warning sensors. If your Clio still has them, these are fitted to the inner pads. Poke the bullet through the hole in the pad backplate, and connect the wires up before the wheel goes back on. If you didn't have wires before, leave 'em off.

11 Smearing a bit of copper grease on the pad backplates shows you're serious about not having annoying squealing brakes. The pads will only fit one way round - and we don't just mean friction-material-to-brake-disc. No pad should have to be forced in - try all four in the box.

12 When they're all in, slide in the pad retaining plate, and peg it in place with a proper wire clip. Or a split pin, if you really must (but proper brake pad fitting kits can be had from Halfords, you know, and they're cheap!).

13 If you're really not going to paint those calipers just yet, brush on a little copper grease where the bottom lips of the pads slide on the caliper body - it all helps to achieve braking perfection.

Remember 2!
New pads of any sort need careful bedding-in (over 100 miles of normal use) before they'll work properly - when first fitted, the pad surface won't have worn exactly to the contours of the disc, so it won't actually be TOUCHING it, over its full area. This will possibly result in very under-whelming brakes for the first few trips, so watch it - misplaced over-confidence in your brakes is a fast track to hospital...

Cool coloured stoppers

One "downside" to fitted massive multi-spoked alloys is that - shock-horror - people will be able to SEE your brakes! This being so, why not paint some of the brake components so they look the biz, possibly to match with your chosen colour scheme (red is common, but isn't the only choice). Red brake calipers are often seen on touring cars, too, which may well be where the initial inspiration came from. Clios with less than 1.8 litres under the hood don't have rear discs, but painting the brake drums is acceptable under the circumstances - but then, do you paint 'em black, to de-emphasise them, or in your chosen colour for the fronts? It's all tough decisions, in modifying. If you're really sad, you can always buy fake rear discs... For the less-sad among you, Renault performance specialists may be able to sell you a rear disc brake conversion kit, but surely that's going a bit far, just to have red calipers front and rear? Remember, the rear brakes don't do much actual stopping...

Tricks 'n' tips
If you have trouble reassembling your brakes after painting, you probably got carried away and put on too much paint. We found that, once it was fully dry, the excess paint could be trimmed off with a knife.

Painting the calipers requires that they are clean - really clean. Accessory stores sell aerosol brake cleaner, which (apart from having a distinctive high-octane perfume) is just great for removing brake dust, and lots more besides! Some kits come complete with cleaner spray. Many of the kits advertise themselves on the strength of no dismantling being required, but we don't agree. Also, having successfully brush-painted our calipers, we wouldn't advise using any kind of spray paint.

We know you won't necessarily want to hear this, but the best way to paint the calipers is to do some dismantling first. The kits say you don't have to, but trust me - you'll get a much better result from a few minutes' extra work. We unbolted the caliper and draped it over the brake disc, with some paper towel to stop the red getting where it shouldn't. If you don't fancy unbolting the calipers (the two bolts have to be re-tightened to 100 Nm, by the way), just take out the pads and lose the disc for a while. Stopping halfway through the new disc fitting process described earlier would be a really sound move for this. Nobody thinks that far ahead, though.

Achtung!
Brake dust from old pads or shoes may contain asbestos. Wear a mask to avoid inhaling it.

Painting **calipers**

01 Get the wire brush out, and attack the rusty old caliper to get rid of all the loose muck. If the caliper's black with brake dust, try not to breathe much of it in. Squirt on your brake cleaner (our Savage kit, from Trillogy, came with its own can), giving the caliper a good dose, and get wiping as soon as possible. Spraying alone will only loosen the muck, and a good scrub is the only answer. If you don't get it spotless, you'll get black streaks in the paint.

02 Even though we're sure you followed our advice, and removed everything except the caliper (!), there's still a bit of masking-up to do, like round the bleed nipples. How much masking you'll need depends on how big a brush you're using, and how steady your hand is!

03 Our Trillogy paint came in two tins - one paint, one hardener. Pour one into the other, stir, and you then have about four hours max before the paint sets hard in the tin, apparently - so get cracking! If you're painting calipers and drums, it's best to do all the prep work, and be totally ready to start painting at all four corners of the car, before you mix the paint.

04 Stick some card or paper under the brake, 'cos this paint's tough to get off your driveway. And, er - get painting! Remember that you only have to paint the bits you'll see when the wheels are on. Once you start painting, it's a job knowing where NOT to paint! It's best to do more than one coat, we found. Follow the instructions with your kit on how long to leave between coats, but remember the time limit before the paint in the tin's useless. Wait 'til the paint's totally dry (like overnight, or longer) before reassembling.

Painting **drums**

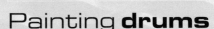

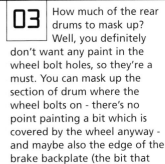

01 At least there's no dismantling with drums - get the rear end jacked up, wheels off (see "Wheels & tyres" if you need jacking info) and just get stuck in with the wire brush, sandpaper (to smooth the surface) . . .

02 . . . then it's spray on the brake cleaner and wipe thoroughly.

03 How much of the rear drums to mask up? Well, you definitely don't want any paint in the wheel bolt holes, so they're a must. You can mask up the section of drum where the wheel bolts on - there's no point painting a bit which is covered by the wheel anyway - and maybe also the edge of the brake backplate (the bit that doesn't turn).

04 Painting the drums is much easier than the rather fiddly calipers. One piece of advice - for the drums, use a thicker, better-quality brush than the one they give you in the kit - you'll get a much smoother paint finish on the drums. Again, two coats of paint seemed like a good idea. Another good idea is to let off the handbrake and turn the drum half a turn every so often until the paint's dry. Nobody likes the runs, after all.

Interiors

The Clio dash is best described as French. Very plastic, very grey, more than slightly wacky - it does the job, and that's about it. It might have no style whatsoever, but at least it doesn't feel like it's about to fall apart, or come off in your hands, unlike certain other French superminis we could mention. Yes, the Clio interior (with the exception of some really awfully-nice seat fabrics - not) is dull as elephant hide. But you need suffer no longer, because the interior really is one area where most of the goodies are pretty easy to fit, and provided you stick to one particular 'theme' (rather than a mixture), the end result can certainly help you forget you're in a base model, if indeed you are...

To be fair to the Clio, not many standard interiors are anything to shout about, particularly when you compare them with the sort of look that can easily be achieved with the HUGE range of product that's out there. As with the exterior styling, though, remember that fashions can change very quickly - so don't be afraid to experiment with a look you really like, because chances are, it'll be the next big thing anyway. Just don't do wood, ok? We've a feeling it's never coming in, never mind coming back...

Removing stuff

Take it easy and break less

Many of the procedures we're going to show involve removing interior trim panels (either for colouring or to fit other stuff), and this can be tricky. It's far too easy to break plastic trim, especially once it's had a chance to go a bit brittle with age. Another 'problem' with the Clio is that the interior trim is pretty well-attached (and the designers have been very clever at hiding several vital screws), meaning that it can be a pig to get off. They also seem to love using Torx

screws - invest in a set or Torx keys (like Allen keys), otherwise you'll come across ONE screw that won't come out using any other type of screwdriver. We'll try and avoid the immortal words 'simply unclip the panel', and instead show you how properly, but inevitably at some stage, a piece of trim won't 'simply' anything.

The important lesson here is not to lose your temper, as this has a highly-destructive effect on plastic components, and may result in a panel which no amount of carbon film or colour spray can put right, or make fit again. Superglue may help, but not every time. So - take it steady, prise carefully, and think logically about how and where a plastic panel would have to be attached, to stay on. You'll encounter all sorts of trim clips (some more fragile than others) in your travels - when these break, as they usually do, know that many of them can be bought in ready packs from accessory shops, and that the rarer ones will be available from a Renault dealer, probably off the shelf. Even fully-trained Renault mechanics aren't immune to breaking a few trim clips!

Door trim panel

You'll find plenty of excuses for removing your door trim panels - fitting speakers, re-trimming the panel, de-locking, even window tinting, so we'd better tell you how ...

01 Open the window, by whatever means you have. Now, if you've got wind-up windows, just pull off the winder handle. Yes, really - you've probably done it a few times by accident, already. Well, at least you don't need any tools.

02 Remove the Torx screw from the door lock interior handle. . .

03 . . . carefully pull the handle out, and unhook the lock operating rod at the back (you'll have to refit this later on, so have a look how it fits, rather than just yanking it out).

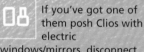

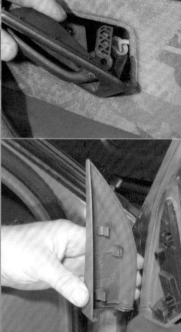

08 If you've got one of them posh Clios with electric windows/mirrors, disconnect the wiring plugs from the switches on the door pocket.

09 The front door speaker covers are also held on by - guess what - more Torx screws. It really is 'game over' on a Clio if you haven't got any Torx keys or bits.

10 The cover, speaker and original housing are all held in by the same four screws - grab the speaker, so it doesn't end up swinging on its own wiring (not good). Unplug the speaker wiring, and we're nearly there.

11 Oh wait - just one last thing - the door mirror panel, which just prises off. What, no Torx screws?

04 Prise off the cover from the door pull handle, trying not to gouge huge chunks of plastic out (use a small screwdriver, carefully) . . .

05 . . . and remove the two Torx screws behind, holding the back part of the handle to the door.

06 Remove the six Torx screws (count 'em) around the edge securing the door pocket . . .

07 . . . and unclip it from the door. It clips into a support halfway along, and hooks in at the front - so first, pull it out at the bottom, and down at the front. Just don't get mad with it. Now pick up your shades/lighter/CDs from the floor, and remember to remove them first, next time!

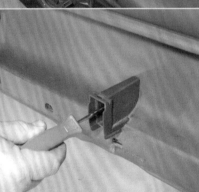

12 Who mentioned Torx screws? Just when we thought we'd seen the last, we find one buried inside the support piece for the door pocket. I blame the EU myself.

13 The trim panel's now held on by several clips around its edge, and also by a bead of nice sticky sealant (these Frenchies - don'tcha just luv 'em?). Careful persuasion with a wide-bladed screwdriver should see the trim panel off without destroying too many of the clips in the process.

14 Lift the panel out of the window channel at the top of the door, and over the door lock button. Phew.

Rear side **panels**

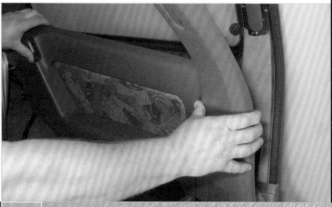

01 There's not an awful lot to removing these, really - they just unclip. Saves you wasting time looking for hidden screws, anyway. But take your time, or they might not re-clip again.

Sill trim panels

01 If all you want to do is feed some wires down behind these, it's easy. Grasp firmly at the front end, and unclip. The panel's quite well tucked-up at the front end, so a little bending may be needed.

02 To remove them completely, the rear side panel's got to come off first, to get access to these two Torx screws at the back. Easy when you know how.

Glovebox

01 Removing the glovebox is slightly easier with the left-hand speaker/vent panel removed, but it's not essential to the plot (the panel is held by three Torx screws - one at the side, two at the base). Prise off the support strap . . .

02 . . . or, if you're really doing the job properly, you can push out the strap mounting peg, from inside the end of the dash.

03 Now there's a crosshead screw at each end to remove . . .

04 . . . and off she comes, ready for painting, filming - whatever.

Dash top panel/column shrouds

See section on white dial kit.

01 Before we get the spanners and screwdrivers out, you might want to disconnect your seat belt tensioners. My what? Fitted to all Phase 2 models from March 1994 (L reg), and not just those with an airbag. Switch off the ignition, pull out the relevant fuse from the fusebox (check your handbook, or decipher the symbols on the fusebox itself - yours may be different to ours), and wait for a minimum of 5 minutes. Then disconnect the tensioner wiring plugs under the front seats. Phew.

02 On Clios with a driver's footrest, remove the two Torx screws . . .

03 . . . and take it out of the way. Nice pedals.

04 Unclip the very nasty old rubber gear gaiter from the centre console, and fold it up around the gear lever.

Centre console

. . . and tip it forwards to access the wiring underneath. Depending on how posh your Clio is, you'll have cigar lighter wiring and a central locking master switch to disconnect.

05 The console's held in by four Torx screws - one each side at the front . . .

06 . . . and two more at the back.

07 Lift the console off the floor, working it over the gear lever . . .

08

Window **winders**

01 Okay, so not everyone's got 'em, but they're never the most attractive door furniture! Removing the old ones is a lot easier on Clios than on most cars - they just pull off. You or your passengers may perhaps have found this out already?

02 The curse of 'universal-fit' falls on us once again with our new handles - very nice items from Richbrook. Before you can fit them to your Clio, you have to pull them to bits. That's right - the new handles contain all the possible fittings required for all different cars, including ones which have a screw in the centre. On a Clio, you have to undo the four Allen screws holding the handle to the base, and remove the centre screw hidden inside . . .

03 . . . before re-assembling and tightening the four Allen screws fully. That's not another free Allen key, to add to our collection?

Spraying stuff

Now slide the handle onto the splines, making sure you've got it at the right angle for when the window's closed, and **04** tighten the grub screw so the handle can't fall off.

Now tell me that chunky chrome item's not miles better **05** than wobbly grey plastic. You can't, can you.

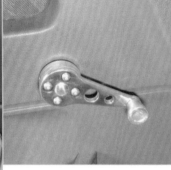

01 This is the sort of result you can get with paint, and a little imagination. Dismantle the door trim panel as described during the removal process - this makes spraying different colours much easier (lots less masking). Otherwise, it's all in the preparation - rough up the panels before hitting them with the spray, and enjoy the results.

Door lock **buttons**

Remove the door trim panel as described earlier. The door lock button is attached to this metal rod, clipped to the door lock mechanism inside the door. A little persuasion with a small screwdriver may be needed to pop the rod out of the clip - but remember, you'll be refitting the new rod and button later, so watch how it comes off.

01

The deal with these is - you cut off the old button, and attach the new one to the stump of rod left, using a screw clamp. Simple enough - but for fairly obvious reasons, the rod must stay roughly the same length with the new button fitted, as it was before you chopped it. Eye the two up, mark and cut.

02

The screw clamp gives you some flexibility with the length of the rod - do it up nice and tight. Looks better already. Cheers to the guys at Richbrook, for supplying these ProLock flashers.

03

Feed the newly-decorated rod into the door, together with the wiring (if you're gonna fit these babies, get flashing ones). Clip the rod back onto the lock mechanism inside the door, and check it goes up and down as expected. Later, when you get the door trim panel back on, also check the button passes freely through the guide hole in the door panel - some 'adjustment' may be needed.

04

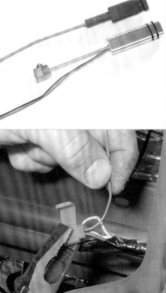
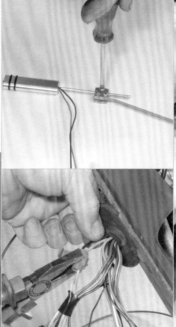

05 Right - back to those wires. If your Clio is of reasonable spec, this won't be tricky - if it's more basic, you'll need to feed some power into those doors, which may mean drilling (but the same holes can be used to feed through decent speaker wiring, so it's not all bad news). Get out the test light, and find an ignition live, and a permanent live. What, no earth? Trust us - we know what we're doing . . .

06 . . . you see, if you feed one LED wire an ignition live, and the other a permanent live, it doesn't blow the LED - it just stops working. This way, when the ignition's on, the door pins DON'T flash. Do you want them going all the time you're driving? Thought not. We found a permanent live on this red wire from the central locking motor . . .

07 . . . and an ignition live from the yellow to the electric window switch. And no, you're quite right - we don't usually approve of this type of connector… Using bullets gives a more reliable connection.

08 Test your flashing buttons, and feel that glow of smug satisfaction. But don't get too carried away just yet. Those doors are full of moving parts, just waiting to slice through your new wiring - so make a decent job of tidying the wiring (with tape and cable-ties) before slapping the door panel back on. You know it makes sense.

Door sill trims

You can get these in any colour you like, as long as it's chrome, but a new trick is getting trims which light up, preferably with the interior lights - these lush items came from Auto Tint Design, who deserve a big shout for all their help with our project Clio. One piece of advice, if you're planning major interior mods - fit the sill trims last. That way, there's less chance of scratching and scuffing 'em up during fitting the rest of the interior.

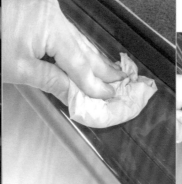

01 Fitting isn't hard, but you will need a steady hand. First, clean the sills with washing-up liquid (or, if they're really filthy, with wicked-strength solvent). Dry them off thoroughly before going any further.

02 Don't even think about peeling off that backing paper yet. Before you get anywhere near that, do a trial fitting, to see where the new sills line up on the car.

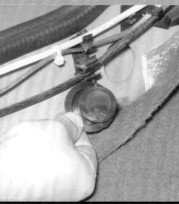

03 With a strip of masking tape in place, measure the distance either end of the sill trim, to get it central.

04 On our illuminated plates, we also needed to mark the position for drilling a wiring hole through (make this hole just inside the marked end of the sill, to hide it).

05 You non-illuminated sill types can now sit back and watch the fun. Drilling holes in your sills is not normally a good idea (ask your MOT tester), but Clios are built slightly better than your average Ford, so one or two small holes won't mean the car falls to bits.

06 Did we say Clios are well built? We weren't wrong. To get a hole inside the sill for feeding the wires into the car, prise off the sill trim (which just unclips at the front) and remove this large grommet . . .

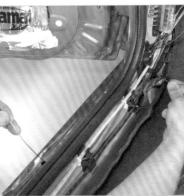

07 . . . are we there yet? No - the inner sills are double-skinned, so you need to drill a hole behind the grommet.

08 Before we start feeding wires through your freshly-drilled holes, spare a thought for electrical safety and fit a grommet, at least to the hole in the inner sill. They're cheap as chips, and should mean your Clio won't go up in smoke. Fitting one to the hole on the outer sill is less easy, so just make sure the wires are well-wrapped with insulating tape, where they go through the metal.

09 To feed your sill plate wiring through, first feed through a thick-ish piece of wire (if you're stuck, unwind a metal coat-hanger). Tie or tape your new wiring to the thick wire, and slowly pull it through. Can take time, especially if you don't attach the wiring properly, and it falls off halfway.

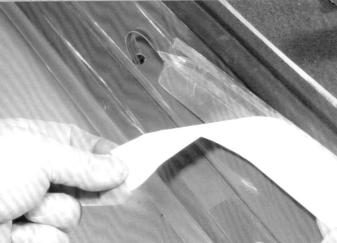

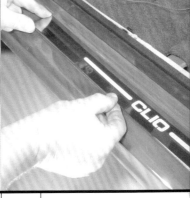

10 At last, we can connect up the sill plates. If you can find a suitable live and earth, you could have a test illumination now.

11 Okay, now you wire-free types can come back in - it's time to stick the plates on at last. Have one last check to make sure you know exactly where they're going (the sticky on the sticky pads is very, very sticky indeed), then peel off the backing . . .

12 . . . and stick it on. Hold the plate at an angle first, and get the back edge pushed right into the back of the sill. When the plate's positioned centrally, 'roll' the trim down flat onto the sill. Notice we did the passenger door first? Always a good idea - you can then make a better job of the one you and everyone else will see most of...

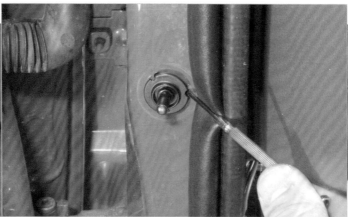

13 Now back to the wiring. If you want your plates to light up with the interior lights, you need to attack the door pin switches first. Prise off this rubber cover . . .

14 . . . then use a thin wire or pointed tool to release the three clips around the edge of the switch . . .

15 . . . and pull it out of the door. Though there's not much wire to join into, you're looking for a pink/yellow wire (or at least, that's what was on our Clio).

16 The sill plates work on a switched-earth principle, meaning you can feed them a permanent live from anywhere, but they'll only work with the door switches if you connect the plates' earth wires (black) to the door switch wiring. We're using a double bullet to join in the passenger plate earth wire to the switch (only just fitted back through the hole in the door pillar).

17 For the live supply to each plate, you need a permanent live supply. We already knew where to find one - at the back of the fusebox, there's a small wiring plug at one end (which is actually the live feed for the interior lights). Pull this plug out, and there's plenty of room to join on your two sill plate red wires.

18 Our plates came with a handy wiring 'junction box', which helps to keep the wiring tidier. We shoved ours inside the space behind the left-hand speaker/grille panel. To feed the driver's-side wiring across the car, take off the dash top panel (see 'white dials') and feed the wires across the car. You'll need to tap into the driver's door pin switch for the remaining black wire.

Anything but black?

The interior trim on the Clio at least hides its age well, and doesn't rattle much. And that's about it - for a lover of elephant-hide grey, it's heaven, but for more normal people, it's something else. Fortunately, there's plenty you can do to personalise it, and there are three main routes to take:

1) Spray paint - available in any colour you like, as long as it's... not black. This Folia Tec stuff actually dyes softer plastics and leather, and comes in a multi-stage treatment, to suit all plastic types. Don't try to save money just buying the top coat, because it won't work! Special harder-wearing spray is required for use on steering wheels. Ordinary spray paint for bodywork might damage some plastics, and won't be elastic - good primer is essential. Make sure you also buy lots of masking tape.

2) Adhesive or shrink-fit film - available in various wild colours, carbon, ally, and, er... walnut (would YOU?). Probably best used on flatter surfaces, or at least those without complex curves, or you'll have to cut and join - spray is arguably better here. Some companies will sell you sheets of genuine carbon-fibre, with peel-off backing - looks and feels the part (nice if you have touchy-feely passengers).

3) Replacement panels - the easiest option, as the panels are supplied pre-cut, ready to fit. Of course, you're limited then to styling just the panels supplied.

If you fancy something more posh, how about trimming your interior bits in leather? Very saucy. Available in various colours, and hardly any dearer than film, you also get that slight 'ruffled' effect on tighter curves.

Get the cans out

For the Clio interior, we found that the spray approach was the most successful - but that's just us, and for our chosen look. For variety, we tried (real) stick-on carbon-fibre for some things, and a Dash Dynamics kit to break up the rest of the cream interior.

Any painting process is a *multi-stage* application. With the Folia Tec system (thanks to Eurostyling for supplying ours), many of you apparently think you can get away just buying the top coat, which then looks like a cheap option compared to film - WRONG! Even the proper interior spray top coat won't stay on for long without the matching primer, and the finish won't be wear-resistant without the finishing sealer spray. You don't need the special foaming cleaner - you could get by with a general-purpose degreaser, such as meths. Just watch the cloth doesn't suddenly turn black - if it does, you're damaging the finish! This might not be too important to you, as it's being sprayed over anyway, but if you take out the black too far on a part that's not being sprayed all over, you'll have to live with a white-black finish to any non-painted surface…

Providing you're a dab hand with the masking tape, paint gives you the flexibility to be more creative. With our interior, we decided to try colour-matching the exterior of the car - could we get ordinary car body paint to work on interior plastics? Only one way to find out…

Choice of paint's one thing, but what to paint? Well, not everything - for instance, you might want to avoid high-wear areas like door handles. Just makes for an easier life. The glovebox lid and dash speaker/vent end panels are obvious first choices, as is the dash top panel (which comes out incredibly easily - see in 'white dials' for just how easily). The centre console's not lighting anyone's fire in standard Renault grey, so hit it with some spray too. The console ashtray and switch panels just pop out, giving you an easy opportunity to go for a contrasting colour (lots less masking needed) - just make sure whatever you're dismantling was meant to come apart, or it'll be out with the superglue instead of the cans.

Don't be afraid to experiment with a combination of styles - as long as you're confident you can blend it all together, anything goes! How about mixing-in carbon-fibre sheet or brushed-aluminium film instead - neutral colours like this, or chrome, can be used to give a lift to dash bits which are too tricky to spray.

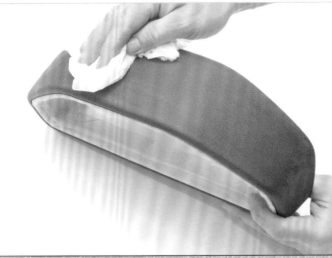

01 Clean up the surface to be sprayed, using a suitable degreaser - we used meths in the end, having tried some thinners initially (this started taking off the black). You must use something fairly evil, to get off any silicone- based products you or the previous owner may have used, as these are death to paint adhesion. If you're not going to paint the whole thing, don't degrease the whole thing, or you might ruin the finish on the black bits.

02 To be even more certain your chosen paint won't peel when the masking comes off, you need to get a bit brutal (no going back If you change your mind). You need some Scotchbrite, which is a bodyshop-spec scouring pad, available in several grades. Try a bodyshop or motor factors - it's not dear, and it's great for roughing-up any surface before spraying, giving the paint a 'key'. Cheaper alternatives may be available in Tesco!

03 Mask up the bits you don't want sprayed, as necessary. Make sure you protect all surfaces from overspray - you can never do too much masking. After masking-up, give it a final wipe over with solvent, then apply a mist coat of primer - this is essential to help the paint 'stick' to the plastic. Allow plenty of time for the primer to dry. If you're using ordinary spray as a topcoat (like we did), you'll need a special primer for plastics, which is available from places like Halfords.

Painting
trim

04 Now for the colour coat - keep shaking the tin between passes, and don't bottle-out halfway across, or the can's nozzle will spit paint on, leaving nasty blobs in the finish. Also, don't try to cover the job in one coat, nor spray too close. You'll be a natural in the end - practice on some scrap card until you've mastered the technique (it's all in the wrist, y'know). Allow time for each coat to dry (a few minutes) before banging some more on.

05 Once you're happy that there's even coverage, let the last top coat dry, then slap on the sealer coat (or lacquer, in our case). This final coat is intended to improve wear-resistance (not much good if your carefully-applied paint rubs off in a few weeks, is it?). You should only need a light coat to finish the job.

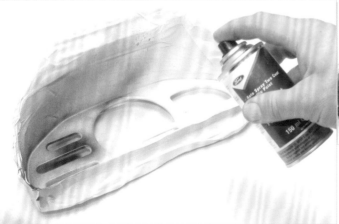

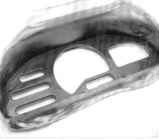

06 Let the paint go tacky (rather than fully dry) before peeling off the masking, and take care when you do - if the paint's too dry, you'll peel some of the paint off with the mask! If you're in any doubt, take your steadiest hand and sharpest knife to the edges of the masking tape before peeling.

Filming your Clio

If you fancy creating a look that's a bit more special than plain paint colours, film is the answer - but be warned - it's not the easiest stuff in the world to use, and so isn't everyone's favourite. If you must have the brushed-aluminium look, or fancy giving your Clio the carbon-fibre treatment, there really is no alternative (apart from the lazy-man option of new panels, of course).

For our Clio, we chose to cover the radio cover flap, and the dash-top 'finger-trays' with carbon-look film (supplied by Eurostyling), just to break up the cream treatment.

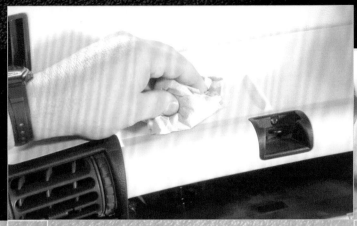

01 Step 1 is cleaning and degreasing - see the advice in Step 1 for painting. On a heavily-grained finish, remember that the grain will show through thin film - this does slightly ruin the effect, and a deep grain means the film won't stick all over the surface. Not a good idea to go mad with the wet-and-dry (or Scotchbrite), to get rid of the grain - you'll destroy the surface totally.

02 Rather than sacrifice your valuable carbon fibre getting it wrong, try using a piece of paper as a template . . .

Applying **film**

03 . . . then use the template on the carbon sheet, and trim it out.

04 Peel off the backing, making sure you don't lose track of which way round your trimmed piece is supposed to go . . .

05 . . . and stick it on straight (carbon fibre and brushed ally both look stupid if you get it stuck on un-straight, so take your time).

Bum notes

There are limitations to using film, and the quality of the film itself has a lot to do with that. We had major problems doing any kind of job with one particular make of brushed-aluminium-look film - it was a nightmare to work with, and the edges had peeled the next day. Buying quality film will give you a long-lasting result to be proud of, with much less skill requirement and LOTS less swearing. But it still pays not to be too ambitious with it.

Ready-made panels

A far easier route to the brushed-ally or carbon look, pre-finished ('here's some we did earlier') panels are available from suppliers. Dash kits are available for the Clio from companies like Dash Dynamics, and offer a simpler way of livening-up the dull Clio dash. Did we say simple? It's sometimes not too obvious where the various kit bits are supposed to go! A trial fitting isn't a bad idea, before peeling off the backing. Make sure your chosen trim piece is lined up nice and square, and keep it square as you press it on - the adhesive's usefully-sticky, meaning it will stay stuck whether you get it right or wrong. Still, it's easier by far than trying to mask up and spray the edges of the vents, which is what you'd have to do otherwise.

Sort your knob out

01 If you're changing the gaiter as well as the knob (and who wouldn't?), remove the centre console as described earlier. We're fitting a chrome surround as well as our new gaiter, so the first job is to make a few holes to fit the surround with. And yes, this is our expensive-looking leather-trimmed console we're violating with the drill. The leather trimming's covered later in this section, in case you were wondering.

02 Before you go too far with the hole-drilling process, it's not a bad plan to pop one or two screws in. With the surround pinned in a couple of places, the rest of the holes you drill will be more accurate.

03 Now to make our posh new gaiter fit. Experience tells us that not all 'universal' gaiters are alike, and some are definitely more work to make fit than others. We've been quite lucky here - this gaiter's flexible enough to stretch into the shape of our surround, and we're able to use the surround screws through the gaiter to secure it. Here, we're using a sharp pointy tool to make those holes.

04 Put the screws through the chrome and the leather, to keep the gaiter in place . . .

05 . . . while you screw it into position. We're so far managing to keep our cream-and-black leather theme going quite nicely.

06 Okay, so the new console and gaiter are shaping up nicely, but the old knob and gaiter still have to be dealt with. The old knob just pulls off. Yes, we know these things usually don't 'just' anything, but this time, it's true. If you have trouble, you may simply not be strong enough - but you could try warming it with a heat gun, and a little careful levering underneath (don't knacker the reverse lift collar, though).

07 The very, very nasty rubber gaiter is fortunately very easy to remove, and very easy to forget. Slip the console and new gaiter back in place, and it's time for that new knob.

08 Providing you choose a knob that's suitable for use with a reverse-gear lifting collar (ask before you buy), this shouldn't even be a 5-minute job. Most knobs come with a selection of rubber sleeves, which you fit over the end of the gear lever to give an initial tight fit. All you have to do then is loosely fit a small grub screw . . .

09 . . . and fit your new knob over its rubber sleeve, onto the gear lever. Using the Allen key they normally give you in the knob kit, tighten the screw until it's... er... tight. Don't want your knob coming off in your hand, now do we?

10 The final act of tidying-up is making a neat job of the top of your new gaiter. As the Clio has a lift collar for reverse gear, you can't use the rather neat screw-on lower collars you get with some gear knobs, to secure the top of the gaiter. We had a trial run with a very skinny cable-tie, not expecting it to look any sense, but when pulled tight, the excess leather could be folded over to hide the tie. But a black shoe lace would probably have been more professional, we admit.

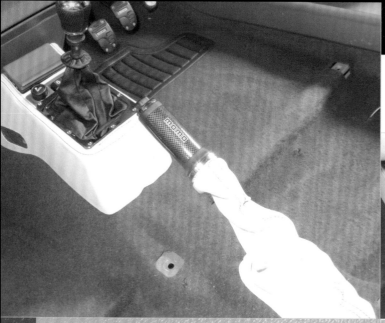

Handbrake
knobs
& gaiters

01 Your sexy new gear knob and gaiter's making the sad black stick behind look even worse, so get it sorted. Being a quality, well-built vehicle, designed to last for years, the deeply-unpleasant plastic handbrake 'gaiter' on the Clio just pulls straight off.

02 But give them their due - the handbrake knob's not coming off without a fight. In fact, we had to slice it with Stanley . . .

∧

Do not play with the handbrake once you've sliced off the old knob, otherwise the operating button and spring drop down, and you're in deep stuff. We know. We found out how much of a pain it is to refit. The first thing we had to hand was a cable-tie, so we used that to tie it up.

You won't find the handbrake gaiter we used in any Demon Tweeks catalogue - oh no. Ours was made for us by our leather-wielding friends at Pipers, to match our leather-trimmed console - cheers, chaps! To stick it to the Clio carpet, we tried sticking on some of the (rough) velcro strips left over from our rear light brows - and it worked a treat.

03 . . . before peeling off the remains. That's one bit that ain't going back to standard in a hurry.

04

05

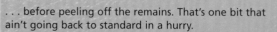

06 Fold up the base of the gaiter, so the velcro doesn't stick to everything, then slide the gaiter over the lever, and stick it down to the carpet.

07 When we first tried to fit our sexy new Momo carbon-fibre handbrake knob, our cunning plan to stop the handbrake lever coming to bits met its first hurdle. With that flippin' cable-tie in the way, the new knob wouldn't go on. So, being very careful not to let everything fly apart, we cut off the tie, and replaced it with some equally-useful tape.

08 Ahh, that's more like it. The handbrake knob's as easy to fit as most gear knobs - loosely fit the grub screws, and tighten them up. On this knob, there are four holes available for screws, but the one underneath wasn't used on our Clio - there's a slot in the lever underneath, so a screw can't be tightened up.

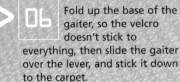

Slide the gaiter down the lever, and use the Allen key provided (another one? We'll have our own collection soon) to tighten the three screws. Make sure you position the new knob so that the handbrake release button can still be used. We know it sounds very obvious, but you might be surprised…

09

Now for a little fiddling with our new gaiter, to achieve that perfect fit. After various attempts, we decided that the gaiter would look best fitted over the back end of the new knob, but how could we secure it, without it looking cack?

10

Once again, it's leftover Velcro that saves the day. This self-adhesive Velcro strip is wonderful stuff - wrap it around the base of the knob, stick some more inside the top of the gaiter, and it's one tidy result to the Haynes crew.

11

The personal touch –
re-trimming

Okay, so you're definitely not happy with how the inside of your Clio looks, but you're not sold on any of the off-the-shelf options for tricking it up, either. You know how you want it to look, though, so get creative!

There are any number of upholstery companies in Yellow Pages, who will be able to create ANY look you want (we got one in our own back yard,

almost - Pipers of Queen Camel, Somerset, who were extremely helpful in their contribution to this section). If your idea of Clio heaven is an interior swathed in black and purple leather, these guys can help. Don't assume that you'll have to go to Carisma, to get a car interior re-trimmed - they might well be the daddies at this, but any upholsterer worth the name should be able to help, even if they normally only do sofas!

Of course, if you're even slightly handy with things like glue and scissors, you might be inspired to get brave and DIY. An upholsterers will still be a useful source for your materials.

Seats

This is really one for a pro upholstery outfit - it involves pulling your seats to bits. For what it's worth, if you're determined to try trimming your seats on your own, our advice is to practice on a seat from the scrapyard first, 'til you've got the hang of it! Good luck, and we salute you! Let's see how the professionals do it.

For info on removing the standard seats, see 'Are you sitting stylishly', further on.

 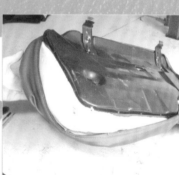

01 Okay, we really are mad. Here we are, with a Clio 1.4 RT, we go to the trouble of sourcing a full 16V leather interior from a scrappy, and now we're going to re-trim it in leather. Huh? Well, it's not quite as mad as it seems - our RT seats were best described as 'comfy'. Not at all sporty, in other words. We would've been mad to re-trim those.

02 If you can't stand seeing a nice leather seat ripped apart, look away now. This, by the way, is one half of the rear seat cushion, but it'll tell you most of what you need to know for any seat. First, the leather cover's clipped into a channel in the metal seat base, using a plastic-covered metal tape stitched to the cover - squash the foam, pull the leather down, and out it pops.

∧

03 On top, the cover's pinned to the foam by a number of 'hog-rings' (a bit like large circular staples), which the pros release using special pliers. So does the old cover get binned, once it's removed? Not a bit. We know it fits perfectly, so it gets 'dismantled' and used as a template for the new leather.

04 See? Nothing gets chucked out - not even the metal tape we mentioned earlier, used to clip the base of the seat cover into the metal seat base.

05 If anyone else were doing this, it would probably be vandalism - but not if it's the skilled hands of the lads at Pipers. Any seat cover worth having is made up of sections, stitched together. Each section now has to be carefully unpicked . . .

06 . . . and laid out for marking-up. Notice how adjoining sections have been marked across each other, in case our man should forget how it's supposed to fit together (no chance).

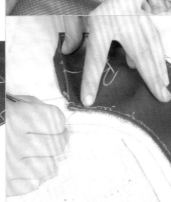

07 At last we get a glimpse of some new leather. We're going for cream, mainly, but with black perforated leather inserts. Here, our man's marking out the piece for the main centre panel. Notice he's not just marking out the size, but also where the centre stitching lines are - we'll see why in a minute.

08 Once the black leather section's have been marked up, it's out with the scissors. And here's another little trick to spot - he's not cutting these pieces right to the lines he's marked. Is he cutting it out roughly, to trim to the lines later? No. Leaving half-an-inch or so outside the required size gives you enough material to stitch to - of course.

09 It's not all straight lines when it comes to re-trimming seats. And it's not all black leather, either - here, a section that's going to be cream's being marked-up, again slightly oversize.

10 Here's some we cut out earlier - but what's that stuff they've been laid on top of? Is it - foam?

>>

Virtually every section of this seat cover's going to end up being foam-backed - here's another section being trimmed up. So why use foam? To make the seat more comfy? Well, it does do that as well, obviously, but the real reason is to improve the visual effect. Leather would look too flat and lifeless without the foam backing, and it's really effective where you have stitching across a large panel, as it 'puffs up'

11 the stitched sections. You'll see what we mean in a minute.

So now it's over to the sewing machine (well, you didn't think all that stitching was fake, did you?) to join the trimmed

12 leather panels to a matching piece of foam.

13 Any excess foam can then be trimmed off . . .

. . . and now any centre-stitching can be added. This is why the original stitch-lines were marked out on the leather, and why using foam backing makes such a huge difference. Now you know

14 for sure this is going to be a quality job.

15 And here we have the finished sections of our rear seat cushion top cover, foam-backed and ready for sewing together . . .

16 . . . which is exactly what happens next. Nothing girly about lads using a sewing machine, either - just serious craftsmanship at work.

17 Believe us now? Not only is it looking lush, it's the right shape to be a seat, too.

18 The next step is to add the 'show-stitching'. The seats are already in effect sewn together - the contrasting black or cream thread going in at this stage is just 'for show', and doesn't necessarily actually do anything. Apart from making the whole job look even sweeter.

Once the seat side and front panels have been added (these are the only bits not to get the foam backing), it's time to refit the bits 'n' pieces originally used by Renault to hold the seat cover to the seat foam. This, for instance, is the rail used to attach those 'hog-rings' we saw coming off earlier . . .

19

. . . while here we've got the metal tape (used to attach the base of the cover) being stitched back on. If it worked before, why ditch it when you could stitch it?

20

By now, we're dying to see whether it's all going to come together (but we've got a good feeling about it). First, the hog-rings - these are used to pull the seat cover into the creases in the foam. A lack of these items is the reason why aftermarket seat covers don't fit properly and look dreadful.

21

And here's a hog-ring in close-up, about to be crimped on using those special pliers.

22

23 Now the seat cover can be stretched over the foam . . .

24 . . . and the metal tape gets shoved back into the guide channel in the seat base to secure it all. If this was a front seat, the seat cover would have metal hooks at the base, to join either onto a wire 'mattress' below the seat, or directly to the seat foam itself.

25 The finished article. Now call us mad if you dare - and the front seats look even better . . .

26 . . . see what we mean?

Headrest

01 Right - you've seen seats, but how would an upholsterers do a headrest? We're about to see for ourselves.

02 On our Clio headrest, there's first of all a plastic guide each side to unclip . . .

03 . . . then we're prising out a few staples. In between the headrest 'posts', where the flaps of the cover meet, there's a catch which you just unhook . . .

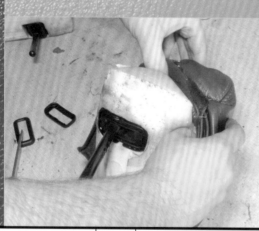

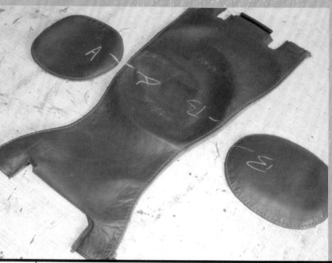

04 . . . before the old cover can be peeled off the foam beneath.

05 Believe it or not, this is what a headrest cover looks like, once you've unpicked all the stitching. As with the seats before, the old headrest cover is going to be used as a template for the new leather.

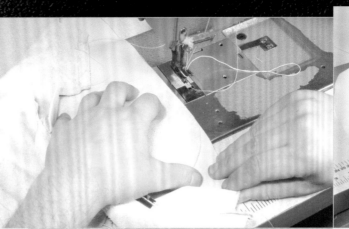

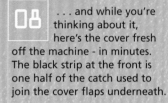

06 The outline of each piece is marked on the cream leather (allowing enough all round for the pieces to be folded and stitched), then cut out . . .

07 . . . before the three bits get transferred to the sewing machine for assembly. Can you imagine the skill and patience required to produce a 3D object on a sewing machine? Think about it . . .

08 . . . and while you're thinking about it, here's the cover fresh off the machine - in minutes. The black strip at the front is one half of the catch used to join the cover flaps underneath.

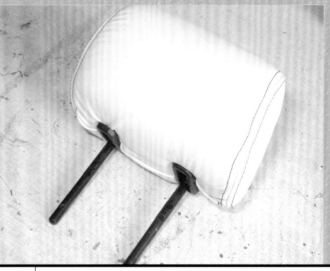

09 Once the 'show-stitching' has been added, we get to the fun part. You wouldn't think the hardest part would be refitting the new cover, but it is - remember, we're trying to slide leather (the rough back-side of leather) over foam, and the two 'stick' very well. To overcome this, our skilled artisans at Pipers use a plastic bag over the foam, which they then pull out once the leather's basically in position. It's called tricks of the trade.

10 A few tacks with the stapler (and this is a pro air-stapler, no less) to tidy up the job around the posts, and with a little trimming and fettling, the plastic guides will be ready to clip back on.

11 Tell me that doesn't look miles better than the grey. Still needs a little stretching and fiddling to get rid of the creases (some people like that in a leather interior), but that's basically the finished job.

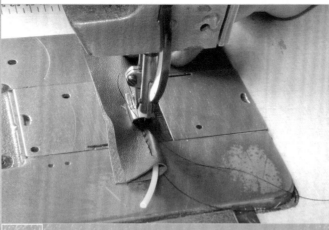

Piping

We've all seen piped seats, of course. But have you ever wondered how exactly piped seats get their piping? Is it glued on, or melted on with heat? Stretched around the finished seat, maybe? And how do you get the different colours? Well, we're about to see the simple truth - our tame upholstery outfit isn't called Pipers for nothing, you know.

01 Here we have the materials required for a small sample of cream leather, piped with black. Already we're beginning to suspect the truth of what goes on, in the mysterious world of piping.

02 Take your chosen strip of leather (or vinyl), in whatever colour takes your fancy, fold it around a strip of thin circular plastic bead (or 'pipe'), and stitch it along, tight.

03 Take your new material strip, and stitch it to one piece of the cream leather . . .

04 . . . then lay the other piece of cream on top, and stitch that too.

05 And that's all there is to it. Apart from a certain skill with materials, ability to use a sewing machine, and a lifetime of experience.

Door trim panels

What applies to seats can also be applied to your door cards.

We wanted a lush look for our sad Clio door trim panels, so we engaged the services of our local upholstery experts, Pipers. So - will we do them in cream and black leather, like the seats? Dismantling the door cards is not the science of rockets - a quick prise with a wide-bladed tool is all that's needed. For some reason, the fabric panels on the rear cards have a plastic backing, while the fronts are mounted on cheap card. Which

01 tears if you're not careful.

Look at that truly disgusting blue fabric - even the card underneath's more attractive. The old fabric piece can be used as a

02 template for cutting out the new leather/alcantara.

How scary is this? Well, not very, actually. Hands

03 up, who can't use spray glue?

If you're gonna DIY, practice on something old first. If you've had your seats trimmed, you'll obviously choose the same stuff for your doors - but here's a tip. Say you've gone for some nice bucket seats, in maybe a red-and-black pattern cloth. Would be nice to match your seats to the door panels here, too, wouldn't it? So how about doing what we did for another of our project cars, and contacting the seat manufacturer for a few square metres of the actual cloth they use to make the seats with? Should match then, shouldn't it? Hand material and cash to your upholstery experts, with cash, and wait. Or do it yourself.

04 Our new piece of black leather has been stretched out and stapled to the bench, before the door card insert gets laid onto it - helps to avoid creases.

05 Now our Pipers crew are using the serious 'I can fly' contact adhesive to do a proper job on the folded-over edges. Well, if you're sniffing leather all day, you need something different occasionally.

06 The straight edges are obviously no problem . . .

07 . . . but this is the proper way to trim up for a decent corner. For the square holes where the door handles will fit through, do two diagonal cuts from corner to corner, and fold the sides in.

Centre console

So we've seen seats and headrests get the leather treatment, and the (flat) door card inserts). What's involved in covering something solid, 3D, that wasn't actually material-covered before? Such as part of the dash, or maybe the centre console?

No interior can claim to have had a 'full' leather re-trim if only the seats and door cards have been done, after all. If your fetish for leather still hasn't been satisfied, read on.

01 With the console removed as described earlier in this section, and stripped of gaiters, switches and ashtrays, the first thing an upholsterer needs to do is visualise how many separate panels will be needed to cover the object, and where the joins will have to be.

02 The spray glue is a temporary measure - here, a roughly-cut side panel is being stuck on for trimming.

03 As with the seats earlier, an allowance of about half an inch has to be made, to leave enough leather to stitch to.

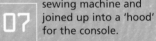

Now the side panel can be cut out, and carefully **04** peeled off the side of the console.

As a centre console is a fairly symmetrical item, the side panel that's just been trimmed up can now be used as a mirror-image **05** template for the other side. Makes life a bit easier, anyway.

The trickiest piece to accurately trim up will be the top section. But for now, all we need is the basic overall size. Plus **06** an allowance for joining.

Once we've got our three main pieces, they get taken to the sewing machine and **07** joined up into a 'hood' for the console.

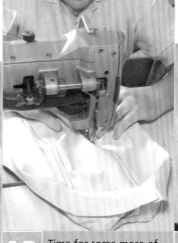

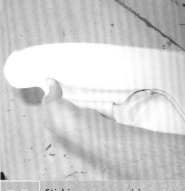

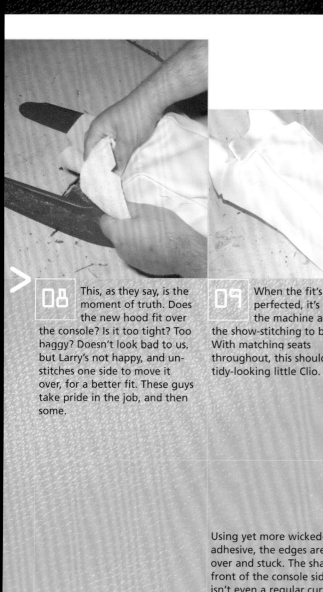

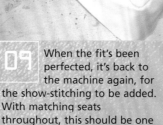

08 This, as they say, is the moment of truth. Does the new hood fit over the console? Is it too tight? Too baggy? Doesn't look bad to us, but Larry's not happy, and un-stitches one side to move it over, for a better fit. These guys take pride in the job, and then some.

09 When the fit's been perfected, it's back to the machine again, for the show-stitching to be added. With matching seats throughout, this should be one tidy-looking little Clio.

10 Time for some more of that high-flying contact adhesive, to be applied to the console and to the leather. Imagine working somewhere you're surrounded by the smell of glue and leather all day… The lads at Pipers reckon they can't smell leather any more - that's what we call an industrial injury.

11 Sticking on a precision-cut leather hood straight, with no lumps or creases, isn't a job for the faint-hearted or unskilled . . .

12 . . . and neither's trimming-up the top section, to accept the gaiter, switches and ashtray.

13 Using yet more wicked-strength adhesive, the edges are folded over and stuck. The shape at the front of the console side panels isn't even a regular curve, but it doesn't phase these boys - snipping-out like this gives you a smooth corner.

14 Not even the side vents get overlooked, in the detailed trimming operation.

15 Now that's one saucy-looking centre console. But you'll have to wait 'til it's had the new gear gaiter fitted, and the ashtray and switch panel sprayed, before you can really judge the finished effect, in-car.

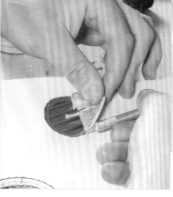

Are your dials all white?

White dial kits aren't that difficult to fit, but you will need some skill and patience not to damage the delicate bits inside your instrument panel - the risk is definitely worth it, to liven up that dreary grey Clio dash, anyway. Just make sure you get the right kit for your car, and don't start stripping anything until you're sure it's the right one - look carefully. Most dial kit makers, for instance, want to know exactly what markings you have on your speedo and rev counter. If they don't ask, be worried - the kit they send could well be wrong for your car, and might not even fit. We were surprised to find that our 1.4 Clio speedo goes to 140 mph - yeah, dream on!!

01 If you haven't yet removed the steering wheel - don't! You don't really need to for this. Of course, if you're fitting a new wheel AND a dial kit, it's a good plan to do both at once - but are you that organised? First, slide back the covers from the radio remotes (one each side, if you've got 'em), and loosen off the Torx screw below.

02 Here we have a worm's eye view of the three Torx screws holding the steering lower shroud . . .

They're having a laugh, getting these clocks out - now we've gotta take off the entire top of the dash, for flip's sake. Luckily, it's quite easy, and only five screws hold it on - three along the top, in the screen vent, and one each side, next to the side window vent.

The top shroud (which is the one we really want to get off, to get at the clocks) is now held on by two more screws, inside those radio remotes we loosened off earlier . . .

. . . and you can see where they came from, by the holes in the shroud.

03 . . . and an equally low-level shot of the shroud coming off. Just to prove we dun it.

04

05

06

07 That's one big piece of naff grey plastic - if it comes off that easy, why not do something with it, while it's off? Hmm

08 At last - light at the end of the clock-removing tunnel. The instrument cluster has two (shorter) Torx screws at the top - those are dead easy to see . . .

09 . . . the two longer screws are in from below, at the angle indicated by our long-shafted Torx screwdriver. You'll just have to trust us that they're there.

10 Now the clocks can be lifted out - slightly. Play around a little bit with the wiring that's still attached, and try to get them out as far as you can without busting anything - for the next bit, you'll need all the room behind you can get.

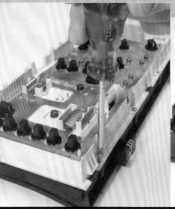

11 Yes, it's time to disconnect that speedo cable - here's one we disconnected just seconds ago. Reach in behind the speedo, then squeeze the white plastic collar and pull the cable end fitting down until it detaches. Take the time to notice how it all fits, 'cos you'll have to reconnect this later, and it's tricky.

12 Lastly, there's four wiring plugs to pull off - something easy, finally. Well-built, these Clios.

13 There's a good reason why Lockwood (makers of our kit) suggest getting a small bowl to keep all the tiny bits in - the first dismantling job involves removing eight tiny cross-head screws . . .

14 . . . which hold the clocks to the panel lens. If it hasn't already fallen off, pull off the trip meter reset knob, and add it to the pile of screws.

15 So this is what your Clio clocks look like, naked. Steady now.

16 The bigger gauges have two screws, the weeny ones have three. Make sense to you? Now would be a good time to replace any instrument panel bulbs which may have packed up - there's over twenty bulbs in ours! And where IS that airbag warning light, so we can take its bulb out altogether?

17 Nurse, the screens - this man's attacking his speedo dial with a scalpel, and he isn't even a proper doctor. The idea is to trim away a decent hole around the needle (which you don't have to take off, so don't try) . . .

18 . . . and then slice through to the edge of the dial so you can peel it off. Predictably, Renault stick these dial faces on quite well.

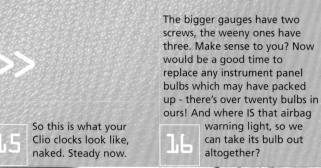

19 Give the gauge surface a good clean-up with some meths, to get rid of the excess sticky.

20 Now let's see - a white needle against a white dial. Not going to see much of it, are we? I think some colour-contrasting might be in order. Make your needles as individual as you like - matching-in the car's basic colour might not be a bad plan, but you call it. Paper or tape behind the needle will keep the paint off the gauge.

21 While the paint's drying, tackle the smaller gauges - three screws each for these . . .

22 . . . okay, so it's pretty obvious which gauge does what, but how long does it take to mark each one on the back, to make sure you don't confuse them? And have you made a note of which small gauge fits where?

The makers of our kit supply a packet of what they charmingly refer to as 'banjos'. These black stick-on bits are meant to go around the needle hubs, and stop the light from the illumination bulbs from shining up through at night. Sounds fair to us. It's all a bit fiddly, though - peel off the backing, then hook them over the needle hub (there's a slit in the banjo) . . .

As with the big dials, the needles don't have to be removed - just slice away enough to get the old dial off.

23

24

. . . use something like a screwdriver to press the banjo onto the gauge.

25

This is what you've paid to see - let's get those white dials on. Peel off the backing from the two rather weedy-looking adhesive strips, then hook the centre of the dial over the needle . . .

26

27 . . . make sure it's all lined up, using the little cut-outs at the edges, and stick it on firmly.

28 When you're refitting the speedo, don't forget this funny rubber pad which fits on behind. No, we don't know what it's for, either. But we're sure it's important.

29 We haven't really mentioned the tacho yet, so here it is being refitted. As you'll have discovered when removing it, the top of the dial has an edge connector, which must be slotted back into its plug when refitting. Or it won't work.

30 And here's that trip reset knob going back on. You didn't 'reset' your mileage while the speedo was out, did you?

Racing starts

Like to have a racing-style starter button on your Clio? Read on! A very cool piece of kit, and not too bad a job to wire up - the most difficult bit's deciding where to mount the button (somewhere easy to get at, but still in full view so's you can impress your passengers!). The idea of the racing starter button is that the ignition key is made redundant, beyond switching on the ignition lights (it'd be a pretty negative security feature, if you could start the engine without the key at all).

This is one job where you'll be messing with big wires, carrying serious current - more than any other electrical job, don't try and rush it, and don't skimp on the insulating tape. Do it properly, as we're about to show you, and there's no worries. Otherwise, at best, you'll be stranded - at worst, it could be a fire.

01 Our Prostart button was supplied by Richbrook, but the instructions here should be good for most makes. First, DISCONNECT THE BATTERY. You may have ignored this advice before. You may not. Don't do so now.

02 Before we got to the 'tricky' wiring, we did the easy bit - mounting the button itself. You could use the centre console, but we liked the idea of using the grille section below the driver's-side dash vent. This panel (which houses the tweeter speaker) is easy to remove - three Torx screws (one to the side, two at the bottom). We wanted to mount our button on a strip of brushed ally - the metal we had, but the 'brushing' we achieved with some Scotchbrite . . .

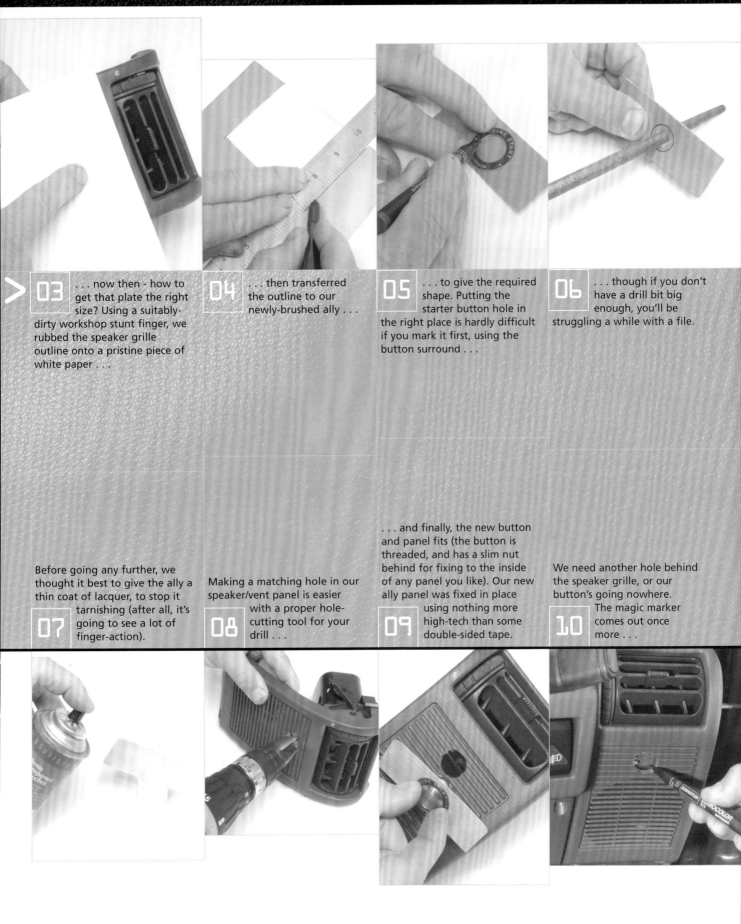

03 . . . now then - how to get that plate the right size? Using a suitably-dirty workshop stunt finger, we rubbed the speaker grille outline onto a pristine piece of white paper . . .

04 . . . then transferred the outline to our newly-brushed ally . . .

05 . . . to give the required shape. Putting the starter button hole in the right place is hardly difficult if you mark it first, using the button surround . . .

06 . . . though if you don't have a drill bit big enough, you'll be struggling a while with a file.

Before going any further, we thought it best to give the ally a thin coat of lacquer, to stop it tarnishing (after all, it's going to see a lot of finger-action).

07

Making a matching hole in our speaker/vent panel is easier with a proper hole-cutting tool for your drill . . .

08

. . . and finally, the new button and panel fits (the button is threaded, and has a slim nut behind for fixing to the inside of any panel you like). Our new ally panel was fixed in place using nothing more high-tech than some double-sided tape.

09

We need another hole behind the speaker grille, or our button's going nowhere. The magic marker comes out once more . . .

10

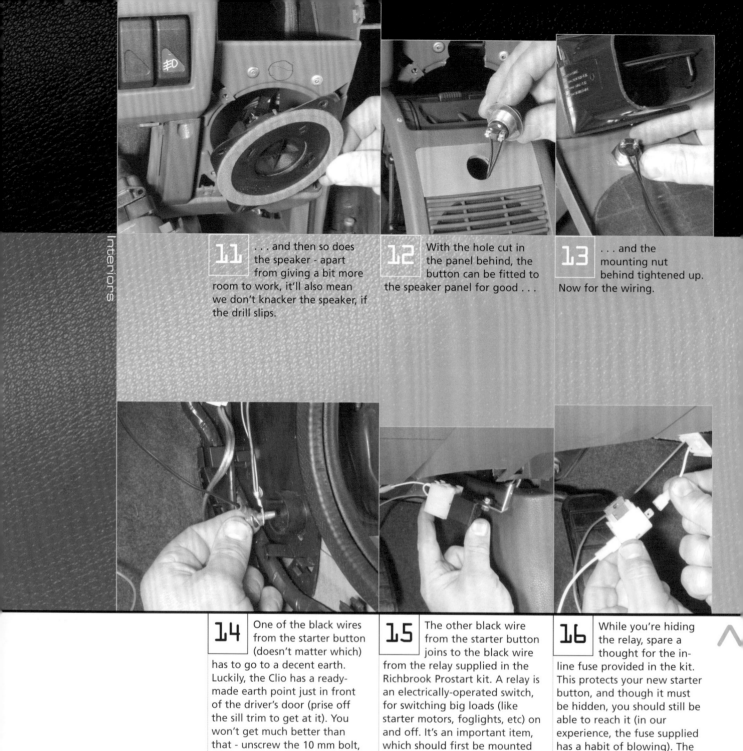

11 . . . and then so does the speaker - apart from giving a bit more room to work, it'll also mean we don't knacker the speaker, if the drill slips.

12 With the hole cut in the panel behind, the button can be fitted to the speaker panel for good . . .

13 . . . and the mounting nut behind tightened up. Now for the wiring.

14 One of the black wires from the starter button (doesn't matter which) has to go to a decent earth. Luckily, the Clio has a ready-made earth point just in front of the driver's door (prise off the sill trim to get at it). You won't get much better than that - unscrew the 10 mm bolt, add your earth (with ring terminal) to the bunch already there, and tighten back up.

15 The other black wire from the starter button joins to the black wire from the relay supplied in the Richbrook Prostart kit. A relay is an electrically-operated switch, for switching big loads (like starter motors, foglights, etc) on and off. It's an important item, which should first be mounted securely, somewhere out of the way (we made a little bracket up for ours, and hid it just below the dash).

16 While you're hiding the relay, spare a thought for the in-line fuse provided in the kit. This protects your new starter button, and though it must be hidden, you should still be able to reach it (in our experience, the fuse supplied has a habit of blowing). The white wire from the relay has a spade connector to join on the fuseholder - get this plugged in before you hide the relay.

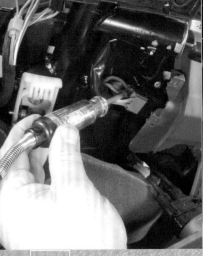

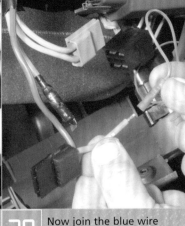

17 The rest of the wiring-up involves getting an ignition live for the relay (white wire), and tapping the relay output (blue wire) into the Clio's starter circuit. What could be easier? Whip off the steering column shrouds (see the section on fitting the white dial kit for details), and carefully probe the wiring plugs on the back of the ignition switch - temporarily reconnect the battery to test the plugs, then leave it off.

18 Our Clio had a grey plug with two yellow wires, and a black plug with a red and an orange. The orange wire turned out to be the one supplying the starter motor feed, and this must be joined to the blue wire from the relay. If you want to disable the ignition switch starting, cut this wire (leaving enough on the plug to play with) . . .

19 . . . and to be safe, crimp a female bullet onto the wire end, and tape it all up. This is what you call overkill. To clarify, we're taping-up the wire which disappears off under the dash - the one still sticking out of the wiring plug, we want next.

20 Now join the blue wire to the stump of orange wire coming out of the wiring plug - we used a double-ended joiner, but you could use blue bullets or even solder. If you want to retain key-operated starting as well as your new button, don't leave the orange wire cut - just splice into it, like we're about to for the ignition live feed.

21 The other wiring plug with the two yellows gave us a small problem - both wires were ignition-switched live, but one was live only with the key in the accessory position (first key click). After once more briefly reconnecting the battery, make sure you identify the wire that's on in the ignition position (ie all dash warning lights on).

22 Even we get nervous about chopping wires as thick (and obviously important) as this, which is why solder was invented. Instead of trying to find a bullet connector big enough to take this phat wire, just strip away a small section of the yellow insulation . . .

23 . . . then strip the end of the wire you want to splice on (in this case, the white wire from the relay), and wrap it round the bared section of the yellow wire. And now, with the aid of a little solder, we'll make our connection permanent - and without disturbing the existing wire, so we know everything else which worked before will still work.

24 Leaving a bare section of live wiring inside the dash is not a good idea, so get to work with the insulating tape when the solder's cooled down. Apply one finger, and the racing Clio bursts into life. Fantastic stuff.

Wheely cool

A new steering wheel is an essential purchase as a first step to personalising your Clio. It's one of the main points of contact between you and the car, it's sat right in front of you, and the standard ones are dull as a very dull thing. Sort it out now!

Don't be tempted to fit too small a wheel if you've not got power steering. Clio steering isn't exactly heavy, but a tiny-rimmed steering wheel will make manoeuvring very difficult, especially with fat tyres.

One bit of good news is that, once you've shelled out for your wheel, it may be possible to fit it to your next car, too. When you buy a new wheel, you usually have to buy a boss (or mount) to go with it - the mounts are less pricey, so one wheel could be fitted to another completely different car, for minimum cost.

A trick feature worth investigating is the detachable wheel/boss. This feature comes in handy when you park up and would rather the car was still there when you come back (something most people find a bonus). It's all very well having a steering wheel immobiliser or steering lock, but I doubt many thieves will be driving off in your car if the steering wheel's completely missing! Also, removing the wheel may remove the temptation to break in and pinch… your wheel!

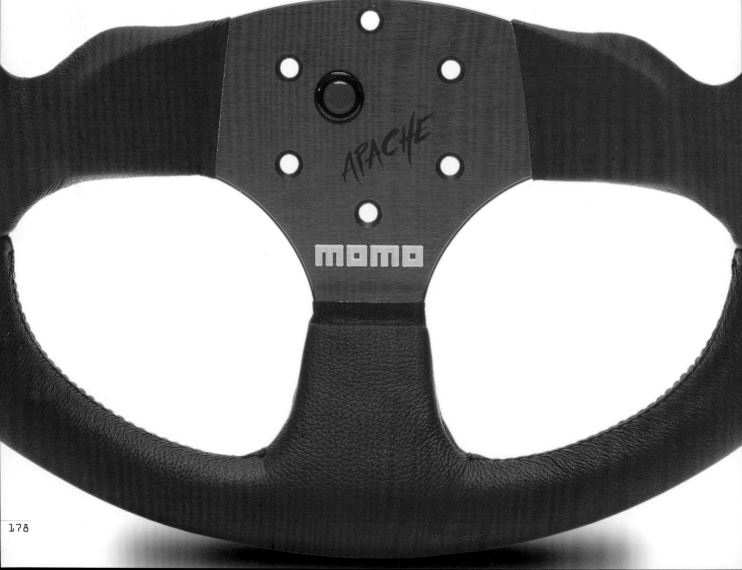

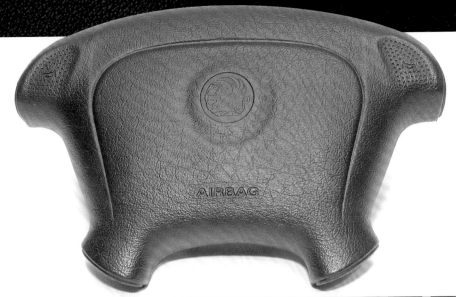

A word about **airbags**

Many Clios will have a driver's airbag fitted to the original wheel. So far, the market for replacement wheels with airbags doesn't seem to have materialised, so fitting your tasty new wheel means losing what some (old) people think is a valuable safety feature.

But the problem with airbags doesn't end with simply disconnecting the damn thing, because all that'll happen then is your AIRBAG warning light will be on permanently. Not only is this extremely irritating, it'll also be one of the reasons your newly-modded motor will fail the MOT (having the airbag itself isn't compulsory, but if the warning light's on, it's a fail - at least at the time this was written). Two ways round this - either take out the clocks (see the section on fitting white dials) and remove the offending warning light bulb, OR bridge the airbag connector plug pins with two lengths of wire attached to either side of a 5A fuse. Bridging the pins this way 'fools' the test circuit (which fires up every time you switch on the ignition) into thinking the airbag's still there, and the warning light will go out as it should.

Disabling the airbag is yet another issue which will interest your insurance company, so don't do it without consulting them first. We're just telling you, that's all.

Warning: Airbags are expensive to replace (several £100s), and are classed as an explosive!!! Funny, that - for a safety item, there's any number of ways they can CAUSE injuries or damage if you're not careful - check this lot out:

a Before removing the airbag, the battery MUST be disconnected (don't whinge about it wiping out your stereo pre-sets). When the battery's off, don't start taking out the airbag for another 10 minutes or so. The airbag system stores an electrical charge - if you whip it out too quick, you might set it off, even with the battery disconnected. True.

b When the airbag's out, it must be stored the correct way up.

c The airbag is sensitive to impact - dropping it from sufficient height might set it off. Even if dropping it doesn't actually set it off, it probably won't work again, anyway. By the way, once an airbag's gone off, it's scrap. You can't stuff it back inside.

d If you intend to keep the airbag with a view to refitting it at some stage (like when you sell the car), store it in a cool place - but bear in mind that the storage area must be suitable, so that if the airbag went off by accident, it would not cause damage to anything or anyone. Sticking it under your bed might not be such a good idea.

e If you're not keeping the airbag, it must be disposed of correctly (don't just put it out for the bin men!). Contact your local authority for advice.

f Airbags must not be subjected to temperatures in excess of 90°C (194°F) - just remember that bit about airbags being an explosive - you don't store dynamite in a furnace, now do you? Realistically in this country, the only time you'll get THAT hot is in a paint-drying oven.

Fitting a
Momo wheel

Clios without airbags have it easy - just prise out the centre section of the steering wheel, and skip to the bit where we undo the steering wheel nut. If you've got an airbag, it's time to reach for those Torx bits again - this time we need a long T30, inserted from behind (sounds painful). There are two screws to undo behind the

01 wheel (turn the wheel to get at them), and they might be tight.

Now that airbag 'pad' can be lifted out of the wheel, and the yellow connector pulled off. Remove the airbag to a safe place. A 'safe place' is not on the pavement, by your car. Get it indoors, in a cupboard, or maybe in the loft. Our workshop (like any decent garage) actually has a wall safe for storing airbags, to

02 meet Health & Safety regs. That's how scary airbags are.

Attention!
If you remove an airbag, you are disabling a safety-related system. Make sure you tell your insurance company.

> **03** Reset the steering wheel back to straight-ahead before undoing the centre bolt. Be warned - this will be very tight and will not undo easily. And of course it's a Torx bolt - it's a Renault. This time it's a size T50 bit you'll need. Don't be lazy and rely on the steering lock to hold the wheel while you undo the bolt - there's a good chance you'll wreck the lock. Use your other hand.

It would be a terrific idea to fit a **new** wheel mounting bolt (but we don't suppose you'll bother). At least tighten it to the proper torque (non-airbag cars - 40 Nm, airbag cars - 45 Nm), if you've got a wrench. If you haven't, do it up like your life depended on it. Which of course, it does. Hold the boss with your other hand - **07** don't rely on the steering lock, or you'll bust it.

04 Even with the bolt undone, you may find that the wheel is stuck on pretty hard. If so, screw the bolt back in a few threads, then grip the wheel at both sides and pull. Why put the bolt back in? Well, when the wheel comes loose it won't smack you full in the face, preserving your looks for Saturday night!

With the boss kit you should **08** find a rubber cover, to make it look pretty - ease this over the boss.

05 If you're keeping the old wheel, to refit at any time in the future, preserve the life of the airbag battery by disconnecting the warning light pin plug.

Having chosen a very sexy Momo wheel, we decided to also fit a Snap Off kit. Apart from making the car harder to steal, no crim's walking off with our wheel, either! The Snap Off mounting boss has two horn contacts, and these wires on the back. The Clio has a perfectly good horn push on the stalk, so the wires kinda disappeared. If you'd like your centre horn button to work, you'll need to connect these to the horn **09** wiring from the stalk control. Good luck.

06 Check that the front wheels are still straight, then slot the new wheel boss on, with the 'TOP' mark - at the top! Our boss had a triangle marking to denote top. Make sure the indicator stalk is in the neutral (off) position, as the self-cancelling lug on the boss has to be in line with the indicator.

>

Six small Allen screws (not Torx, **10** for a change) hold the mounting boss in place . . .

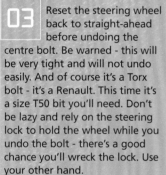
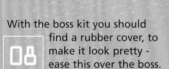

11 . . . and they also supply two anti-tamper shear-head pins, which you can use to 'plug' two of the Allen screw heads with. Push the head of the shear pin into the screw head (tap it in with a hammer, to make sure it's in there), then twist off the larger portion of the pin. These Snap Off boys think of everything.

12 Time for a quick practice of the Snap Off routine. Place the quick-release plate on top of the boss, with the keys at the top right, then pull out the release knobs and position the quick-release plate onto boss. When satisfied this is in place, let go of the knobs and the plate should sit firmly into place.

13 The Snap Off kit comes with an adapter plate, so you can fit almost any make of steering wheel to your car - good thinking Mr Snap Off! No problem mating it to our rather nice Momo wheel, then. Place the adapter plate on top of the quick-release system, and tighten the Allen screws.

Inside the box our kit came in, we found two weird and wonderful metal plates. Diagrams from Snap Off showed us that these plates were guides to retain the horn button - check to see if you need the other plate, if you're not fitting a Momo wheel. Place the metal ring on the adapter plate, and **14** check that the holes are in alignment with the ones in the wheel.

Place your steering wheel on top of the metal ring, ensuring the wheels are still straight, and (d'oh) it's the right way up! Allen screw the steering wheel into place - and do it up tight, won't you? This Momo Commando wheel was supplied **15** by our good friends at Brown & Geeson - thanks, guys.

Final touch - push the horn button (centre badge, in our case) onto the steering wheel, and you're all done - go forth and show all those lovely ladies your gorgeous fifth wheel. If **16** they want a better look, of course, you can just pop it off.

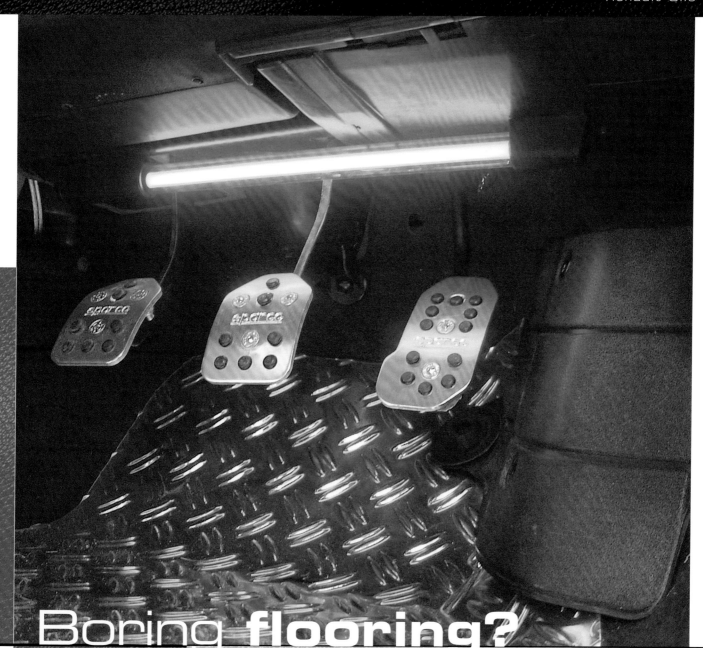

Boring flooring?

Alright, so carpets have always been a dull colour because they have to not show the dirt - when was the last time you heard of a car with white carpets? What goes on the floor needn't be entirely dull, though, and can still be easy to clean, if you're worried.

Ripping out the old carpets is actually quite a major undertaking - first, the seats have to come out (you might be fitting new ones anyway), but the carpets and underfelt fit right up under the dashboard, and under all the sill trims and centre console, etc. Carpet acts as sound-deadening, and is a useful thing to hide wiring under, too, so don't be in too great a hurry to ditch it completely.

A popular halfway-house measure to a fully decked-out chequerplate interior are the tailored footwell 'plates available from some suppliers - these are a big improvement on even the coolest carpet mats, and because they're a tailored fit, they should stay put, not slide up under your pedals.

Chequerplate is the current fashion in cool flooring, and it's easy to see why it'll probably have an enduring appeal - it's tough but flexible, fairly easy to cut and shape to fit, has a cool mirror finish, and it matches perfectly with the racing theme so often seen in the modified world, and with the ally trim that's widely used too.

Fully-tailored
chequer mats

The halfway-house to a fully-plated interior is to make up your own tailored mats (hell, you can buy ready-mades if you're not allowed to play with sharp knives). Unless you buy real ally chequer, what you'll get is actually plastic, and must be supported by mounting it on hardboard. Take one of the lovely 'Granny' mats your car might have come with, and use it as a template to mark the shape onto the hardboard (you could always make a template from some thin card).

01

With the shape marked out, it's time for the jigsaw - next to a cordless drill, this has to be one of the most useful tools ever invented for the modder.

02

To make the hardboard fit better into the footwells, score it at the bend where it goes up under the pedals . . .

03

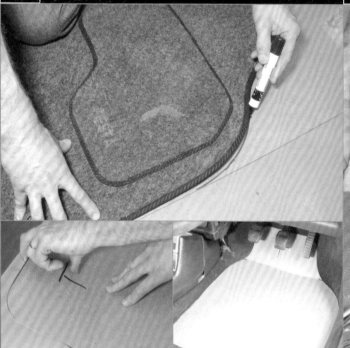

04 . . . then carefully 'fold' the hardboard back to the required shape - trust us, this will make your new chequer mats fit superbly.

05 Not unlike this in fact. Try your hardboard mat in place, and trim the corners and edges as necessary to get it fitting as flat as poss.

06 Now you can use your hardboard as a template, for cutting out the chequer. Try to make the chequer fractionally bigger overall than the hardboard, so you don't see the wood edge (you shouldn't anyway, if your board is a tidy fit). Stick the chequer to the board, using some decent glue - spray glue's convenient, but usually not quite up to the job. You can't beat good old brush-on Evo-Stik (and no, we're not being paid to say that).

07 Do it right, and you too can have a floor like this - looks sweet, and the mats don't slip. Sorted.

Tips 'n' tricks
If you're completely replacing the carpet and felt with, say, chequerplate throughout, do this at a late stage, after the ICE install and any other electrical work's been done - that way, all the wiring can be neatly hidden underneath it.

Under neon light...

So how much of a poser are you? How'd you like to show off all this funky chequer floor and sexy pedals to full effect, in the midnight hour? You need some neons, baby! Yeah!

01 There's not a great deal to this, really - decide where you want 'em, where you're going to get a live and an earth (and a switch, if necessary), then fit 'em. We wanted our neons up under the dash, to light up the footwells. The kit we had came with these plastic mounting clips, which didn't seem up to the job, so we screwed on some metal brackets from the local DIY store . . .

One beauty of the Clio is that the dash top panel comes off really easily (see how by looking in the white dial kit section). Why is this a bonus? Because it makes it very easy to feed wires across the car - and we need to get all our neon wiring in the same place, for the switch. Feed the first neon wires up behind the dash, and across the car . . .

. . . then down to the location we've chosen for our neon switch - there's a blank switch on our Clio, next to the steering wheel, and it just prises out. Asking for it, really.

02 . . . then out came the drill . . .

03 . . . and in went the passenger-side neon. Hey, it works, and we're halfway there.

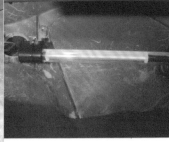

04 . . . and across the car . . .

05

Bum notes

It appears that interior neons have recently been declared ILLEGAL, and this means, in the first place, you're unlikely to find anywhere that even sells them any more. Exterior neons have been illegal from day one (though loads of people fit them). If you fit interior neons, make sure they're at least easily switched off, should you get pulled. Remember that driving at night with a brightly-lit interior makes it even harder to see out. Neons are best used for show purposes.

06 To get our driver's-side neon in place, the lower dash panel has to come out - it's held by two Torx screws at the front edge . . .

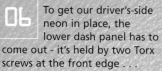

07 . . . then the headlight aim adjuster knob pulls off . . .

08 . . . for access to the two adjuster securing screws behind . . .

09 . . . with these undone, the back part of the adjuster comes away from the dash panel . . .

10 . . . and the panel itself lifts out (it's hooked into the base of the dash, at the bottom).

11 At last, we can try our other neon in place. Obviously, it mustn't interfere with the pedals, or the brake light switch, so it's got to be positioned pretty carefully, and fitted securely (if it drops down while you're driving, it could be a tad inconvenient).

12 After a few different approaches, we hit on the ideal DIY bracket. Yes, it's another winner from B&Q, fitted with two speed clips (which just clip over the bracket, and give you something for the self-tapping screws to bite into).

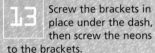

13 Screw the brackets in place under the dash, then screw the neons to the brackets.

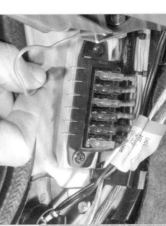

14 Well, now the neons are in, but it's still a no-glow situation, which means we're missing some power and some earth. The live we can get from our auxiliary fusebox (which we fitted in the security section). If you don't have one, you might need to probe around at the back of the standard fusebox for a permanent live feed. Join the two red wires from the neons together, and connect in the live feed (run the wires across the top of the dash as necessary).

15 The earth's altogether easier to sort. Yes, it's our favourite Clio earth point once again - the bolt down in front of the door, which you get to by unclipping the sill trim panel at the front. Unscrew the 10 mm bolt, add your earth wire (with ring terminal fitted), and tighten back up. Run the earth wire up behind the dash to your switch location.

Connect the live and earth to the back of the switch (experiment if you're not sure, until something works). This is a switch which lights up itself when the neons are on - to get the switch to light, we need another live wire for the middle terminal. Just splice one from the lives you've already got for the neons - add another small piece of wire to the connector for the neon red wires, and feed it to the middle terminal.

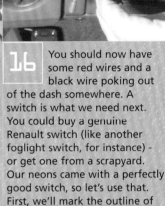

16 You should now have some red wires and a black wire poking out of the dash somewhere. A switch is what we need next. You could buy a genuine Renault switch (like another foglight switch, for instance) - or get one from a scrapyard. Our neons came with a perfectly good switch, so let's use that. First, we'll mark the outline of the new switch on the blank panel we prised out of the dash earlier . . .

One very tidy little switch, which lights up in the dark, like the neons themselves. But you have to admit a genuine Renault switch would be more discreet on your dash...

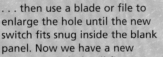

. . . then use a blade or file to enlarge the hole until the new switch fits snug inside the blank panel. Now we have a new switch that'll fit nicely in the dash. Quality job.

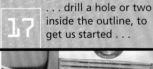

17 . . . drill a hole or two inside the outline, to get us started . . .

18

19

20

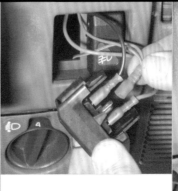

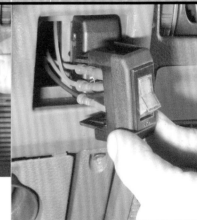

Pedalling your Clio

A very nice race-equipment touch to your modded machine, pedal extensions really look the part when combined with full chequerplate mats - available in several styles and (anodised) colours. Not sure how well the anodising will wear, though… The only other issue with pedals is that they must have some kind of rubbers fitted - this is first of all sensible (so your feet don't slip off them at an awkward moment) and it's also a legal requirement. Don't buy extensions without.

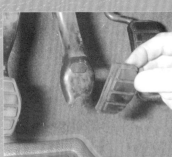  

01 Let's start with the all-important brake pedal. The first step's a doddle - prise off the old rubber.

02 These Sparco extensions have a backplate - offer it in place first, and see if the two holes up the middle line up with the pedal. On our Clio, there's already two large holes in the pedal, so no drilling was needed at first . . .

03 . . . using the nuts and bolts supplied (and some large washers we had lying about), we managed to mount the backplate on half-sensibly . . .

Achtung!
Check your insurance company's position regarding pedal extensions. A while ago there was a big fuss after a couple of cars fitted with pedal extensions crashed, which resulted in pedal extensions being withdrawn from sale at a lot of places.

04 . . . but just to make sure, we drilled and screwed a third mounting - extensions that could slip are well-dangerous.

05 We reckon these saucy red Sparcos are the perfect choice for our red Clio - the top plates just mount onto the backplates . . .

06 . . . and secure with the Allen bolts in the kit. Would be slightly more tasteful if the bolt heads were red too, don't you think? How about it, Mr Sparco?

07 The clutch pedal extension fits in much the same way (we're sure you've got the hang of it by now). One very important point is that the pedal spacing must be maintained with the new extensions in place - fitting the plates centrally on the pedal will ensure you've done all you can. Saxos and 106s have pedals which are too close together as standard - this kind of 'upgrade' you don't need.

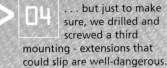

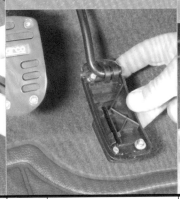

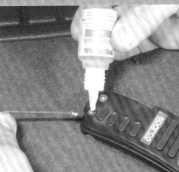

08 Considering how much right-foot abuse it's likely to get, it's incredible how easy the throttle pedal is to remove - but it makes fitting an extension dead simple. Just unclip the pedal at the top, by pulling it forwards, and slide it off the throttle arm to the right.

09 This pedal does have to be drilled - we decided to try mounting the top plate straight onto the pedal, which seemed to work fine . . .

10 . . . until we found that no way could we fit the top left-hand mounting bolt, because the throttle arm clips in right behind, leaving no room for a nut. We'll deal with that in a minute - at least one of the other bolts had to be cut off shorter too, for the same sort of reason. Did we say the throttle pedal was easy? We might just have lied.

11 To cover up the gaping hole in the extension where we couldn't fit the top left bolt, we chopped off the Allen bolt head, and glued it in place. Nice touch. As long as an extension (or a backplate) is firmly held on by at least three bolts, there should be no probs - worth checking every so often that the nuts haven't come loose, on the back.

Are you **sitting stylishly?**

The perfect complement to your lovingly-sorted suspension, because you need something better than the standard seats to hold you in, now that you can corner so much faster… and they look brutal, by way of a bonus. Besides the seat itself, remember to price up the subframe to adapt it to the mounting points in your car. Most people also choose the three- or four-point harnesses to go with it (looks a bit daft to fit a racing seat without it), but make sure the harness you buy is EC-approved, or an eagle-eyed MOT tester might make you take 'em out.

Reclining seats are pricier than non-recliners, but are worth the extra. With non-adjustable seats, how are your mates meant to get in the back? Through the tailgate? Or maybe there is no back seat… You can get subframes which tilt, so that non-reclining seats can move forward. Non-reclining racing seats should be tried for fit before you buy.

An alternative to expensive racing seats would be to have your existing seats re-upholstered in your chosen colours/fabrics, to match your interior theme. You might be surprised what's possible, and the result could be something truly unique. If you've got a basic model, try sourcing 16V (Clio or 19) seats from a breakers. A secondhand interior bought here will be a lot cheaper than buying new goodies, and you know it'll fit easily (all Clios are the same underneath) - but - it won't have that unique style. Specialist breakers may be able to supply something more rad, such as a wicked leather interior from a top-spec Laguna - might take some persuading to get it in, though!

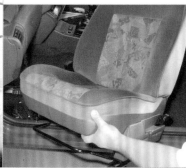

01 If your Clio has an airbag, bad luck - chances are you've also got seat belt tensioners, which must be deactivated before you start ripping out the seats. Actually, the deactivation process isn't hard - just find the airbag/tensioner fuse in the fusebox, and pull it out. If you're not sure, feel under the front of the seat for a plug (see Step 3).

02 There are two bolts holding the seat outer rail in place, and they're easy to reach - one at the front, and one at the back. These we can easily show you - the other two nuts are only accessible under the car, and are right next to the exhaust. Jack the car up safely, and watch you don't burn yourself (see 'Wheels & tyres'.

03 The tensioner wiring plug's at the front of the seat - tip it on its side without straining the wiring, and disconnect it.

04 That's one less standard chair to worry about. On the offensive seat pattern scale, this rates about a six (some Clios are eight and up).

Removing
seats

The rear seat cushions have to be about the most easily-removed of any car we've seen - they're just hinged into the floor. Swing forward, lift out. **05**

Not too much difficulty removing the seat back, either - fold forward, then flip up the little catch on either side at the base . . . **06**

07 . . . and lift the whole backrest out - it's so easy, no wonder he looks happy.

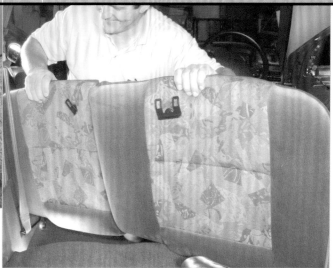

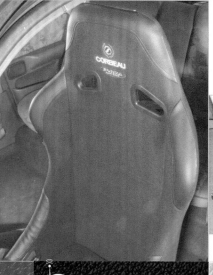

Tricks 'n' tips

During fitting, the seats will have to slide forwards or back, for access to the mounting bolts. Make sure the bases are bolted in firmly before you slide the seat, or there's a risk of twisting the seat relative to the base, and it will jam up solid. Trust us - we've been there.

01 The first job (apart from working out which base is for left and right) is to try the bases in the car, and make sure they line up with your floor holes - if not, it's game over immediately. Fortunately, ours were spot-on.

02 Now fit the bases to the new seats. As we're talking about a fairly important safety item, which we wouldn't want to come loose, we felt that a drop of thread-lock on the frame-to-seat bolts was a good move . . .

03 . . . especially since it's also not easy to tighten a cheese-head screw really tight, as you should - ideally, use a screwdriver which has a hex fitting below the main handle, and tighten it with a spanner.

Fitting new Corbeaus

The new chairs are now ready to fit - hopefully, the bolt holes in the new bases will line up with the holes in the floor . . .

04

. . . if one side fits and the other doesn't, all that's probably happened is that you've accidentally 'released' one of the seat runners, and let it slide. If you checked before and they were fine, they should be again. Do not panic - just reset the runner . . .

05

. . . and drop in the bolts.

06

The seat mounting bolts are, of course, the old ones you took out. Which are probably rusty as hell, so treat them to some copper grease, instead of just bunging them straight back in. Tighten the bolts to 20 Nm, but if you haven't got a torque wrench handy, just do them up good 'n' tight.

07

How strapped are you?

It's true that not everyone likes racing harnesses, but the majority of those who don't are FAT. And boring. You don't fit sexy race seats and then not fit race belts, do you?

The only problem with harnesses is caused by where you have to mount them. Even with a three-point harness, you end up using one of the rear seat belt mounts, and it seriously reduces your ability to carry bodies in the back seats (webbing everywhere). The MOT crew say that, if you've got rear seats, you must have rear seat belts fitted, so you either 'double-up' on your rear belt mounts (use the same mounts for your harnesses and rear belts), or you take the back seats out altogether. Removing the rear seats leaves the rear deck free for chequerplate, speakers, roll cages - whatever you like.

It's just important to understand how fundamental harnesses can end up being, to the whole look of your car - there's almost no half-measures with race belts, so you've got to really want 'em.

One thing you must **not** do is to try making up your own seat belt/harness mounting points. Renault structural engineers spent plenty of time selecting mounting points and testing them for strength. Drilling your own holes and sticking bolts through is fine for mounting speakers and stuff, but you're heading for an interview with the Grim Reaper if you try it with seat belts. The forces in a big shunt are immense. We're not convinced either that the practice of slinging harnesses round a rear strut brace is kosher, from the safety angle - the strut braces available are so flimsy (they're usually ally) you can bend them in your hands. Nuts to trusting MY life to one of those!

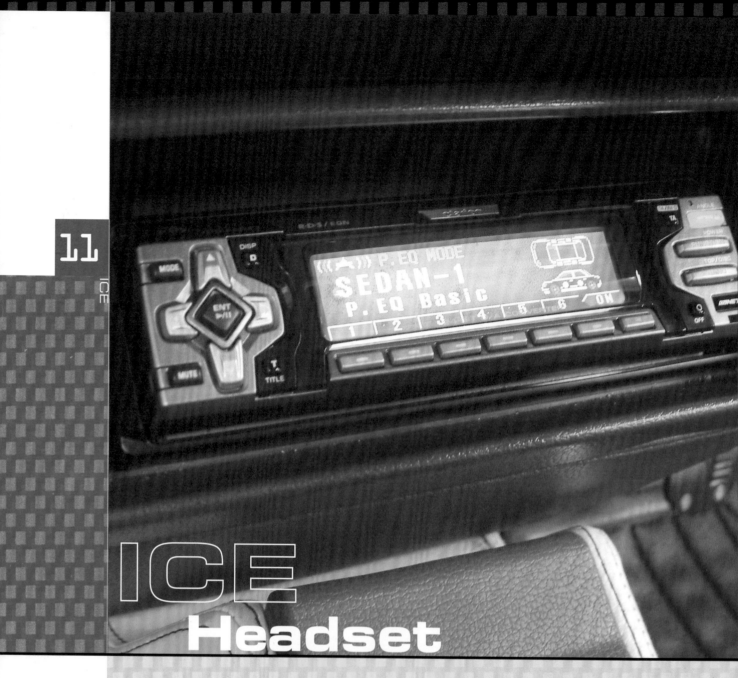

11

ICE

ICE
Headset

The cheaper your Clio, the nastier your standard head unit's going to be - you really do get what you pay for. Fine if all you want to do is aimlessly listen to the radio with your arm out the window, but not - definitely not - if you want to impress your mates with the depth and volume of your bass. Or, of course, if you want to listen to CDs. It's got to go - and there's plenty of decent headsets out there which will give you a night-and-day difference in sound quality and features. The headset is the heart of your new install - always go for the best you can afford. Ask the experts which features matter most, if you're building a full system.

Our headset wasn't a make many people think of when choosing ICE - how about Clarion? Yeah, that's what we thought as well. But this is a top-notch set, with a full-colour screen and 24-bit digital sound - and it really does sound amazing. Even the hardened Alpine-o-philes at Liquid ICE were very impressed, so give it some thought. Big shout to the guys at Bass Junkies (www.bassjunkies.com) for opening our minds, and ears, to Clarion.

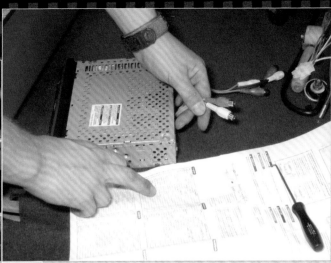

01 First, the old set's got to be shifted. Resist the urge to just crowbar the thing out of the dash - you'll be needing two of the standard radio removal tools to do the job with less damage. And you could always sell it, or keep it, to stick back in when you sell the car? The first thing to go in is the new 'cage' - no, you can't just use the old one. Feed through all the wires required, and slide the new cage in place - try not to distort it as it goes in.

02 To make sure it doesn't just slide out again (which slightly defeats the idea of having special security removal tools), you need to bend up the cage securing lugs, to pin it inside the radio hole in the dash. Don't bend them all up - just two top and bottom, and one each side, will do the job nicely.

03 So what wire goes where? Again, there's nothing like reading those instructions. Our Clio had an ISO connector, which makes a lot less work, taking care of the power, remote/p-cont and speakers. Some high-power sets require a separate fused supply direct from the battery - rig this in when you run the supply through for the amps.

Our Clarion set has three sets of RCA pre-outs - those rather handy instructions tell us which does what. Don't overlook the red/white colour-coding on the RCA connections - Red is for Right, usually. When it's all connected up, it pays to tidy the wiring as much as poss, looming it with a few strips of tape, instead of just **04** stuffing it all into the dash. Don't forget the aerial lead... common mistake... or your CD changer lead...

It's not a bad idea to test that everything's working at this point, before pushing the unit right into its cage. If all's well, push the headset home until the cage clips click in. Sounds easy, but you'll almost certainly have to reach in behind the set, and straighten out the wiring before the set will go in. Do not force it in, or you could end up having a very bad day. Success! Now get **05** out the instruction manual again, and set those levels properly. Enjoy.

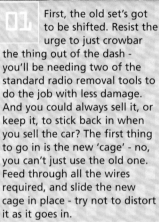

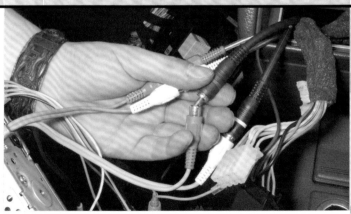

Front **speakers**

The standard items in the Clio speak volumes (hur-hur) about any car manufacturer's desire to build things down to a price - ie spend as little as poss. What does it cost Renault for the speakers in a Clio? If it's more than a fiver a set, they're being robbed. Low on power, and with nasty paper cones which disintegrate after a few years, fitting ANY aftermarket speakers is going to be an upgrade. But we don't want to give you that - how about showing you how to fit some tasty Alpine components?

01 Once you've got the door trim panel off, and have removed (and burnt) the old speaker, it's time to think vibration. If you don't want all that kicking power to set your door panel tizzing, you need to invest in some Dynamat. Expensive? Yes. For perfectionists? Yes. Worth it, all the same? Hell, yes. Clean up the door panel with some decent solvent . . .

02 . . . then cut it, and get it onnn. Real pro's will sound-deaden the outer door panel, too - for the best results, you'll need to budget for at least a sheet of 'mat per door, if not more.

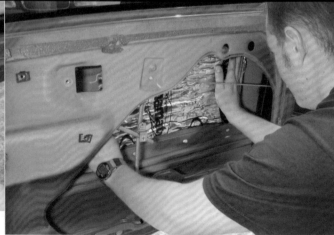

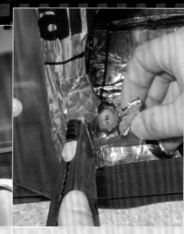

03 This stuff works best when fully attached, and although its sticky stuff is very sticky indeed, helping it on with a roller is the true professional touch.

If you're going for high-power front speakers, re-using the Renault speaker wiring is not an option. But - this might well mean drilling holes in your doors, to get decent speaker wire (oxygen-free) through. Our Alpine components are only worth about 70 a channel, so our installers at Liquid ICE opted for the easy life, and tapped into the wiring just before the door. This means taking out the dash tweeters under the vent trim panel . . .

07

04 If nothing else, do the section of door around where the speaker will sit. When the Dynamat's on, slice it across the speaker hole and tuck in the excess behind. Two things about Dynamat - use it warm (warm it up with a heat gun, on a cold day), and watch your fingers (the metal foil edges are sharp!).

. . . and disconnecting the wiring plug. This plug has four wires running to it - two for the tweeters, and another two for the door speakers.
Finding out which wire does what is the next step.

08

05 If you got a little carried away in your quest for sonic perfection, you might find you've covered up some useful door features - like the screw holes for the original speakers, which we're planning on re-using (the holes, not the speakers). Trim round with a sharp knife to re-liberate your holes, door trim panel clips, etc.

Using a multi-meter, do a continuity test from the tweeter plug terminals to the door speaker plugs, and find the two wires which go to the door speakers. Chop these two out of the plug, and fit (male) bullets. Another testing method is to reconnect the old speaker, and check for speaker resistances on the tweeter plug - move the speaker cone, and the resistance reading will change.

09

06 Mind you, a fully-Dynamatted door looks almost too good to cover up with the door trim!

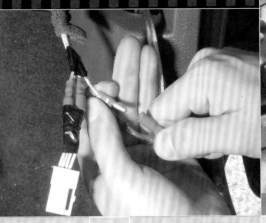

10 Though we've cheated by re-using the door wiring, it's oxygen-free all the way back to the amp in the boot. Decide which "half" of your oxygen-free is going to be "pos" (+) first - most wire has one part with writing on, and the other without, for identification. Stick to the same rule with all the new wiring you're putting in the car. As a general rule, on Renault speaker wiring, the lighter colour is negative.

11 Next, we've got to fit our new tweeters to the door panel. Choose where to mount them carefully - a large chunk of the panel ends up tight against the end of the dash, when the door's shut. A hole saw, especially one you can mount in a drill chuck, makes the job of making a hole easier and neater.

12 Most tweeters have a separate mounting plate, which fits to the door panel. Our hole was such a precision job that it made a good push-fit, but you might want to use a hot glue gun to secure yours. With the plate in, feed through the speaker wires, and pop in the tweeter itself.

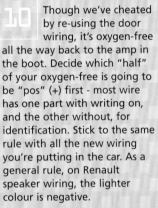

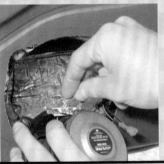

13 The old door speaker wiring plug can now go for good, then it's on with the new speaker terminals - the new tweeter wires will need some too. On our Clio, the standard speaker wiring was purple-positive, cream-negative.

14 This is what we like to see - a man reading the instructions. Wiring your speakers up backwards is not something we'd recommend.

15 Our Alpine components are actually dead easy to install on our Clio - the tweeters connect to "crossover" terminals at the top of the main speaker, and incredibly, the main speaker mountings line up with the holes already in the door. The only fiddly bit is holding the speaker in place while you put the screws in, through the original grille. But we know you like a challenge.

Amplifiers

01 Decide where you'll mount the amp carefully. One factor to consider is that it must be adequately cooled - don't cover it up, and don't hang it upside-down from your shelf. Our two Alpine amps are going either side of a centrally-mounted sub box, so the first job is to make sure the various wires reach. Here, we've got the earth (more on that later), p-cont/remote, live (from the distribution block behind), and speaker wiring - the RCAs go in the other side.

02 Make an earth cable from the same-thickness wire as you've used for your live feed. In our case, it was eight-gauge, in black. For an earth point, you can use any handy bolt, but seat and seat belt mounting bolts must be re-done up tight, of course. You can always make your own hole (just don't go through the fuel tank).

So, how many amps do we want in our car? One school of thought says each pair of speakers, and each sub, should have an individual amp - by setting the output from each amp separately, you can control each aspect of the sound, before you even need to think about adding a graphic equaliser. You can also better match your speakers to the level of power they need, to work best. Trouble is, running several amps means doubling-up on wiring, and you could end up drawing an awful lot of power from that battery.

Any starter system can be made to seriously kick, using just one 400W four-channel amp - choose the right one carefully (and the components to go with it), and just one will do. With the right kind of amp, you could run your front components off one pair of channels, bridge the other two for a sub, and run some 6x9s off the head unit. Don't forget that many decent modern headsets chuck out fifty-per-channel now, so don't assume you'll need separate amps for everything.

Unusually, our Clarion headset was so top-of-the-range, it didn't have a built-in amp (RCA pre-outs only), so we ended up with a four-channel amp for the main speakers, and a bridged two-channel for the sub.

03 Read the amp's instruction book carefully when connecting any wires, or you might regret it, especially if you're using the amp in bridged or tri-mode. Make sure you're happy about your speaker pos and neg/left and right wires, and get them screwed on. It's not essential to use ring terminals on speaker wiring, but, on a hefty and important wire like the live feed (and even the earth), a ring terminal is a must, and wrap the end with tape, to prevent it shorting across the other connections.

04 The last job is to connect up the RCA leads (red-to-red, white-to-white). Time to re-check everything, before connecting up the live feed to the battery, and trying it out. Turn the volume well down on the headset to start with, in case something's not right - very few systems work 100%, first time. If the amp LEDs don't light up, for instance, are they getting power? Are the p-cont/remote wires connected properly? If the sub doesn't kick, is the amp switch set to bridged or tri-mode, not stereo? RTFM.

05 A good tip is to leave the amps loose until after you've set them up - if you can, leave good access to the gain adjustment (volume) screws after final fitting, too. Starting at normal listening volume, with the amp gain turned down, put on a kicking track, then turn the gain up until the speakers just start to distort. Turn the gain down a tad from there, and you've a good basic setting. Amp gain and headset faders can now be tweaked to give a good balanced sound - or whatever tickles your lugholes.

01 First job with our new ready-made shelf is to mark the speaker positions. Not tricky.

Rear shelf & speakers

You can always try hacking your rear side panels about for speakers, but that means leaving them in there when you sell the car on. Speakers work best when rigidly mounted, so shelf-mounting is the simplest and best option. If you don't want to butcher your standard shelf (always a flimsy item), either make a new one from MDF, using your stock shelf as a template, or buy a ready-made acoustic shelf. Either way, make hiding your new speakers a priority - tasty speakers on display in the back window could soon mean no rear window, and no speakers...

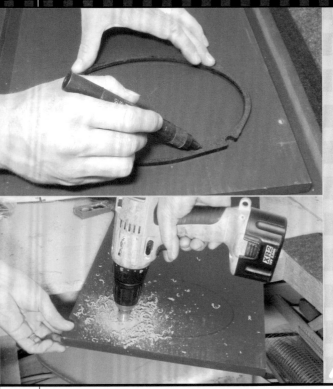

02 With a speaker outline marked, remove the wood from the rest of the shelf, and drill a nice big hole somewhere inside it . . .

Achtung!
MDF dust is nasty stuff to breathe in. Wear a mask when you're cutting, drilling or sanding it.

03 . . . then get busy with the jigsaw.

Use the speaker mounts (or even the speakers themselves) as a template to **04** drill the mounting holes . . .

. . . then screw on the speakers themselves. Don't forget that 6x9s can be run off the headset, to provide a little "rear fill" - if you have them amped-up, you **05** might find that the sound's too biased to the back of the car.

06 One useful feature of a ready-made shelf is that it comes with hinge pins, and even with pre-drilled holes to take them. A few light taps with the hammer, and the shelf's ready to fit. If you're putting a sub box in the boot as well, it's not a bad idea to plonk the box and shelf in, to check your speaker magnets will clear above the box. Just a thought...

07 Remember that the length of wire to each speaker should be the same (as near as poss), or you might find the speakers run slightly out of phase. Crimp on the right terminals, and connect up your speakers.

08 For max neatness, use P-clips screwed along the edge of the shelf. If you plan on being able to take the shelf out easily, you'll be needing a Neutrik plug and socket, which allows quick and easy wiring disconnection. Using the instructions provided with the connector, connect up your pos and neg speaker wires, and assemble the plug. Ordinary folk just fit bullet connectors at the side of the shelf, which work just as well (but don't look as flash).

Subs & boxes

ICE

No system's complete without that essential deep bass boom and rumble. Don't muck about with bass tubes - get the real thing to avoid disappointment. So you lose some of your boot space - so what? Is getting the shopping in an issue? We think not.

Most people opt for the easy life when it comes to boxes, at least until they're ready for a full-on mental install. The Clio at least has a roomy boot, so most standard boxes will fit easily. Making up your own box isn't hard though, especially if you were any good at maths and geometry. Oh, and woodwork. Most subs come with instructions telling you what volume of box they work best in, but ask an expert (or a mate) what they think - the standard boxes are just fine, and none are pricey. The only real reason to build your own is if you've got an odd-shaped boot (or just like a challenge).

Another plus with a ready-made box is that the speaker connection plate is usually pre-fitted, meaning all you have to do is connect speaker wire to it,

01 and to the speaker connections on the sub itself.

Lining, and then filling, your new box with Dacron, is thought to be a good way to smooth out the bass sound. Makes a bit of a nonsense of all your precise volume calculations, if you built your

02 own box, but we won't argue with the experts.

03 All that's left is to drill (the left-hand technique shown here, apparently, is to stop the drill from damaging the speaker cone if it slips, but we're sure you're not that nervous) . . .

04 . . . and screw your sub into place. Make sure you fit the gasket (or sections of gasket) between the speaker and box, and do the screws up tight - vibration might just be a bit of a problem here…

Wiring-up

For most people, this is the scariest part of an install - just the thought of masses of multi-coloured spaghetti sticking out of your dash might have you running to the experts (or a knowledgeable mate). But - if you do everything in a logical order, and observe a few simple rules, wiring-up isn't half as brain-numbing as it seems.

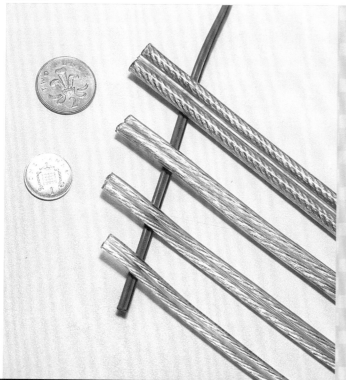

Live feeds

If you're running a modern head unit, or a brace of amplifiers, you'll be needing a new live feed, taken straight off the battery. Re-using any of the standard Renault stereo wiring could be a bad move - the stock wire is probably only good for about 15 amps, tops, so don't go fitting a bigger fuse, or you'll have a meltdown (and maybe, a fire).

Get some decent "four-gauge" wire (which is about as thick as battery cable - serious stuff) and a matching fuseholder. If you're running more than one item off this feed wire, get a distribution block too, which splits the feed up, with a separate fuse for each item - who'd have thought electrical safety can look trick too?

Pub trivia:

Hands up, who knows what 'RCA' stands for? We use it every day in ICE-speak, but WHAT does it really mean? Really Clever Amplifier lead? Remote Control Acoustic lead? Well, the answer's a strange one. RCA leads and connectors are also known as 'phono' connectors in the world of TV and hi-fi, and they've been around a long, long time. How long, exactly? We're talking back in the days when you could only get radios - big suckers with valves in them, and long before anyone thought of putting one in a car. RCA actually stands for Radio Corporation of America, who hold the patent on this type of connector and lead. Not a lot of people know that.

Speaker and RCA wiring

As with virtually all wiring, the lesson here is to be neat and orderly - or - you'll be sorry! RCA leads and speaker wires are prone to picking up interference (from just about anywhere), so the first trick to learn when running ICE wiring is to keep it away from live feeds, and also if possible, away from the car's ECUs. Another favourite way to interference-hell is to loop up your wiring, when you find you've got too much (we've all been there). Finding a way to lose any excess lengths of wire without bunching can be an art - laying it out in a zig-zag, taping it to the floor as you go, is just one solution.

Another lesson in neatness is finding out what kinds of cable clips are available, and where to use them. There's various stick-on clips which can be used as an alternative to gaffer tape on floors, and then "P-clips", which look exactly as their name suggests, and can be screwed down (to speaker shelves, for instance). "Looming"

your wiring is another lesson well-learned - this just means wrapping tape around, particularly on pairs of speaker wires or RCAs. As we've already said, don't loom speaker wire with power cables (or even with earths).

The last point is also about tidiness - mental tidiness. When you're dealing with speaker and RCA wiring, keep two ideas in mind - positive and negative. Each speaker has a pos (+) and neg (-) terminal. Mixing these up is not an option, so work out a system of your own, for keeping positive and negative in the right places on your headset and amp connections. Decent speaker cable is always two wires joined together - look closely, and you'll see that one wire has writing (or a stripe) on, and the other is plain. Use the wire with writing for pos connections throughout your system, and you'll never be confused again. While we're at it, RCA leads have red and white connector plugs - Red is for Right.

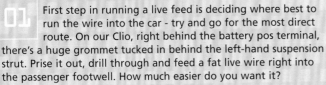

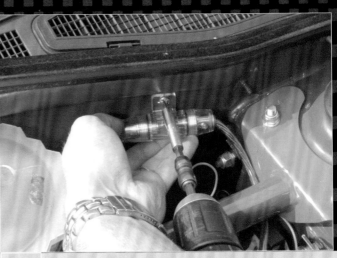

01 First step in running a live feed is deciding where best to run the wire into the car - try and go for the most direct route. On our Clio, right behind the battery pos terminal, there's a huge grommet tucked in behind the left-hand suspension strut. Prise it out, drill through and feed a fat live wire right into the passenger footwell. How much easier do you want it?

02 Kit yourself out with a decent fuseholder - ones like this not only look good, they're really excellent to use. Get a fuse the same rating as your amp, or the total load on your distribution block - ask a pro for advice. The fuseholder ought to be securely mounted, and somewhere you can get at it, if there's ever a meltdown

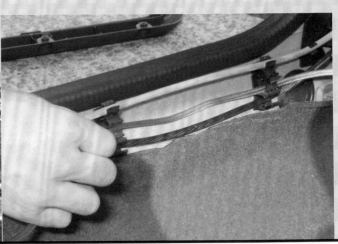

03 We're using eight-gauge wire, but for mega amounts of power, four-gauge is the way (thicker than normal battery cable). Crimp on a ring terminal big enough to deal with such hefty wire. Don't get carried away and connect up your live feed until you're ready - remember, this feed is NOT ignition-switched!

04 Here's where your live feed could end up - a distribution block. Here, your power can be split off, usually to separate amps - each amp gets its own fuse (downrated from the large one in the holder up front). This all makes for excellent electrical safety, and the blocks themselves look the nuts too, as a bonus. The wire ends are pinned in by chunky Allen grub screws, and the whole thing has a tidy plastic cover (which must be on tight, or lives will touch earths, and sparks will fly).

05 Okay, so no-one's gonna see it, once all the trim's back on, but try and keep all wiring neat and tidy - one day, you'll be glad you did. Renault helpfully provide clips down the insides of the door sills, just gagging to have wires clipped into them. If you're going to run power and speaker wires near each other, make sure 'near' doesn't become 'touching' . . .

06 . . . don't rely on the sill clips alone for this - here, we've found some luminous-yellow cable-ties to make the point clearer - separate your wires, and keep it all tidy.

07 As they're most prone to picking up interference, we ran the RCA leads down the centre of the car. With strips of gaffer tape to keep it all neatly tied down, this is how a professional wiring install should look.

08 Sooner or later, some of those wires will have to be bundled up using good old-fashioned insulating tape - this is a process known as 'looming'. Real looming addicts take this very seriously, and go all-out to wrap all their new wires in black tape, like the car makers do. You and I make do with a small piece every six inches.

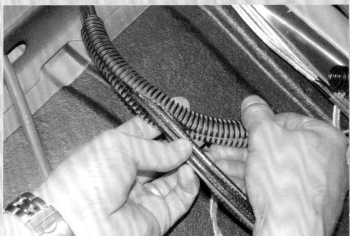

09 Another approach, which is especially effective for wires which will be on display, is to shroud the wiring inside plastic convoluted tubing. This stuff's really neat - it's split open along its length, so you slip the wires inside, then use just a little tape to seal it up. Looks smart, and offers some protection/insulation too . . .

10 . . . here, our Liquid ICE guys are using 'convolute' to make a neater job of a sharp right-hand 'turn' in the wiring. Just cut the convolute to length, bend the wires round the corner, then loom them up and fit some more tubing. The professional touch.

12 Engines

Faster, faster!

So now your car talks the talk, but does it walk the walk, as in walking away from everything at the next set of lights... Not everyone's into mega-performance, which is why the bolt-on goodies like induction kits and big-bore exhausts are such big business. Serious engine tuning costs, and not just in the initial expense - it goes without saying that your insurance company will throw a wobbly at a gas-flowed head, and might refuse to cover you altogether if you go for that 2.0 litre Williams conversion.

The induction kit and sports exhaust are an essential first choice, and are as far as you can really go before your insurance company disowns you, or before you need another bank loan to afford the mods in the first place. Both mods help the engine to 'breathe' better, which helps when you go for the accelerator initially, improving the response you feel, while you also get a crowd-pleasing induction roar and rasp from the back box, so everyone's happy.

Now for the harsh and painful truth. On their own, an induction kit and back box will not gain you much extra 'real' power. Sorry, but it's a myth. Time and again, people fit induction kits and back boxes, expecting huge power gains, and those 'in the know' have a quiet chuckle. All these things really do is make the car sound sportier, and improve the response - accept this, and you won't be disappointed. Ask yourself why most insurance companies don't generally increase premiums for the likes of a performance rear box or induction kit. The answer is - because (on their own) they don't make enough difference!

The 'bolt-on' performance goodies have more effect as part of an engine 'makeover' package, and setting-up the engine properly after fitting these parts can make a huge difference. If you're halfway serious about increasing the go of your Clio, talk to someone with access to a rolling road, so you can prove that what's been done HAS actually made a useful gain. If you've spent time and a ton of money on your car, of course you're going to think it feels faster, but is it?

Fitting all the performance goodies in the world will be pretty pointless if the engine's already knackered, but it might not be as bad as you think. One of the best ways to start on the performance road is simply to ensure that the car's serviced properly - new spark plugs, HT leads, and an oil and filter change, are a good basis to begin from. Correct any obvious faults, such as hoses or wiring plugs hanging off, and look for any obviously-damaged or leaking components, too.

Breathe with me...

Replacement element

One of the simplest items to fit, the replacement air filter element has been around for years - of course, now the induction kit's the thing to have, but a replacement element is more discreet (if you're worried about such things).

While we're at it, don't listen to your mates who tell you to simply take out the air filter completely - this is a really lame idea. The fuel system's air intake acts like a mini vacuum cleaner, sucking in air from the front of the car, and it doesn't just suck in air, but also dust, dirt and leaves - it's also designed to suck in oil fumes from the engine itself (through the 'breather' connection). Without a filter, all this muck would quickly end up in the sensitive parts of the fuel injection system, and will quickly make the car undriveable. Worse, if any of it makes it into the engine, this will lead to engine wear. Remember too, that cheaper performance filters can be of very suspect quality - if your new filter disintegrates completely inside six months, it'll do wonders for the airflow, but it'll also be letting in all sorts of rubbish!

Some performance filters have to be oiled before fitting - follow the instructions provided; don't ignore this part, or the filter won't be effective. If the filter won't fit, check whether you actually have the right one - don't force it in, and don't cut it to fit, as either of these will result in gaps, which would allow unfiltered air to get in.

01 This is a man who obviously hasn't fitted a strut brace yet. How do we know this? Because he can still get to his air cleaner, that's how. There's one screw (a cross-head, not a Torx, for a change) . . .

02 . . . and two bolts to undo, followed by . . .

03 . . . about six over-centre clips to release round the edge, before finally . . .

04 . . . the air cleaner lid comes off, and we can take out the nasty paper element. Before you fit your new K&N, it's worth cleaning out any dust, leaves or small furry mammals lurking in the air cleaner housing. Make sure that none of it goes down the middle, as that's into the engine - best to use a damp cloth (the muck will stick to it better).

05 The new filter goes in like the old one came out - check for any markings which show which way up the filter's meant to fit. Refit the lid as before, then (and this is the most important bit) find a prominent spot to display your K&N sticker.

Induction kit

With an induction kit, the standard air filter housing and ducting are junked, and the new filter bolts directly to the airflow meter or throttle body. Most kits also feature special air inlet ducting (hoses) to feed the new filter with the coldest possible air from the front of the car - cold air is denser, and improves engine power. Feeding the filter with cold air is in theory good for maximum performance with a hot engine or in hot weather, but in colder conditions with a cold engine, driveability and fuel economy might suffer.

The fuelling arrangements for fuel injection are based largely on the volume of incoming air. If you start feeding the injection system an unusually large amount of air (by fitting an induction kit, for instance), the management system will compensate by throwing in more fuel. This could result in some more power - or the car will drink petrol and your exhaust emissions will be screwed up, inviting an MOT failure. We're not saying "don't do it", just remember that power gains can be exaggerated, and that there can be pitfalls.

What no-one disputes is that an induction kit, which operates without all the normal ducting provided as standard, gives the engine a real throaty roar when you go for the loud pedal. So at least it sounds fast. Jubbly.

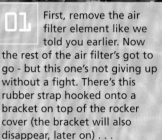

01 First, remove the air filter element like we told you earlier. Now the rest of the air filter's got to go - but this one's not giving up without a fight. There's this rubber strap hooked onto a bracket on top of the rocker cover (the bracket will also disappear, later on) . . .

05 . . . there's just the breather hose connection to the rocker cover to pull off . . .

06 . . . and at last, the whole disgusting mess can be chucked. Or 'recycled', if you're being PC, but recycled into what?

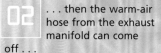

02 . . . then the warm-air hose from the exhaust manifold can come off . . .

03 . . . as can the cold-air inlet, which disconnects just in front of the battery.

04 Various clips are used to hold all the unsightly hosework in place, but don't be put off . . .

The breather hoses are something you can't overlook when fitting any kind of new filter - just ripping them off will make the engine run lumpy, and an eagle-eyed MOT tester will rightly fail your car on emissions. Yup, 'fraid so. With our K&N, they supply a longer section of hose, into which you plug the plastic joiner, and then reconnect to the stub on the rocker cover . . .

>>

07 Look, the last remnant of the old order - that bracket and its rubber band can be unbolted and thrown out. We're not recycling that into anything.

08

09 . . . while to get the engine fumes up into the filter cone, there's another weird-shaped section of hose, which goes onto the other side of the plastic joiner . . .

10 . . . and the whole lot can then be fed in through and around the existing pipes, wires, etc. It's no good if the breather pipe's just stuffed in, kinked up and effectively blocked - it won't so much breathe as choke.

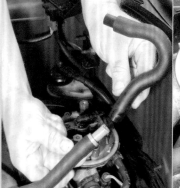

11 On this single-point injection motor, the filter cone sits on top of the throttle body - on multi-point models, you'd have a mounting bracket to fix in for the cone. Don't forget to plug in the breather hose, into the hole provided in the base of the cone . . .

12 . . . and do up the huge Jubilee clip nice and tight - an inlet air leak will really screw up the running.

13 The only thing left is to feed the new filter with the coldest-possible air. You have two choices. Re-using the old cold-air inlet stub in front of the battery is easy, and will work well enough. Doing it properly might mean taking the bonnet off, to make a new inlet hole. The bonnet's held on by two hinge bolts either side - don't try taking it off (or refitting it) without some help.

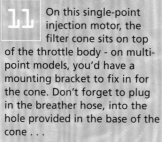

With a combination of a drilled hole first, and a hacksaw later, we end up with a hole large enough to poke the (supplied) section of air trunking through - mind that radiator. You could almost convince yourself you'll get some motorbike-style ram-air effect with this (just makes it easier to justify taking off that bonnet). **14**

With the front end of the hose in its new hole, feed the rest round the engine, and fix the other end close to the filter cone. Cable-tie the hose to a convenient point, like one of the coolant hoses - it's no good if that icy blast of power-giving air ends up pointing at the bulkhead, is it? **15**

Finally...

Once you've fitted your new filter or induction kit, even if you don't take the car to a rolling road for setting up, at least take it to a garage and have the emissions checked - any minor adjustments should ensure that the engine will, if nothing else, still tick over okay, and should ensure an MOT emissions pass.

Other air filter-type mods

One old favourite, if you've got a square filter box and haven't gone for an induction kit, is drilling holes in the air filter box. Only drill the air filter box below the level where the filter element sits, or the air going into the engine won't be filtered. Making your airbox look like a Swiss cheese won't make the car faster, but it does give you the nice throaty induction roar at full throttle.

No quicker
but it looks nice

Of course, if you're embarrassed about how your engine looks, you could always claim your bonnet pull's knackered, and only open the bonnet while no-one else is around. But come on, even a boggo Clio's engine bay can be made to look well smart, with just a few simple mods.

First up - try cleaning the engine, for heaven sake! How do you expect to emulate the show-stopping cars if your gearbox is covered in grot? Get busy with the degreaser (Gunk's a good bet), then get the hosepipe out. You can take it down to the local jetwash if you like, but remember your mobile - if you get carried away with the high-power spray, you might find the car won't start afterwards!

When it's all dry (and running again), you can start in. Get the polish to all the painted surfaces you reasonably can, and don't be afraid to unbolt a few of the simpler items to gain better access. We're assuming you've already fitted your induction kit, but if not, these nicely do away with a load of ugly plastic airbox/air cleaner and trunking, and that rusted-out exhaust manifold cover, in favour of decent-looking product. Take off the rocker cover (or engine cover), and paint it to match your chosen scheme (heat-resistant paint is a must, really, such as brake caliper paint), set off with a funky oil filler cap. A strut brace is a tasty underbonnet feature, especially chromed. Braided hose covers (or coloured hose sets), ally battery covers and bottles, mirror panels - all give the underbonnet a touch of glamour.

Brighten up the underbonnet, and maybe (if you believe what it says on the tin) make your car go better too? Gotta be worth a punt, to find out. First, make sure the ignition's off - take out the key, to be certain. Work on one lead at a time here - pull this end off the spark plug . . .

01

. . . then unclip it from the rocker cover, and off the distributor cap.

02

Lay the new leads out, and choose the lead closest in length to the one you've just pulled off. Our Megaleads set was actually for a Megane 1.4, as the Clio 1.4 set originally supplied had leads which were way too short. Always pays to check these things, before you get too far in - and don't wreck the box they came in, when you open it up.

03

Push the new lead home onto the spark plug, then clip it into the rocker cover . . .

04

Coloured HT leads

. . . and finally, onto the distributor. Might not be quite the same on your Clio (16-valvers have a centre cover, held on by two screws, to remove first), but the principle's just the same - do one lead at a time, or regret it later. Worth spraying each end of the lead with some WD-40 (or similar stuff) to keep the damp out.

05

And here's one we did earlier. Don't like red? Well, they also come in blue, yellow...

06

Adjustable fuel
pressure regulator
(power boost valve)

Generally only available for Clios with multi-point injection (1.8/2.0 litre engines mainly), these valves allow the fuel system pressure to be increased over the standard regulator valve. Contrary to what you might think, they don't actually provide much more fuel (this is regulated separately by the injection ECU). The effect of increasing the injection pressure is to improve the injector spray pattern, which helps the fuel to burn more efficiently, and has the effect of increasing engine power while actually reducing emission levels.

To see the true effect of these valves, they must be set up using emission test gear and ideally a rolling road - merely turning the pressure up to the maximum level might not produce the desired effect. Fitting one of these valves involves breaking into the high-pressure fuel line, which is potentially dangerous for the inexperienced - also, if the valve is poorly fitted (or the fuel lines are in poor condition), you could end up with fuel spraying out under pressure onto a hot engine. Make sure you know what you're doing - take great care when dealing with petrol, and watch carefully for any sign of fuel leakage after fitting, even if this is done by a professional.

Braided hoses

Turning your engine bay into something resembling that of a racing machine should only be done when the engine's completely cold to start with - like first thing in the morning, NOT when you've just got back from the cruise. With the state of the NHS these days, visiting the burns unit should be avoided wherever possible. Depending on which hoses you decide to treat, you could be removing ones containing hot coolant or fuel, and you don't play games with either, so be smart.

01 First step is to remove your chosen hose. If supplies of braiding are limited, go for the hoses at the top of the engine first, then the ones underneath you can't see won't matter so much. Renault tend to use spring-type clips, best released using pliers . . .

02 . . . but you'll also find clips which there appears to be no tool for removing, apart from a large screwdriver - ie removal by destruction. Make sure you've got a handy source of new Jubilee clips available, just in case.

03 If the hose is stuck, be careful how you free it, or you could snap the pipe stub underneath (some are only plastic). This sort of thing can really ruin your day. Careful prising with a screwdriver is usually enough to loosen a stubborn hose end.

Engines

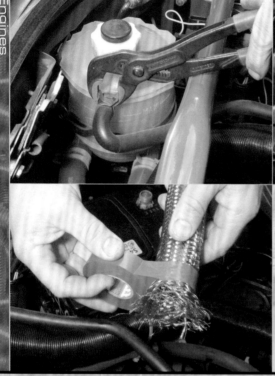

08 . . . then (and this bit's optional, but it worked well for us) wrap round a little insulating tape - we had some colour-coded red stuff lying about - to tidy the end . . .

09 . . . before trimming off the excess braiding (and not the hose).

10 Slide a new Jubilee clip over the braiding at one end, then slip one of the coloured end fittings over the clip.

Achtung!

If you're braiding coolant hoses, feel them up first (oo-er) to make sure they're COLD. Have a bowl ready to catch the coolant in (antifreeze is poisonous despite its sweet smell, and will make a mess of your paintwork if you douse the engine bay and front wings with it!). Also, don't forget to top-up the coolant level before heading out in your newly-braided-up machine.

If you're planning to braid your fuel lines, disconnect the hoses very carefully - have some rags wrapped around the pipes, so you don't spray high-pressure fuel everywhere.

04 Unroll your braiding, check the length against your freshly-removed hose . . .

05 . . . and trim it roughly to length - you might need something heftier than scissors for this.

06 Now expand the braiding to the right size using a suitable blunt object. Like a screwdriver handle, we mean - what were you thinking of?

07 Once the braiding's roughly the right size, you can slip your pipe in (lovely). Smooth out the braiding round the bends, as it tends to gather up and look naff otherwise . . .

11 Repeat this process at the other end of your chosen hose, and it'll be ready to fit back on.

12 When you're sure the hose is fully onto its fitting, tighten the hose clip securely to avoid embarrassing leakage. If any of the end fittings rattle annoyingly, you can put a stop to it by packing the fittings with silicone.

13 If you've got an awkward (kinky) hose to do, make life easier for yourself by spraying on a little WD-40 before trying to slip the braiding on . . .

14 . . . and use something like a screwdriver (or a socket extension piece) to straighten out those bends while you're fitting.

Chrome
battery cover

You'd really think there wouldn't be much to this, wouldn't you? Get a chrome battery cover, stick it on your battery, job done. Well, yes, except that you'd quite likely have a fire if you did just stick it on. Any cover worth having's made of metal, which will do a great job of shorting-out your battery terminals if you let it. We chose the safe option of fitting a piece of hardboard inside (you can use anything non-conductive - like cardboard, if you want). Measure up . . .

01

. . . then get out the jigsaw (or scissors), and try the finished article in place for size.

02

We thought it might be nice if our hardboard terminal protector didn't fall off, so out came the sticky double-sided tape . . .

03

. . . before the hardboard was finally stuck in position.

04

And now, safe in the knowledge that our battery won't suffer meltdown, we can fit our shiny new cover. Except that our Clio has a very protruding positive terminal, which will mean further chopping, this time of the chrome itself - mark it up . . .

05

. . . and cut it out. Pretty saucy - now, has anyone seen red anodised covers?

06

ECU "chipping"

All Clios have fuel injection, which is controlled by an engine management system with a 'computer' at its heart, known as the ECU, or Electronic Control Unit. The ECU contains several computer chips, at least one of which has programmed onto it the preferred fuel/air mixture and ignition advance setting for any given engine speed or load - this information is known as a computer 'map', and the system refers to it constantly while the car's being driven. Obviously, with the current trend towards fuel economy and reducing harmful exhaust emissions, the values in this 'map' are set, well, conservatively, let's say (read 'boring'). With a little tweaking - like richening-up the mixture, say - the engine can be made to produce more power, or response will be improved, or both. At the expense of the environment. Oh well.

Companies like Superchips offer replacement computer chips which feature a computer map where driveability and performance are given priority over outright economy (although the company claims that, under certain conditions, even fuel economy can be better, with their products). While a chip like this does offer proven power gains on its own, it's obviously best to combine a chip with other enhancements, and to have the whole lot set up at the same time. By the time you've fitted an induction kit, four-branch manifold, big-bore pipe, and maybe even a fast-road cam, adding a chip is the icing on the cake - chipping an already-modified motor will liberate even more horses, or at least combine it with majorly-improved response. Renault tuning specialists like Hill Power are best placed to advise you on the most effective tuning mods.

Another feature programmed into the ECU is a rev limiter, which cuts the ignition (or fuel) progressively when the pre-set rev limit is reached. Most replacement chips have the rev limiter reset higher, or removed altogether. Not totally sure this is a good thing - if the engine's not maintained properly (low oil level, cambelt changes neglected), removing the rev limiter and running beyond the red line would be a quick way to kill it. But a well-maintained engine with a rally cam fitted could rev off the clock, if the ECU would let it, so maybe not a bad thing after all...

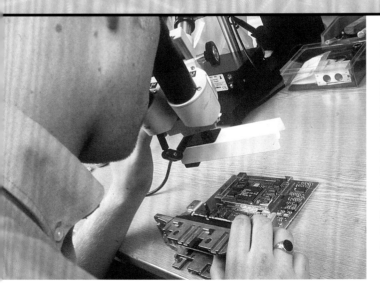

Now the bad news

Chipping is often thought of as an easy, 'no-tell' route to increased performance and driveability - after all, the ECU is well-buried inside the car, not on show under the bonnet, so who's gonna know? Needless to say, the insurance companies have been wise to this trick for a long time. A sure way to tell whether a 'performance' product does what it says on the tin is to see what it'll do to your premium - telling them you're fitting a sports ROM chip will cost. Big-time. But, in the event of a claim, if they suspect your car's been 'chipped', rest assured, they will make efforts to find out, because if you haven't told them about it, it means they save on paying out. What's an insurance assessor's salary for one day, compared to the thousands you could be claiming in case of an accident or theft? Do it by all means, but at least be honest.

Gaining access to the ECU

On all Clios, the ECU (brain) is in a rather bizarre spot - it's under the jack. The jack storage hole under the driver's side of the windscreen can fill up with water, if the bulkhead drains get blocked (with leaves, say). Quite a good place for an expensive Electronic Control Unit, then - not. Take out the jack by

01 undoing the securing bolt . . .

02 . . . and lifting it out. Still can't see an ECU in there.

03 Now there's three nuts to undo - two you can see, with the third slightly buried . . .

04 . . . and out comes the jack mounting plate. Well. there's a black box in there, but it don't look much like an ECU.

05 Well, let's take that black box out, anyway, and have a look. It won't come out far - there's a thick wiring harness attached. Are we getting warm?

06 Ah - a rubber strap. Let's unhook it, and see what happens . . .

07 . . . the strap hooks onto an upper metal plate, and loops round to hold a plastic box underneath (we turned ours over, so we didn't drop the box on the floor).

08 The plastic box is in two halves, and clips together around the edge. Unclip the lid, and an ECU is revealed at last - the brain behind your Clio (don't worry, this won't hurt a bit).

09 Slide off the red locking clip from the ECU multi-plug . . .

10 . . . and making certain that the ignition's switched off (take out the key), disconnect the plug. The ECU is now at your mercy. Treat it with some respec' once it's out (not dropping it on the floor is a good place to start, as is not 'having a go' yourself with a soldering iron). If you want it to work again, send it away for professional chippery.

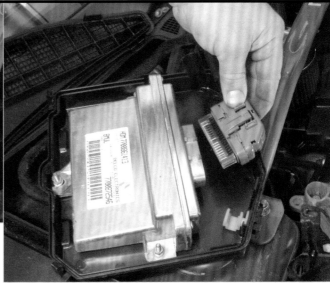

Engine tuning

So you've done the induction kit, exhaust and chip - what's next, short of going for a complete engine swap? Assuming you've got a capacity-challenged Clio, there's not much more you can, or should, sensibly do before thinking about going for a 'valver' (16V) conversion next. You'll have an easier time extracting more oomph from a 16V engine, mostly because there's far more available from specialists.

One of the premier Renault tuning wizards, Prima Racing will sell you almost anything your heart desires in 16-valve tuning bits, from an upgraded ECU to a turbo conversion. That's right - for those of you still mourning the passing of the R5 GT Turbo, you can relive the whole where's-the-power-cripes-hold-on kick in the back, torque-steer experience (at a price). Another Renault tuning outfit, 5 Alive, recently stuck a 5 GT Turbo engine straight into a Clio, but it wasn't exactly the work of an afternoon... Somewhere in between, we find gas-flowed heads, road/race/rally cams and throttle bodies. If you're prepared to blow upwards of two grand on your 16V lump, you can quite easily be looking at approaching 200 bhp - which is Cosworth power, in a Clio. The word 'awesome' springs to mind.

Here's another tasty little morsel to chew over. To create the Clio Williams 2.0 litre engine, what exactly did our French friends do? Design a new engine from scratch, for a limited-edition model? *Je crois que non* (I think not). Actually, it was easy - dipping into the Renault parts bin, they found a long-stroke crankshaft from - the Clio diesel! Add that to a 1.8 16V block, season with some forged pistons and extra cooling, *et voilà* (as they say in Fr) you have cooked up a long-stroke 2.0 litre version of the same engine. Further proof of this fact is that the 2.0 litre motor has a lower red line than the 1.8 litre,

because of the longer-throw crankshaft. And has anyone done their own Clio V6 conversion, using the 3.0 litre 24-valve motor from the Laguna/Safrane (170 bhp, must be tuneable), or a turbo conversion using the lump from the 21 Turbo (200 bhp!) - if not, why not be first?

And finally tonight - the bad news. Any major engine mods means telling those nice suits who work for your insurance company, and it's likely they'll insist on a full engineer's report (these aren't especially expensive - look one up in the Yellow Pages, under *'Garage Services'* or *'Vehicle Inspection'*).

Exhausts

It's gotta be done, hasn't it? Your rusty old exhaust lacks the girth to impress, and doesn't so much growl as miaow. Don't be a wimp and fit an exhaust trim - they'll fool nobody who really knows, and they certainly won't add to your aural pleasure (oo-er). Sort yourself out a decent back box upgrade, and even a timid 1.2 litre Clio can begin to cut it at the cruise.

What a back box won't do on its own is increase engine power - although it'll certainly sound like it has, provided you choose the right one, and fit it properly. Check when you're buying that it can be fitted to a standard system - you'll probably need something called a reducing sleeve for a decent fit, which is a section of pipe designed to bridge the difference between your small-diameter pipe and the larger-diameter silencer. Try and measure your standard pipe as accurately as possible, or you'll have major problems trying to get a decent seal between the old and new bits - don't assume that exhaust paste will sort everything out, because it won't.

Fashion has even entered the aftermarket exhaust scene, with different rear pipe designs going in and out of style. Everyone's done the upswept twin-pipe "DTM" style pipes, while currently the trend in single pipes is "the bigger the better", or fat oval (or twin-oval) designs. If you must have the phattest Clio on the block, you can't beat a twin-exit system, even though it'll mean losing your

Know your enemy - this is what your cat looks like inside. Is it any wonder they restrict gas flow?

spare wheel in the fitting process. Well, when was the last time you had a puncture? And what are mobiles and breakdown cover for, anyway? In case you needed reminding, the daddy of all Clios (the Mk 2 V6) sports a rather nifty centre twin-exit system...

If you've got a capacity-challenged Clio, you might need to lightly modify even your standard rear bodywork/bumper to accommodate a bigger rear pipe; if you're going for a bodykit later, your back box will have to come off again, so it can be poked through your rear valance/mesh.

You'll see some useful power gains if you go for the complete performance exhaust system, rather than just the back box. Like the factory-fit system, the sports silencer again will only work at its best if combined with the front pipe and manifold it was designed for! Performance four-branch manifolds alone can give very useful power gains. Watch what you buy, though - cheap exhaust manifolds which crack for a pastime are not unknown, and many aftermarket systems need careful fitting and fettling before you'll stop it resonating or banging away underneath. A sports rear box alone shouldn't attract an increased insurance premium, but a full system probably will.

Most Clios have a catalytic converter (or "cat"), which acts like a restrictor in the exhaust, inhibiting the gas flow and sapping some engine power (maybe 5 to 10%). Several companies and exhaust specialists market replacement sections which do away with the cat (a "de-cat pipe"), and get you your power back. You could easily have one made up, if you know someone handy with the welder - all you need is the two flanges and some half decent pipe (from a scrapyard or motor factors). Unfortunately, by taking off or disabling the cat, your car won't be able to pass the emissions test at MOT time, so you'll have to "re-convert" the car every 12 months. This fact, arguably, means that the car is illegal on the road with a de-cat pipe fitted - you'd have no defence for this, if questions were asked at the roadside, and potentially no insurance if the unthinkable happens. Sorry, but we have to say it...

One other point to consider, if your Clio's been slammed to the floor - will your big new sports system be leaving behind a trail of sparks as it scrapes along the deck? Shouldn't do, if it's been properly fitted, but will the local multi-storey be out-of-bounds for your Clio, from now on? And - pub trivia moment - you can actually be done for causing damage to the highway, if your exhaust's dragging. Well, great.

You probably couldn't give a stuff if your loud system's a very loud major public nuisance, but will that loud pipe start interfering with your sound system? If you rack up many motorway miles, you might find the constant drone of a loud pipe gets to be a real pain on a long trip, too...

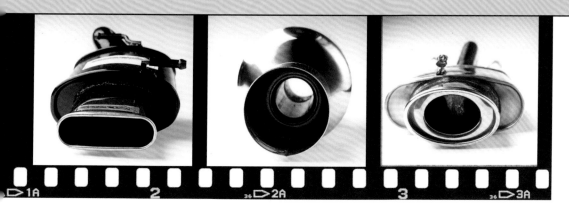

Fitting a **sports back box**

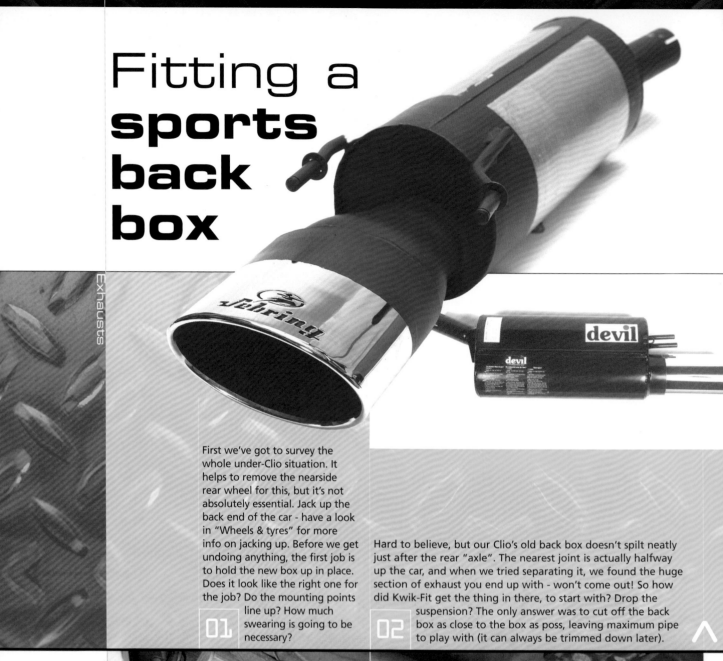

First we've got to survey the whole under-Clio situation. It helps to remove the nearside rear wheel for this, but it's not absolutely essential. Jack up the back end of the car - have a look in "Wheels & tyres" for more info on jacking up. Before we get undoing anything, the first job is to hold the new box up in place. Does it look like the right one for the job? Do the mounting points line up? How much swearing is going to be necessary?

01

Hard to believe, but our Clio's old back box doesn't spilt neatly just after the rear "axle". The nearest joint is actually halfway up the car, and when we tried separating it, we found the huge section of exhaust you end up with - won't come out! So how did Kwik-Fit get the thing in there, to start with? Drop the suspension? The only answer was to cut off the back box as close to the box as poss, leaving maximum pipe to play with (it can always be trimmed down later).

02

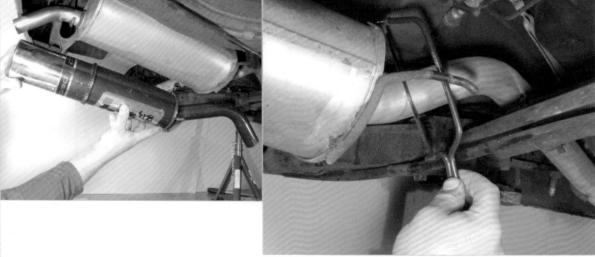

03 To join on our new box, we used a short sleeve (just another bit of pipe, slightly bigger bore) and two clamps. Not a bad idea to use some Firegum on the joints, to make sure it all ends up gas-tight and phart-free. Don't tighten the clamps yet - some wiggling will be needed.

04 Is that the worst bit over with? Depends. Peco at least supply decent, well-thought-out mounting clamps , which appear to've been designed for the job. Excellent. Just slip it over loose . . .

05 . . . and lift the box into place.

So here we are, lying on our backs, working in the dark. This is where a well-designed clamp is a major bonus. Hook one half of the rubber onto the clamp, over the mount provided at the back, then slip the other half home. Stress factor? Zero.

06

07 Now tighten those clamps fully . . .

. . . and stand back to admire the Peco Big Bore effect. Nice. You might want, or need, to modify the rear bumper slightly, to avoid melting plastic.
Or to emphasise the phatness of your new pipe.

08

Safety and tools

Safety

We all know that working on your car can be dangerous - and we're not talking about the danger of losing your street cred by fitting naff alloys or furry dice! Okay, so you'd be hard-pushed to injure yourself fitting some cool floor mats or a tax disc holder, but tackle more-serious mods, and you could be treading dangerous ground. Let's be honest - we have to put this safety section in to cover ourselves, but now it's in, it would be nice if you read it…

Burning/scalding

The only way you'll really burn yourself is if your car's just been running - avoid this, and you won't get burned. Easy, eh? Otherwise, you risk burns from any hot parts of the engine (and especially the exhaust - if you've got one, the cat runs very hot), or from spilling hot coolant if you undo the radiator hoses or filler cap, as you might when you're braiding hoses.

Fire

Sadly, there's several ways your car could catch fire, when you think about it. You've got a big tank full of fuel (and other flammable liquids about, like brake fluid), together with electrics - some of which run to very high voltages. If you smoke too, this could be even worse for your health than you thought.

a Liquid fuel is flammable. Fuel vapour can explode - don't smoke, or create any kind of spark, if there's fuel vapour (fuel smell) about.

b Letting fuel spill onto a hot engine is dangerous, but brake fluid spills go up even more readily. Respect is due with brake fluid, which also attacks paintwork and plastics - wash off with water.

c Fires can also be started by careless modding involving the electrical system. It's possible to overload (and overheat) existing wiring by tapping off too many times for new live feeds. Not insulating bare wires or connections can lead to short-circuits, and the sparks or overheated wiring which results can start a fire. Always investigate any newly-wired-in kit which stops working, or which keeps blowing fuses - those wires could already be smouldering…

Reference

Crushing

Having your car land on top of you is no laughing matter, and it's a nasty accident waiting to happen if you risk using dodgy old jacks, bricks, and other means of lifting/supporting your car. Please don't.

Your standard vehicle jack is for emergency roadside use only - a proper trolley jack and a set of axle stands won't break the overdraft, and might save broken bones. Don't buy a cheap trolley jack, and don't expect a well-used secondhand one to be perfect, either - when the hydraulic seals start to fail, a trolley jack will drop very fast; this is why you should always have decent stands in place under the car as well.

Steering, suspension & brakes

Screwing up any one of these on your car, through badly-fitted mods, could land you and others in hospital or worse. Nuff said? It's always worth getting a mate, or a friendly garage, to check over what you've just fitted (or even what you've just had fitted, in some cases - not all "pro" fitters are perfect!). Pay attention to tightening vital nuts and bolts properly - buy or borrow a torque wrench.

To be absolutely sure, take your newly-modded machine to a friendly MOT tester (if there is such a thing) - this man's your ultimate authority on safety, after all. Even if he's normally a pain once a year, he could save your life. Think it over.

Even properly-fitted mods can radically alter the car's handling - and not always for the better. Take a few days getting used to how the car feels before showing off.

Wheels

Don't take liberties fitting wheels. Make sure the wheels have the right stud/bolt hole pattern for your car, and that the wheel nuts/bolts are doing their job. Bolts which are too long might catch on your brakes (especially rear drums) - too short, and, well, the wheels are just waiting to fall off. Not nice. Also pay attention to the bolt heads or wheel nuts - some are supposed to have large tapered washers fitted, to locate properly in the wheel. If the nuts/bolts "pull through" the wheel when tightened, the wheel's gonna fall off, isn't it?

Asbestos

Only likely to be a major worry when working on, or near, your brakes. That black dust that gets all over your alloys comes from your brake pads, and it may contain asbestos. Breathing in asbestos dust can lead to a disease called asbestosis (inflammation of the lungs - very nasty indeed), so try not to inhale brake dust when you're changing your pads or discs.

Airbags

Unless you run into something at high speed, the only time an airbag will enter your life is when you change your steering wheel for something more sexy, and have to disable the airbag in the process. Pay attention to all the precautionary advice given in our text, and you'll have no problems.

One more thing - don't tap into the airbag wiring to run any extra electrical kit. Any mods to the airbag circuit could set it off unexpectedly.

Exhaust gases

Even on cars with cats, exhaust fumes are still potentially lethal. Don't work in an unventilated garage with the engine running. When fitting new exhaust bits, be sure that there's no gas leakage from the joints. When modifying in the tailgate area, note that exhaust gas can get sucked into the car through badly-fitting tailgate seals/joints (or even through your rear arches, if they've been trimmed so much there's holes into the car).

Tools

In writing this book, we've assumed you already have a selection of basic tools - screwdrivers, socket set, spanners, hammer, sharp knife, power drill. Any unusual extra tools you might need are mentioned in the relevant text. Torx and Allen screws are often found on trim panels, so a set of keys of each type is a wise purchase.

From a safety angle, always buy the best tools you can afford - or if you must use cheap ones, remember that they can break under stress or unusual usage (and we've all got the busted screwdrivers to prove it!).

DO Wear goggles when using power tools.

DO Keep loose clothing/long hair away from moving engine parts.

DO Take off watches and jewellery when working on electrics.

DO Keep the work area tidy - stops accidents and losing parts.

DON'T Rush a job, or take stupid short-cuts.

DON'T Use the wrong tools for the job, or ones which don't fit.

DON'T Let kids or pets play around your car when you're working.

DON'T Work entirely alone under a car that's been jacked up.

Legal modding?
No such thing!!

The harsh & painful truth

The minute you start down the road to a modified motor, you stand a good chance of being in trouble with the Man. It seems like there's almost nothing worthwhile you can do to your car, without breaking some sort of law. So the answer's not to do it at all, then? Well, no, but let's keep it real.

There's this bunch of vehicle-related regulations called Construction & Use. It's a huge set of books, used by the car manufacturers and the Department of Transport among others, and it sets out in black and white all the legal issues that could land you in trouble. It's the ultimate authority for modifying, in theory. But few people (and even fewer policemen) know all of it inside-out, and it's forever being updated and revised, so it's not often enforced to the letter at the roadside - just in court. Despite the existence of C & U, in trying to put together any guide to the law and modifying, it quickly becomes clear that almost everything's a "grey area", with no-one prepared to go on record and say what is okay to modify and what's not. Well, brilliant. So if there's no fixed rules (in the real world), how are you meant to live by them? In the circumstances, all we can promise to do is help to make sense of nonsense...

Avoiding roadside interviews

Why do some people get pulled all the time, and others hardly ever? It's often all about attitude. We'd all like to be free to drive around "in yer face", windows down, system full up, loud exhaust bellowing, sparks striking, tyres squealing - but - nothing is a bigger "come-on" to the boys in blue than "irresponsible" driving like this. Rest assured, if your motor's anywhere near fully sorted, the coppers will find something they can nick you for, when they pull you over - it's a dead cert. Trying not to wind them up too much before this happens (and certainly not once you're stopped) will make for an easier life. There's showing off, and then there's taking the pee. Save it for the next cruise.

The worst thing from your point of view is that, once you've been stopped, it's down to that particular copper's judgement as to whether your car's illegal. If he/she's having a bad day anyway, smart-mouthing-off isn't gonna help your case at all. If you can persuade him/her that you're at least taking on board what's being said, you might be let off with a warning. If it goes further, you'll be reported for an offence - while this doesn't mean you'll end up being prosecuted for it, it ain't good. Some defects (like worn tyres) will result in a so-called "seven-day wonder", which usually means you have to fix whatever's deemed wrong, maybe get the car inspected, and present yourself with the proof at a police station, inside seven days, or face prosecution.

If you can manage to drive reasonably sensibly when the law's about, and can ideally show that you've tried to keep your car legal when you get questioned, you stand a much better chance of enjoying your relationship with your modded beast. This guide is intended to help you steer clear of the more obvious things you could get pulled for. By reading it, you might even be able to have an informed, well-mannered discussion about things legal with the next officer of the law you meet at the side of the road. As in: "Oh really, officer? I was not aware of that. Thank you for pointing it out." Just don't argue with them, that's all...

Documents

The first thing you'll be asked to produce. If you're driving around without tax, MOT or insurance, we might as well stop now, as you won't be doing much more driving of anything after just one pull.

Okay, so you don't normally carry all your car-related documents with you - for safety, you've got them stashed carefully at home, haven't you? But carrying photocopies of your licence, MOT and insurance certificate is a good idea. While they're not legally-binding absolute proof, producing these in a roadside check might mean you don't have to produce the real things at a copshop later in the week. Shows a certain responsibility, and confidence in your own legality on the road, too. In some parts of the country, it's even said to be a good idea to carry copies of any receipts for your stereo gear - if there's any suspicion about it being stolen (surely not), some coppers have been known to confiscate it (or the car it's in) on the spot!

Number plates

One of the simplest mods, and one of the easiest to spot (and prove) if you're a copper. Nowadays, any changes made to the standard approved character font (such as italics or fancy type), spacing, or size of the plate constitutes an offence. Remember too that if you've moved the rear plate from its original spot (like from the tailgate recess, during smoothing) it still has to be properly lit at night. You're unlikely to even buy an illegal plate now, as the companies making them are also liable for prosecution if you get stopped. It's all just something else to blame on speed cameras - plates have to be easy for them to shoot, and modding yours suggests you're trying to escape a speeding conviction (well, who isn't?).

Getting pulled for an illegal plate is for suckers - you're making it too easy for them. While this offence only entails a small fine and confiscation of the plates, you're drawing unwelcome police attention to the rest of your car. Not smart. At all.

Sunstrips and tints

The sunstrip is now an essential item for any modded motor, but telling Mr Plod you had to fit one is no defence if you've gone a bit too far. The sunstrip should not be so low down the screen that it interferes with your ability to see out. Is this obvious? Apparently not. As a guide, if the strip's so low your wiper(s) touch it, it's too low. Don't try fitting short wiper blades to get round this - the police aren't as stupid as that, and you could get done for wipers that don't clear a sufficient area of the screen. Push it so far, and no further!

Window tinting is a trickier area. It seems you can have up to a 25% tint on a windscreen, and up to 30% on all other glass - but how do you measure this? Er. And what do you do if your glass is tinted to start with? Er, probably nothing. Of course you can buy window film in various "darknesses", from not-very-dark to "ambulance-black", but being able to buy it does not make it legal for road use (most companies cover themselves by saying "for show use only"). Go for just a light smoke on the side and rear glass, and you'd have to be unlucky to get done for it. If you must fit really dark tints, you're safest doing the rear side windows only.

Some forces now have a light meter to test light transmission through glass at the roadside - fail this, and it's a big on-the-spot fine.

Single wiper conversion

Not usually a problem, and certainly not worth a pull on its own, but combine a big sunstrip with a short wiper blade, and you're just asking for trouble. Insufficient view of the road ahead. There's also the question of whether it's legal to have the arm parking vertically, in the centre of the screen, as it obscures your vision. Probably not legal, then - even if it looks cool. Unfortunately, the Man doesn't do cool.

Lights

Lights of all kinds have to be one of the single biggest problem areas in modifying, and the police are depressingly well-informed. Most people make light mods a priority, whether it's Morette conversions for headlights or Lexus-style rear clusters. If they fit alright, and work, what's the problem?

First off, don't bother with any lights which aren't fully UK-legal - it's just too much hassle. Being "E-marked" only makes them legal in Europe, and most of our Euro-chums drive on the right. One of our project cars ended up with left-hand-drive rear clusters, and as a result, had no rear reflectors and a rear foglight on the wrong side (should be on the right). Getting stopped for not having rear reflectors would be a bit harsh, but why risk it, even to save a few quid?

Once you've had any headlight mods done (other than light brows) always have the beam alignment checked - it's part of the MOT, after all. The same applies to any front fogs or spots you've fitted (the various points of law involved here are too many to mention - light colour, height, spacing, operation with main/dipped headlights - ask at an MOT centre before fitting, and have them checked out after fitting).

If Plod's really having a bad day, he might even question the legality of your new blue headlight bulbs - are they too powerful? Keeping the bulb packaging in the glovebox might be a neat solution here (60/55W max).

Many modders favour spraying rear light clusters to make them look trick, as opposed to replacing them - but there's trouble in store here, too. One of the greyest of grey areas is - how much light tinting is too much? The much-talked-about but not-often-seen "common sense" comes into play here. Making your lights so dim that they're reduced to a feeble red/orange glow is pretty dim itself. If you're spraying, only use proper light-tinting spray, and not too many coats of that. Colour-coding lights with ordinary spray paint is best left to a pro sprayer or bodyshop (it can be done by mixing lots of lacquer with not much paint, for instance). Tinted lights are actually more of a problem in daylight than at night, so check yours while the sun's out.

Lastly, two words about neons. Oh, dear. It seems that neons of all kinds have now been deemed illegal for road use (and that's

interior ones as well as exteriors, which have pretty much always been a no-no). If you fit neons inside, make sure you rig in a switch so you can easily turn them off when the law arrives - or don't drive around with them on (save it for when you're parked up). Distracts other road users, apparently.

ICE

Jungle massive, or massive public nuisance? The two sides of the ICE argument in a nutshell. If you've been around the modding scene for any length of time, you'll already know stories of people who've been done for playing car stereos too loud. Seems some local authorities now have by-laws concerning "music audible from outside a vehicle", and hefty fines if you're caught. Even where this isn't the case, and assuming a dB meter isn't on hand to prove the offence of "excessive noise", the police can still prosecute for "disturbing the peace" - on the basis of one officer's judgement of the noise level. If a case is proved, you could lose your gear. Whoops. Seems we're back to "do it - but don't over-do it" again. If you really want to demo your system, pick somewhere a bit less public (like a quiet trading estate, after dark) or go for safety in numbers (at a cruise).

Big alloys/tyres

One of the first things to go on any lad's car, sexy alloys are right at the heart of car modifying. So what'll interest the law?

Well, the first thing every copper's going to wonder is - are the wheels nicked? He'd need a good reason to accuse you, but this is another instance where having copies of receipts might prove useful.

Otherwise, the wheels mustn't rub on, or stick out from, the arches - either of these will prove to be a problem if you get stopped. And you don't need to drive a modded motor to get done for having bald tyres…

Lowered suspension

Of course you have to lower your car, to have any hope of street cred. But did you know it's actually an offence to cause damage to the road surface, if your car's so low (or your mates so lardy) that it grounds out? Apparently so! Never mind what damage it might be doing to your exhaust, or the brake/fuel lines under the car - you can actually get done for risking damage to the road. Well, great. What's the answer? Once you've lowered the car, load it up with your biggest mates, and test it over roads you normally use - or else find a route into town that avoids all speed bumps. If you've got coilovers, you'll have an easier time tuning out the scraping noises.

Remember that your new big-bore exhaust or backbox must be hung up well enough that it doesn't hit the deck, even if you

haven't absolutely slammed your car on the floor. At night, leaving a trail of sparks behind is a bit of a giveaway…

Exhausts

One of the easiest-to-fit performance upgrades, and another essential item if you want to be taken seriously on the street. Unless your chosen pipe/system is just too damn loud, you'd be very unlucky to get stopped for it, but if you will draw attention this way, you could be kicking yourself later.

For instance - have you in fact fitted a home-made straight-through pipe, to a car which used to have a "cat"? By drawing Plod's attention with that extra-loud system, he could then ask you to get the car's emissions tested - worse, you could get pulled for a "random" roadside emissions check. Fail this (and you surely will), and you could be right in the brown stuff. Even if you re-convert the car back to stock for the MOT, you'll be illegal on the road (and therefore without insurance) whenever your loud pipe's on. Still sound like fun, or would you be happier with just a back box?

It's also worth mentioning that your tailpipe mustn't stick out beyond the very back of the car, or in any other way which might be dangerous to pedestrians. Come on - you were a ped once!

Bodykits

The popular bodykits for the UK market have all passed the relevant tests, and are fully-approved for use on the specific vehicles they're intended for. As long as you haven't messed up fitting a standard kit, you should be fine, legally-speaking. The trouble starts when you do your own little mods and tweaks, such as bodging on that huge whale-tail spoiler or front air dam/splitter - it can be argued in some cases that these aren't appropriate on safety grounds, and you can get prosecuted. If any bodywork is fitted so it obscured your lights, or so badly attached that a strong breeze might blow it off, you can see their point. At least there's no such thing as Style Police. Not yet, anyway.

Seats and harnesses

Have to meet the UK safety standards, and must be securely bolted in. That's about it. It should be possible to fasten and release any seat belt or harness with one hand. Given that seat belts are pretty important safety features, it's understandable then that the police don't like to see flimsy alloy rear strut braces used as seat harness mounting points. Any other signs of bodging will also spell trouble. It's unlikely they'd bother with a full safety inspection at the roadside, but they could insist on a full MOT test/engineer's report inside 7 days. It's your life.

While we're on the subject of crash safety, the police also don't like to see sub boxes and amps just lying on the carpet, where the back seat used to be - if it's not anchored down, where are these items gonna end up, in a big shunt? Embedded in you, possibly?

Other mods

We'll never cover everything else here, and the law's always changing anyway, so we're fighting a losing battle in a book like this, but here goes with some other legalistic points we've noted on the way:

a It's illegal to remove side repeaters from front wings, unless they're "replaced" with Merc-style side repeater mirrors. Nice.
b All except the most prehistoric cars must have at least one rear foglight. If there's only one, it must be fitted on the right. We've never heard of anyone getting stopped for it, but you must also have a pair of rear reflectors. If your rear clusters ain't got 'em, can you get trendy ones? Er, no.
c Fuel filler caps have to be fitted so there's no danger of fuel spillage, or of excess fumes leaking from the top of the filler neck. This means using an appropriate petrol-resistant sealer (should be supplied in the kit). Oh, and not bodging the job in general seems a good idea. Unlikely to attract a pull, though.
d Front doors have to retain a manual means of opening from outside, even if they've been de-locked for remote locking. This means you can't take off the front door handles, usually. It seems that rear door handles can be removed if you like.
e Tailgates have to have some means of opening, even if it's only from inside, once the lock/handle's been removed. We think it's another safety thing - means of escape in a crash, and all that.
f You have to have at least one exterior mirror, and it must be capable of being adjusted somehow.
g If you fit new fog and spotlights, they actually have to work. No-one fits new lights just for show (or do they?), but if they stop working later when a fuse blows, relay packs up, or the wiring connectors rust up, you'd better fix 'em or remove 'em.
h Pedal extensions must have rubbers fitted on the brake and clutch pedals, and must be spaced sufficiently so there's no chance of hitting two pedals at once. This last bit sounds obvious, but lots of extension sets out there are so hard to fit that achieving this can be rather difficult. Don't get caught out.
i On cars with airbags, if you fit a sports wheel and disconnect the airbag in the process, the airbag warning light will be on permanently. Apart from being annoying, this is also illegal.
j Pace-car strobe lights (or any other flashing lights, apart from indicators) are illegal for road use. Of course.
k Anything else we didn't think of - is probably illegal too. Sorry.

Any questions? Try the MOT Helpline (0845 6005977). Yes, really.

Thanks to Andrew Dare of the Vehicle Inspectorate, Exeter, for his help in steering us through this minefield!

Thanks to:

We gratefully acknowledge all the help and advice offered from the following suppliers, without whom, etc, etc. Many of those credited below went way beyond the call of duty to help us produce this book - you know who you are. Cheers, guys! Roll the credits...

AS Design, France
(body styling kits)
00 33 03 81 65 37 03
www.as-design-france.com

Autopoint Car Care
(accessories)
01458 440011

AutoTint Design
(styling accessories)
0113 289 1500
www.autotintdesign.com

Bass Junkies
(ICE)
www.bassjunkies.com

BK Racing
(wheels)
01932 203044
www.bkracing.co.uk

Brown & Geeson
(Momo)
01268 764411
www.brownandgeeson.com

Corbeau Seats
01424 854499
www.corbeau-seats.co.uk

Dash Dynamics
0870 127 0003
www.dashdynamics.co.uk

Demon Tweeks
(accessories)
01978 664466
www.demon-tweeks.co.uk

Eurostyling
(Folia Tec)
01908 324950
www.eurostyling.com

Fennland Breakers
01354 651949

Halfords
08457 626 625

K & N Filters
(Induction kits)
01925 636950
www.knfilters.co.uk

LA & RW Piper
(upholstery & re-trimming)
01963 441431

Red Dot Racing
(brake discs & pads)
0208 888 2354

RGM
(light style & accessories)
01525 853888
www.rgmstyling.com

Richbrook
(sport auto accessories)
020 8543 7111
www.richbrook.co.uk

Ripspeed at Halfords
0845 609 1259

Spax
(suspension)
01869 244771
www.spaxperformance.com

A special thank you to:
Jon Hill (cover shots)
Bryn Musselwhite

Editorial Director	Matthew Minter
Designer	Simon Larkin
Page Build	James Robertson
Workshop	Paul Buckland Pete Trott
Editorial Assistant	Emmeline Willmott
Editor	Ian Barnes
Project Co-ordinator	Carole Turk
Production Control	Kevin Heals

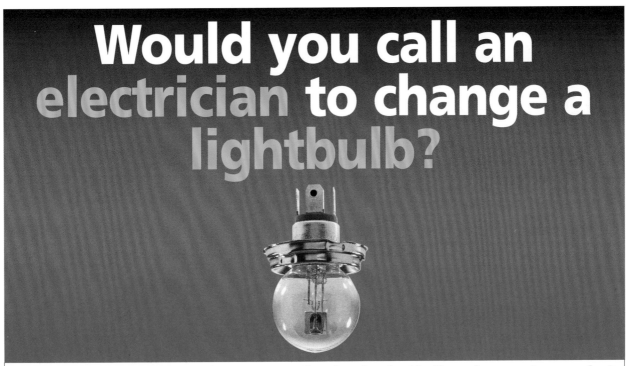

HaynesMaxpower

Haynes Car Manuals

Haynes Manuals

Title	No.
Alfa Romeo Alfasud/Sprint (74 - 88)	0292
Alfa Romeo Alfetta (73 - 87)	0531
Audi 80, 90 (79 - Oct 86 & Coupe (81 - Nov 88)	0605
Audi 80, 90 (Oct 86 - 90 & Coupe (Nov 88 - 90)	1491
Audi 100 (Oct 82 - 90 & 200 (Feb 84 - Oct 89)	0907
Audi 100 & A6 Petrol & Diesel (May 91 - May 97)	3504
Audi A4 (95 - Feb 00)	3575
Austin A35 & A40 (56 - 67) *	0118
Austin Allegro 1100, 1300, 1.0, 1.1 & 1.3 (73 - 82) *	0164
Austin/MG/Rover Maestro 1.3 & 1.6 (83 - 95)	0922
Austin/MG Metro (80 - May 90)	0718
Austin/Rover Montego 1.3 & 1.6 (84 - 94)	1066
Austin/MG/Rover Montego 2.0 (84 - 95)	1067
Mini (59 - 69)	0527
Mini (69 - 01)	0646
Austin/Rover 2.0 litre Diesel Engine (86 - 93)	1857
Austin Healey 100/6 & 3000 (56 - 68) *	0049
Bedford CF (69 - 87)	0163
Bedford/Vauxhall Rascal & Suzuki Supercarry (86 - Oct 94)	3015
BMW 316, 320 & 320i (4-cyl) (75 - Feb 83)	0276
BMW 320, 320i, 323i & 325i (6-cyl) (Oct 77 - Sept 87)	0815
BMW 3-Series (Apr 91 - 96)	3210
BMW 3- & 5-Series (sohc) (81 - 91)	1948
BMW 520i & 525e (Oct 81 - June 88)	1560
BMW 1500, 1502, 1600, 1602, 2000 & 2002 (59 - 77) *	0240
Citroën 2CV, Ami & Dyane (67 - 90)	0196
Citroën AX Petrol & Diesel (87 - 97)	3014
Citroën BX (83 - 94) A to L	0908
Citroën C15 Van Petrol & Diesel (89 - Oct 98)	3509
Citroën CX (75 - 88)	0528
Citroën Saxo Petrol & Diesel (96 - 01)	3506
Citroën Visa (79 - 88)	0620
Citroën Xantia Petrol & Diesel (93 - 98)	3082
Citroën XM Petrol & Diesel (89 - 00)	3451
Citroën Xsara Petrol & Diesel (97 - Sept 00)	3751
Citroën ZX Diesel (91 - 98)	1922
Citroën ZX Petrol (91 - 98)	1881
Citroën 1.7 & 1.9 litre Diesel Engine (84 - 96)	1379
Fiat 126 (73 - 87) *	0305
Fiat 500 (57 - 73)	0090
Fiat Bravo & Brava (95 - 00)	3572
Fiat Cinquecento (93 - 98)	3501
Fiat Panda (81 - 95)	0793
Fiat Punto Petrol & Diesel (94 - Oct 99)	3251
Fiat Regata (84 - 88)	1167
Fiat Tipo (88 - 91)	1625
Fiat Uno (83 - 95)	0923
Fiat X1/9 (74 - 89)	0273
Ford Anglia (59 - 68) *	0001
Ford Capri II (& III) 1.6 & 2.0 (74 - 87)	0283
Ford Capri II (& III) 2.8 & 3.0 (74 - 87)	1309
Ford Cortina Mk III 1300 & 1600 (70 - 76) *	0070
Ford Cortina Mk IV (& V) 1.6 & 2.0 (76 - 83) *	0343
Ford Cortina Mk IV (& V) 2.3 V6 (77 - 83) *	0426
Ford Escort Mk I 1100 & 1300 (68 - 74) *	0171
Ford Escort Mk I Mexico, RS 1600 & RS 2000 (70 - 74) *	0139
Ford Escort Mk II Mexico, RS 1800 & RS 2000 (75 - 80) *	0735
Ford Escort (75 - Aug 80) *	0280
Ford Escort (Sept 80 - Sept 90)	0686
Ford Escort & Orion (Sept 90 - 00)	1737
Ford Fiesta (76 - Aug 83)	0334
Ford Fiesta (Aug 83 - Feb 89)	1030
Ford Fiesta (Feb 89 - Oct 95)	1595
Ford Fiesta (Oct 95 - 01)	3397
Ford Focus (98 - 01)	3759
Ford Granada (Sept 77 - Feb 85)	0481
Ford Granada & Scorpio (Mar 85 - 94)	1245
Ford Ka (96 - 02)	3570
Ford Mondeo Petrol (93 - 99)	1923
Ford Mondeo Diesel (93 - 96)	3465
Ford Orion (83 - Sept 90)	1009
Ford Sierra 4 cyl. (82 - 93)	0903
Ford Sierra V6 (82 - 91)	0904
Ford Transit Petrol (Mk 2) (78 - Jan 86)	0719
Ford Transit Petrol (Mk 3) (Feb 86 - 89)	1468
Ford Transit Diesel (Feb 86 - 99)	3019
Ford 1.6 & 1.8 litre Diesel Engine (84 - 96)	1172
Ford 2.1, 2.3 & 2.5 litre Diesel Engine (77 - 90)	1606
Freight Rover Sherpa (74 - 87)	0463
Hillman Avenger (70 - 82)	0037
Hillman Imp (63 - 76) *	0022
Honda Accord (76 - Feb 84)	0351
Honda Civic (Feb 84 - Oct 87)	1226
Honda Civic (Nov 91 - 96)	3199
Hyundai Pony (85 - 94)	3398
Jaguar E Type (61 - 72)	0140
Jaguar MkI & II, 240 & 340 (55 - 69) *	0098
Jaguar XJ6, XJ & Sovereign; Daimler Sovereign (68 - Oct 86)	0242
Jaguar XJ6 & Sovereign (Oct 86 - Sept 94)	3261
Jaguar XJ12, XJS & Sovereign; Daimler Double Six (72 - 88)	0478
Jeep Cherokee Petrol (93 - 96)	1943
Lada 1200, 1300, 1500 & 1600 (74 - 91)	0413

Title	No.
Lada Samara (87 - 91)	1610
Land Rover 90, 110 & Defender Diesel (83 - 95)	3017
Land Rover Discovery Petrol & Diesel (89 - 98)	3016
Land Rover Freelander (97 - 02)	3929
Land Rover Series IIA & III Diesel (58 - 85)	0529
Land Rover Series II, IIA & III Petrol (58 - 85)	0314
Mazda 323 (Mar 81 - Oct 89)	1608
Mazda 323 (Oct 89 - 98)	3455
Mazda 626 (May 83 - Sept 87)	0929
Mazda B-1600, B-1800 & B-2000 Pick-up (72 - 88)	0267
Mazda RX-7 (79 - 85) *	0460
Mercedes-Benz 190, 190E & 190D Petrol & Diesel (83 - 93)	3450
Mercedes-Benz 200, 240, 300 Diesel (Oct 76 - 85)	1114
Mercedes-Benz 250 & 280 (68 - 72)	0346
Mercedes-Benz 250 & 280 (123 Series) (Oct 76 - 84)	0677
Mercedes-Benz 124 Series (85 - Aug 93)	3253
Mercedes-Benz C-Class Petrol & Diesel (93 - Aug 00)	3511
MGA (55 - 62) *	0475
MGB (62 - 80)	0111
MG Midget & AH Sprite (58 - 80)	0265
Mitsubishi Shogun & L200 Pick-Ups (83 - 94)	1944
Morris Ital 1.3 (80 - 84)	0705
Morris Minor 1000 (56 - 71)	0024
Nissan Bluebird (May 84 - Mar 86)	1223
Nissan Bluebird (Mar 86 - 90)	1473
Nissan Cherry (Sept 82 - 86)	1031
Nissan Micra (83 - Jan 93)	0931
Nissan Micra (93 - 99)	3254
Nissan Primera (90 - Aug 99)	1851
Nissan Stanza (82 - 86)	0824
Nissan Sunny (May 82 - Oct 86)	0895
Nissan Sunny (Oct 86 - Mar 91)	1378
Nissan Sunny (Apr 91 - 95)	3219
Opel Ascona & Manta (B Series) (Sept 75 - 88)	0316
Opel Kadett (Nov 79 - Oct 84)	0634
Opel Rekord (Feb 78 - Oct 86)	0543
Peugeot 106 Petrol & Diesel (91 - 02)	1882
Peugeot 205 Petrol (83 - 97)	0932
Peugeot 206 Petrol and Diesel (98 - 01)	3757
Peugeot 305 (78 - 89)*	0538
Peugeot 306 Petrol & Diesel (93 - 99)	3073
Peugeot 309 (86 - 93)	1266
Peugeot 405 Petrol (88 - 97)	1559
Peugeot 405 Diesel (88 - 97)	3198
Peugeot 406 Petrol & Diesel (96 - 97)	3394
Peugeot 505 (79 - 89)	0762
Peugeot 1.7/1.8 & 1.9 litre Diesel Engine (82 - 96)	0950
Peugeot 2.0, 2.1, 2.3 & 2.5 litre Diesel Engines (74 - 90)	1607
Porsche 911 (65 - 85)	0264
Porsche 924 & 924 Turbo (76 - 85)	0397
Proton (89 - 97)	3255
Range Rover V8 (70 - Oct 92)	0606
Reliant Robin & Kitten (73 - 83)	0436
Renault 4 (61 - 86) *	0072
Renault 5 (Feb 85 - 96)	1219
Renault 9 & 11 (82 - 89)	0822
Renault 18 (79 - 86)	0598
Renault 19 Petrol (89 - 94)	1646
Renault 19 Diesel (89 - 96)	1946
Renault 21 (86 - 94)	1397
Renault 25 (84 - 92)	1228
Renault Clio Petrol (91 - May 98)	1853
Renault Clio Diesel (91 - June 96)	3031
Renault Clio Petrol & Diesel (May 98 - May 01)	3906
Renault Espace Petrol & Diesel (85 - 96)	3197
Renault Fuego (80 - 86) *	0764
Renault Laguna Petrol & Diesel (94 - 00)	3252
Renault Mégane & Scénic Petrol & Diesel (96 - 98)	3395
Renault Mégane & Scénic Petrol & Diesel (Apr 99 - 02)	3916
Rover 213 & 216 (84 - 89)	1116
Rover 214 & 414 (89 - 96)	1689
Rover 216 & 416 (89 - 96)	1830
Rover 211, 214, 216, 218 & 220 Petrol & Diesel (Dec 95 - 98)	3399
Rover 414, 416 & 420 Petrol & Diesel (May 95 - 98)	3453
Rover 618, 620 & 623 (93 - 97)	3257
Rover 820, 825 & 827 (86 - 95)	1380
Rover 3500 (76 - 87)	0365
Rover Metro, 111 & 114 (May 90 - 98)	1711
Saab 95 & 96 (66 - 76) *	0198
Saab 99 (69 - 79) *	0247
Saab 90, 99 & 900 (79 - Oct 93)	0765
Saab 900 (Oct 93 - 98)	3512
Saab 9000 (4-cyl) (85 - 98)	1686
Seat Ibiza & Cordoba Petrol & Diesel (Oct 93 - Oct 99)	3571
Seat Ibiza & Malaga (85 - 92)	1609
Skoda Estelle (77 - 89)	0604
Skoda Favorit (89 - 96)	1801
Skoda Felicia Petrol & Diesel (95 - 01)	3505
Subaru 1600 & 1800 (Nov 79 - 90)	0995

Title	No.
Sunbeam Alpine, Rapier & H120 (67 - 76) *	0051
Suzuki Supercarry & Bedford/Vauxhall Rascal (86 - Oct 94)	3015
Suzuki SJ Series, Samurai & Vitara (4-cyl) (82 - 97)	1942
Talbot Alpine, Solara, Minx & Rapier (75 - 86)	0337
Talbot Horizon (78 - 86)	0473
Talbot Samba (82 - 86)	0823
Toyota Carina E (May 92 - 97)	3256
Toyota Corolla (Sept 83 - Sept 87)	1024
Toyota Corolla (80 - 85)	0683
Toyota Corolla (Sept 87 - Aug 92)	1683
Toyota Corolla (Aug 92 - 97)	3259
Toyota Hi-Ace & Hi-Lux (69 - Oct 83)	0304
Triumph Acclaim (81 - 84) *	0792
Triumph GT6 & Vitesse (62 - 74) *	0112
Triumph Herald (59 - 71) *	0010
Triumph Spitfire (62 - 81)	0113
Triumph Stag (70 - 78)	0441
Triumph TR2, TR3, TR3A, TR4 & TR4A (52 - 67) *	0028
Triumph TR5 & 6 (67 - 75) *	0031
Triumph TR7 (75 - 82) *	0322
Vauxhall Astra (80 - Oct 84)	0635
Vauxhall Astra & Belmont (Oct 84 - Oct 91)	1136
Vauxhall Astra (Oct 91 - Feb 98)	1832
Vauxhall/Opel Astra & Zafira Diesel (Feb 98 - Sept 00)	3797
Vauxhall/Opel Astra & Zafira Petrol (Feb 98 - Sept 00)	3758
Vauxhall/Opel Calibra (90 - 98)	3502
Vauxhall Carlton (Oct 78 - Oct 86)	0480
Vauxhall Carlton & Senator (Nov 86 - 94)	1469
Vauxhall Cavalier 1300 (77 - July 81) *	0461
Vauxhall Cavalier 1600, 1900 & 2000 (75 - July 81)	0315
Vauxhall Cavalier (81 - Oct 88)	0812
Vauxhall Cavalier (Oct 88 - 95)	1570
Vauxhall Chevette (75 - 84)	0285
Vauxhall Corsa (Mar 93 - 97)	1985
Vauxhall/Opel Corsa (Apr 97 - Oct 00)	3921
Vauxhall/Opel Frontera Petrol & Diesel (91 - Sept 98)	3454
Vauxhall Nova (83 - 93)	0909
Vauxhall/Opel Omega (94 - 99)	3510
Vauxhall Vectra Petrol & Diesel (95 - 98)	3396
Vauxhall/Opel Vectra (Mar 99 - May 02)	3930
Vauxhall/Opel 1.5, 1.6 & 1.7 litre Diesel Engine (82 - 96)	1222
Volkswagen 411 & 412 (68 - 75) *	0091
Volkswagen Beetle 1200 (54 - 77)	0036
Volkswagen Beetle 1300 & 1500 (65 - 75)	0039
Volkswagen Beetle 1302 & 1302S (70 - 72)	0110
Volkswagen Beetle 1303, 1303S & GT (72 - 75)	0159
Volkswagen Beetle Petrol & Diesel (Apr 99 - 01)	3798
Volkswagen Golf & Bora Petrol & Diesel (April 98 - 00)	3727
Volkswagen Golf & Jetta Mk 1 1.1 & 1.3 (74 - 84)	0716
Volkswagen Golf, Jetta & Scirocco Mk 1 1.5, 1.6 & 1.8 (74 - 84)	0726
Volkswagen Golf & Jetta Mk 1 Diesel (78 - 84)	0451
Volkswagen Golf & Jetta Mk 2 (Mar 84 - Feb 92)	1081
Volkswagen Golf & Vento Petrol & Diesel (Feb 92 - 96)	3097
Volkswagen LT vans & light trucks (76 - 87)	0637
Volkswagen Passat & Santana (Sept 81 - May 88)	0814
Volkswagen Passat Petrol & Diesel (May 88 - 96)	3498
Volkswagen Passat 4-cyl Petrol & Diesel (Dec 96 - Nov 00)	3917
Volkswagen Polo & Derby (76 - Jan 82)	0335
Volkswagen Polo (82 - Oct 90)	0813
Volkswagen Polo (Nov 90 - Aug 94)	3245
Volkswagen Polo Hatchback Petrol & Diesel (94 - 99)	3500
Volkswagen Scirocco (82 - 90)	1224
Volkswagen Transporter 1600 (68 - 79)	0082
Volkswagen Transporter 1700, 1800 & 2000 (72 - 79)	0226
Volkswagen Transporter (air-cooled) (79 - 82)	0638
Volkswagen Transporter (water-cooled) (82 - 90)	3452
Volkswagen Type 3 (63 - 73) *	0084
Volvo 120 & 130 Series (& P1800) (61 - 73) *	97010
Volvo 142, 144 & 145 (66 - 74)	0129
Volvo 240 Series (74 - 93)	0270
Volvo 262, 264 & 260/265 (75 - 85) *	0400
Volvo 340, 343, 345 & 360 (76 - 91)	0715
Volvo 440, 460 & 480 (87 - 97)	1691
Volvo 740 & 760 (82 - 91)	1258
Volvo 850 (92 - 96)	3260
Volvo 940 (90 - 96)	3249
Volvo S40 & V40 (96 - 99)	3569
Volvo S70, V70 & C70 (96 - 99)	3573

* = Classic Reprints